Disclaimer

SEMAIS

3350 Riverwood Pkwy., Suite 1900

Atlanta, Georgia 30339

Website: www.semais.net

Phone: 800-497-3376

Table of Contents

1. SEMAIS Background

Secure Managed Instructional Systems, LLC (SEMAIS) is a leading Cybersecurity and Workforce Development company consisting of one principal officer with a combined government and military experience of 30 years. The company resides in Atlanta, Georgia, and provides a broad range of cybersecurity solutions to the Department of Defense (DoD, military service branches, commercial entities, strategic alliances, global partners, contractors, and organizations dependent upon data privacy, reducing risks and safeguarding assets.

The core competencies mature customers' business model, risk management program, and security readiness. SEMAIS builds security controls early into System Development Life Cycle (SDLC) and introduces define roles and structured processes to guide the development, authorization, operation, and subsequent security operations. We help clients predict, prevent, detect, and respond to cyber risk via the following core competencies:

SEMAIS Business Domains

Cyber Security Engineering (CySEC)	Cyber Workforce Development (CyWD)	Enterprise Security Services (Esec)	Security and Risk Management (SecRM)

Cyber Security Engineering

- ACAS, HBSS, & DISA STIGS
- Security Implementation
- Security Architecture Services
- Security Development & Testing
- Trusted Internet Connection

Enterprise Security Services

- Configuration Management
- Data Security
- End-Point Security Integration
- Security Tools
- Security Policies

Cyber Workforce Development

- CISSP Prep Course
- Customized Training
- Cyber Awareness Workshop
- Security Plus
- Vulnerability Scanning & Remediation

Security and Risk Management

- FISMA & FedRAMP Guidance
- Governance Risk & Compliance
- NIST Risk Management Framework
- Vulnerability Management
- Software Assurance

Our solutions provide strategic value through assessing and aligning cybersecurity workstreams for business growth, cost savings, and risk reduction. This includes integrating safeguards, engineering a continuous monitoring strategy, designing practices to implement ePHI, PII, and streamlining security-related tasks.

These workstreams also support technology innovation and changes. SEMAIS is heavily engaged in cybersecurity technology best practices and constantly developing **"out-of-box"** solutions that reduce risks.

2. CISSP Certification Background and Approach

- The SEMAIS CISSP study guide aims to help testing candidates synthesize and summarize relevant CISSP information. Therefore, a certification candidate might think of this studyguide as a mini CISSP examination.

- It is especially useful for difficult or complex IT Security concepts or subject areas.

- The primary advantage of using this guide is that it organize the amount of information to belearned. Also, learning is improved through applying the 8-domain knowledge to real-time IT Security experience.

- A certification candidate will grasp several concepts related to the CISSP 8 domains for driving IT Security best practices and industry standards in this guide.

- A candidate may use more than one organizing strategy when assessing questions in thisstudy guide.

- Remember, PROFICIENCY in a SMALLER amount of information is your goal.

3. Why Become A CISSP

International Information System Security Certification Consortium (ISC)² CISSP course is essential if you pursue a senior role in Information Security. CISSP provides an extensive overview of the Common Body of Knowledge (CBK), a compendium of information security practices and standards compiled and continually updated (ISC)².

CISSP is integral in developing an extensive understanding of information security and has gained importance as a critical component in the selection process for management-level information security positions. For familiarity, here are two reasons why CISSP is the certification to choose, now more than ever.

Worldwide Recognition

A certification is only as good as its recognition. Unlike many standard certs, CISSP boasts industry-wide recognition, and it was acknowledged in 2015 by SC Magazine for the fifth time as the 'Best Professional Certification Program.

This Gold Standard credential is not only recognized by the world's leading multinationals - such as Google, IBM, and P&G - it's also deemed a requirement in 56% of cyber jobs in the contracting industry. So if an IT Professional motivation is to resolve the complicated world of IT security, a CISSP certification is a must-have.

Bureau of Labor Statistics

Information Security Analysts
Percent change in employment, projected 2014-24

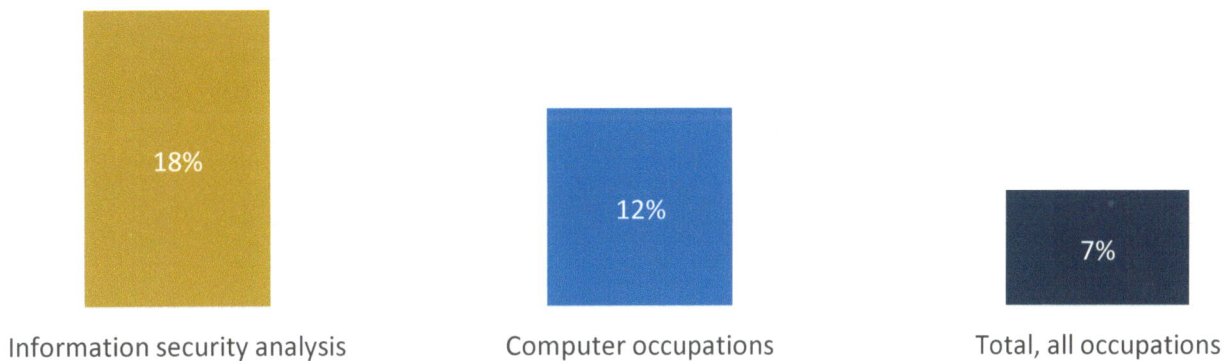

Information security analysis	Computer occupations	Total, all occupations
18%	12%	7%

Diagram – 1 Bureau of Labor Statistics

The Bureau of Labor constantly updates and post statistics and trends for various labor and career skills. Diagram – 1 provides a brief overview of where the IT Security industry is headed. The Cybersecurity market requires workforce development support due to the expected 28% growth rate.

The industry is comprised of private companies, servicemembers, federal contractors, and regular employees. By reviewing the BOL projected 28% growth rate survey, Cybersecurity career development is a requirement and employment necessity. Along with those demands and statistics, training, certification, and job outlook requires certified Cybersecurity professionals.

The BOL survey proves that a CISSP certified candidate will pursue specialized job roles. Examples of such specialist positions include Security Consultant, Security Architect, Information Assurance Manager, or Security Advisor.

4. SEMAIS Training Methodology

In the past, most training companies focused on providing "Teaching-the-Test," and not "Teaching-the-Student." SEMAIS employs a different methodology by aligning concepts with applicative theories. This core practice ensures that candidates receive the most relevant training. In addition, the methodology incorporates methods from practice tests, recognized technical publications, or students' and instructors' practical experience.

SEMAIS service and training combine industry practices and various regulations and frameworks such as FISMA, NIST, and ISO 27002. SEMAIS CISSP training and examination preparation is based upon experience and understanding of information technology standards and workforce development programs. We are registered as a National Training Provider by the Department of Homeland Security.

Candidate Approach and Achievement for CISSP

CISSP's core content, seen in the domains listed below, actively seeks to develop this wide range of information and security management. The CISSP CBK consists of the following eight domains:

Security and Risk Management
Addresses a broad spectrum of general information security and risk management topics.

Asset Security
Addresses the collection, handling, and protection of information throughout its life cycle.

Security Engineering
It is the practice of building information systems and related architecture that continue to deliver the required functionality in the face of threats that malicious acts may cause.

Communication and NetworkSecurity
It encompasses the network architecture, transmission methods, transport protocols, control devices, and the securitymeasures used to maintain the confidentiality, integrity, and availability ofinformation transmitted over privateand public communication networks.

Identity and Access Management
Involves provisioning and managing the identities and access used in the interaction of humans and information systems, disparate information systems,and even between individual componentsof information systems.

Security Assessment and Testing
Involves evaluating information assets and associated infrastructure using various tools and techniques to identify and mitigate risk.

Security Operations
Involves the application of information security concepts and best practices to the operation of enterprise computing systems.

Software Development Security
Involves the application of security concepts and best practices to production and development softwareenvironments.

- Certification testing can become a very overwhelming experience without the proper training. At SEMAIS,we utilize a solution package that integrates Knowledge, Comprehension, and Application (KCA) as a training evaluator for candidates pursuing certifications.

- To align certification and skills, we employ "Application and Theory Based" learning. The overall approachensures that CISSP learning is achieved to gain the certification, which is a successful approach to certification testing. We do not sell generic test questions!

- Our questions are developed by Cybersecurity experts and leading Cybersecurity professionals and mirror the structure and approach for the official examination test questions.

- Many of the leading companies will sell you 2,000 questions that are "not" focused on the exam content.Does this sound familiar? Our methodology to address "Curriculum Content" over "Exam Content" for training material.

- Many of the leading online examination packages focus on "What questions are on the test" and this practice fails the IT Security community.

5. Knowledge, Comprehension, and Application (KCA) Tools

The initial approach to any CISSP examination is to extract the ambiguous information and answers or areas that are not applicable. Using the KCA principle can help foster a more realistic approach to the examination.

Level 1
Knowledge

Knowledge is defined as remembering previously learned CISSP information. This is a recall of the appropriate information. Knowledge represents the lowest level of approaching a test question in the cognitive domain. Objectives at this level require candidates to demonstrate their knowledge of the question.

Level 2
Comprehension

Comprehension is defined as the ability to grasp the question's meaning. These learning outcomes are more complex than simple recall of information and represent the lowest level of understanding.

Level 3
Application

Application is the ability to apply learning in new and concrete ways. The application differs from comprehension in that application shows that students can use (apply to learn correctly.

Example:

SEMAIS has just completed a significant assessment and wants to plan its security remediation strategy across multiple platforms. While examining the report, a manager notices that its major weakness is access control, user isolation, and authentication by-pass settings. While conducting an extended analysis, the manager notices that 25% of its risks are related to illegitimate access control by the network administrators group. When remediating the network administrator group's illegitimate access to the system, which of the following will not be your primary consideration?

A should be given maximum privilege across all systems and IT infrastructure.

B SEMAIS network administrators' duties should be separated.

C Activities of the network administrator should be monitored.

D System/network administrators should be subject to job rotation.

Knowledge
Access privileges provide users the right to information based on their job roles.

Comprehension
The question wants to know the process to prevent network administrators from having illegitimate access.

Application
Question A would be a low priority based on the question asking for the primary consideration and preventing access by separation of duties, continuous monitoring, and job rotation. In addition, question A would be a low priority since it provides full rights and negates the ability to prevent illegitimate access.

Question "A" is the correct answer. Using this strategy for the test questions in this guide will better prepare a candidate to examine. As a candidate become proficient with using KCA, they will master the CISSP examination.

6. Domain 1: Security and Risk Management - Questions

1. When policies are constructed that separate groups and users, the overall objective should consist of information that addresses accepted practices and standards to change data. Which of the following addresses this security concept.

   A. The least privilege to access data corresponds to the availability of resources.

   B. The use of modification principles will ensure well-formed transactions are authorized.

   C. Disaster recovery supports service loss to viable resources.

   D. The confidentiality, integrity, and availability (CIA) triad can be applied across multiple domains to know the primary concern for all functions.

2. The overall relationship for Confidentiality, Integrity, and Availability should address the SDLC's concern for developing and implementing security-related functions. Which answer supports this statement?

   A. The detailed design constraints for security integration and requirements.

   B. The overall assumptions and risks for confidentiality, integrity, and availability within trade-offs and design considerations.

   C. Service solutions for accessing information and resources during the testing and verification stage.

   D. Budget constraints that impose system design changes.

3. One of the most fundamental practices for Security is to ensure management provides oversight and direction for Security. Based on the statement presented, how would this apply to a strong governance strategy? Choose the best answer.

   A. Implementing enterprise auditing and risk standards would reduce risks associated with system changes.

   B. Maintain visible knowledge of new changes to access control features.

   C. Evaluate vendor risk concepts for compliance reviews.

   D. Manage high-level risks and ensure awareness training aligns with compliance issues.

4. Which of the following is considered a well-instituted practice for security management within an organization?

   A. Maintain previous risk-related data for compliance.

   B. Integrate a continuous monitoring program that accepts risk factors and promotes the concept through annual training.

   C. Separate policies and procedures from controls.

   D. Balance risks and control implementation standards for an organization's risk program.

5. SEMAIS has decided to change its organization security policy to reflect changes within its operations. The company has discovered many data breaches and an increasing number of vulnerable applications. What would be the first action to pursue based on the information presented?

   A. Examine the threats associated with the application and update risk concerns.

   B. Implement the change control procedures for vulnerabilities that affect its applications.

   C. Update the security policies and align concepts and practices at defending against data breaches.

   D. Implement new concepts to the governance committee.

6. The Information Security Officer (ISO) has mandated that all departments exercise a new policy for the organization's risk management program. The approach is designed to discover potential weaknesses within the security program. As the Information Security Officer, what would you expect the Policy to cover?

   A. Immediate needs of the organization's security program based on new vulnerabilities.

   B. Change control concepts and practices for risk implementation.

   C. Computer Emergency Readiness Team (CERT) implementation for new security team members.

   D. Standards that are aligned to the baseline.

7. Who would communicate data classification and backup of critical resources status for an organization governance team?

   A. Data custodian and business owners

   B. Information and data owner

   C. Information Steward and Security Administrator

   D. Information System Auditor and Business Owner

8. As a security assessor, you have been tasked to evaluate a control framework for your organization. What are some standard evaluation practices that would help in determining the value of the frameworks?

   A. Determine whether governance programs can survive.

   B. Measuring the standard steps to implement and refine solutions.

   C. Determine whether the controls perform above the minimum standards.

   D. Observing risk and privacy controls for consistency.

9. The continual effort of making sure that the correct policies, procedures, and standards are in place and being followed is described as what?

   A. Use due practice and implement policy standards.

   B. Due diligence

   C. Due concern and

   D. Due care

10. **When corrective action has been instituted for background and credit checks that failed, what action has a company pursued Security?**

    A. A due care philosophy coupled with the due protect process.

    B. Due diligence combined with do correct.

    C. Due concern for security and organization safety.

    D. Due care for organization safety.

11. **A well-developed and implemented risk-management program can achieve the Payment Card Industry-Data Security Standard (PCI-DSS). What does this statement relate to?**

    A. Successful compliance with laws and regulations.

    B. Fraud prevention and consumer risk safety for PCI data loss.

    C. Regulatory laws that support control analysis.

    D. Threat and Risk Management programs.

12. **When an organization decides to implement a safe harbor practice, what are some actual outcomes?**

    A. The success to implement pre-existing laws with scrutiny.

    B. Protection from different laws that may occur.

    C. Governance and Risk Management for compliance.

    D. Legal practices that protect the organization from risks.

13. **SEMAIS has decided to outsource control assessments to a third-party auditing firm. The Chief Executive Officer (CEO) and the Security team have made it clear that privacy and control standards are the primary concern for the organization. The assessor arrives at the corporate office, and the security guard escorts him to the datacenter. Upon arriving at the datacenter, the assessor notices that employees' copyright data and personal information are openly available. What security mythology addresses the assessor gathering personal data and using it for financial gain?**

    A. Data diddling, which means he changed the personal data to gain access to a victim's account.

    B. Data breach constitutes stealing of trade secrets.

    C. Trademark violations for SEMAIS proprietary data on employees.

    D. Violation of a need-to-know principle could constitute a data breach.

14. **SEMAIS has decided to outsource control assessment to a third-party auditing firm. The CEO and the Security team have made it clear that privacy and control standards are the primary concern for the organization. The assessor arrives at the corporate office, and the security guard escorts him to the datacenter. Upon arriving at the datacenter, the assessor notices copyright data and personal information for employees. What would constitute a violation of copyright infringement based on the scenario?**

    A. Using SEMAIS security standards for financial gain.

    B. Copying data from the datacenter for financial reasons.

C. Using SEMAIS contract proposals for business development.

D. Any use of registered information that relates to SEMAIS computer programs.

15. **SEMAIS has decided to outsource control assessment to a third-party auditing firm. The CEO and the security team have made it clear that privacy and control standards are the primary concern for the organization. The assessor arrives at the corporate office, and the security guard escorts him to the datacenter. Upon arriving at the datacenter, the assessor notices copyright data and personal information for employees. As a reference to understanding personal data, SEMAIS could make what organizational decision?**

A. Create user regulations that address corporate goals.

B. Enforce regulatory compliance for all employees.

C. Institute a company-wide training on Data Protection Directive 95/46/EC.

D. Create Data protection guidelines that are feasible.

16. **You decide to log onto your computer, and a banner displays that states: "Please pay the amount of $750 to unlock your computer." You have 10 minutes to make the payment, or your computer will lock. What type of computer crime is being used against you?**

A. Scareware tactics to prevent you from logging onto your system.

B. A Ransomware that requires a payment.

C. Anti-virus software advertisement which is normal.

D. A serious data breach that requires attention.

17. **Violation of Intellectual property rights can best be described as which of the following?**

A. The unauthorized use of another person's artistic work without written consent.

B. The transfer of copyright information and its rights to a third party.

C. Using a new publicly accessible invention without consent from the patent approval authority.

D. Extending licenses and their coverage.

18. **As a consultant, you have been hired to travel to a foreign location to perform security tasks for SEMAIS. After conducting your work, you have been required to transfer scientific and technical information for military applications. Which program proposes the highest concern based on the information provided?**

A. Trans-Border regulations are designed to prevent transparency.

B. The Wassenaar agreement clause to conceal information.

C. Control of import and export based on International Traffic in Arms Regulations.

D. Propriety information for SEMAIS.

19. SEMAIS Human Resource (HR) department has mandated that all personal data concerning clients be guarded with the highest level of Security. Two months later, the security team discovered personal data that identified clients' financial and home addresses being emailed to partnering companies. Later that day, the company found hackers gained access to the central database server and exported personal information about 15 clients' financial records to criminals. What security principle would address the misuse of personal data for SEMAIS?

    A. Privacy as it relates to the collection and retention of private information.

    B. Confidentiality due to the need-to-know principle.

    C. Ethics as a result of unauthorized access to resources.

    D. Data breach where hackers gather personal information.

20. SEMAIS HR department has mandated that all personal data concerning clients be guarded with the highest level of Security. Two months later, the security team discovered personal data that identified clients' financial and home addresses being emailed to partnering companies. Later that day, the company realizes that hackers gained access to the central database server and exported personal information about 15 clients' financial records to criminals. What two security principle addresses the unauthorized disclosure of financial data based on the scenario provided?

    A. Privacy as it relates to the collection and retention of private information and integrity of data resources.

    B. Confidentiality for data breaches and the need-to-know principle.

    C. Ethics and unauthorized access to resources.

    D. Data breach where hackers gather personal information, release the information to criminals; and need to know principles.

21. As a consultant, you have been hired to travel to a foreign location to perform security tasks for SEMAIS. After conducting your tasks, you must transfer scientific and technical information for military applications through a cloud solution within a foreign country. Which program would you be concerned about based on data transmittal through cloud service while in unfamiliar territory?

    A. Trans-border regulations are designed to control the free flow of data.

    B. The Wassenaar agreement clause to conceal information.

    C. Control of import and export based on International Traffic in Arms Regulations.

    D. Propriety information for SEMAIS.

22. Which of the following statements about the International Information System Security Certification Consortium (ISC) is 2 Code of Ethics incorrect?

    A. All information systems security professionals certified by (ISC)2 recognize that such a certification is a privilege that must be earned and maintained.

    B. All information systems security professionals certified by (ISC)² shall provide diligent and competent service to principals.

    C. All information systems security professionals certified by (ISC)² shall discourage such behavior as associating or preparing to associate with criminals or criminal behavior.

D. All information systems security professionals certified by (ISC)² shall promote the understanding and acceptance of prudent information security measures.

23. **As the new Information System Security Officer, you have been tasked to assess the code of ethics for your organization. To better assist your evaluation process, you decide to research various programs such as Health Insurance Portability and Accountability Act (HIPPA), Computer Crimes, and the Gramm-Leach-Bliley Act (GLBA). The CIO has requested that he receives feedback on the status and recommendations for the organization. What would be the best description to convey your situation to the CIO concerning ethics and regulatory compliance based on the scenario?**

A. Financial disclosure is our leading ethical practice, and following GLBA will keep the company in compliance. Employees can request the company policies and code of conduct via a formal request.

B. The ethical standards employees follow are all based on the employee handbook and policies created for the organization. HIPPA laws are addressed for patient information; GLBA protects clients' financial information, and computer crimes are considered a violation of policies.

C. HIPPA is far more critical when it comes to ethical practices. Our code of conduct policy for computer crimes will address this concept and more.

D. Ethical practices are all covered as employees on board, which is sufficient for our organization's policies on ethics. Regulatory standards do not change unless a new Chief Information Officer (CIO) boards the company.

24. **When a security team decides to implement a baseline configuration change, what are some key components to successfully fulfill the shift in organization requirements?**

A. Designs policies and step-by-step practices to ensure it is appropriately implemented.

B. Examine the current minimum security controls and omit and procedural items.

C. Update policies that pertain to baseline compliance.

D. Use a single guideline to ensure baseline controls comply.

25. **The use of HIPPA would best be described as which of the following as it relates to management?**

A. A baseline to medical practice and protection of health records.

B. Procedures that mandate standards of practice.

C. A bottom-up approach to development and implementation.

D. Top-down relationship with business owners to implement the policies.

26. **Which of the following would not support Business Continuity Project Plan (BCP)?**

A. Establish timelines and schedules for deliverables.

B. Define a project Scope and what must be archived based on the BCP activities.

C. Rely on the BCP coordinator to move forward with the plan.

D. Consider resources required for the project.

27. During the re-development of a BCP Project Scope, the team discovers that various servers will require additional operational support. Which of the following pertains to this issue?

   A. The team will have to assess the impact analysis and verify whether changes are required.

   B. There will be a requirement to adjust the Alternate Site location for possible changes.

   C. Resource assignments will change based on the critical functions.

   D. Recovery point must be escalated to support operations.

28. Which of the following is true concerning a business impact analysis?

   A. The recovery point objective should be longer than the recovery time objective.

   B. The maximum tolerable downtime is a very long process.

   C. The Mean Time Between Failures should be greater than the Mean Time to Repair.

   D. Mean Time to Repair should be less than the Mean Time Between Failure.

29. SEMAIS has requested all employees to provide private information about their previous jobs, including credit and critical legal matters. Employee "A" did not provide the information, but he was still able to work. A new employee checks on board, and the same process occurs. What should SEMAIS do to correct the issue?

   A. Gain permission from the CEO to conduct a background investigation for the new employee.

   B. Create a policy where private information would be kept secret for all company actions.

   C. Develop a policy to thoroughly screen employee's employment history and related job information.

   D. Verify that the employee is a CISSP, which shows the employee is ethical.

30. User "A" has requested to gain privileged access to a database server. The company policies only allow the developers to have access to the server. As a Security Manager, how would you address this concern to "User A?"

   A. Explain the concept of separate roles, duties, and privilege escalation as it relates to access control.

   B. Enforce a mandatory vacation to help offset the issue.

   C. Request a non-disclosure agreement (NDA) to address risks and concerns.

   D. Make a recommendation to change roles.

31. When an employee has been terminated, the security team should proceed to what technical action they are notified?

   A. Collect token devices and smart cards.

   B. Delete all accounts and audit the system for possible data breaches.

   C. Check the company policy to ensure the termination process was legal before changing account settings.

   D. Disable all accounts and review system access for additional charges.

32. A Security Engineer from an external partner has been hired to configure new firewall settings. When the individual arrives at the organization, what would be the proper security approach?

    A. Perform account reviews for the Security engineers to perform their tasks.

    B. Omit non-disclosure agreements from the relationship.

    C. Conduct personnel investigations and provide oversight to external business relationships.

    D. Require three forms of identification from the Security Engineer.

33. The overall goal of personnel security policies is to establish compliance for employees to meet corporate security goals. Which of the following supports the statement?

    A. Investigative Security should emphasize employee audits for compliance.

    B. Policies should require an organization to conduct preliminary checks on potential employees.

    C. Ensure all individuals are qualified for employment.

    D. Perform random job rotation duties to cross-train employees.

34. To implement privacy for physical controls, an organization must consider what potential issue?

    A. Whether the policies align with the organization's goals and privacy objectives.

    B. Does the Policy enforce investigative rights for issues outside regular working hours?

    C. Whether the company facility requires particular policies.

    D. How often criminals break privacy policies and regulations.

35. An assessor has completed a security assessment for a significant application and decides to draft a report on its outcome. During the review, he discovered several active malware programs. As part of his report, which is the best solution to present the information?

    A. Examine human threats for inducing vulnerabilities.

    B. Perform a new security assessment after the vulnerability scans are executed.

    C. Examine a new framework to address the risk.

    D. Address the malware issue and all exploitation patterns while considering vulnerable access points.

36. As a CIO, you need to develop a decision on risk and budget constraints for your organization. You receive a report that states the Single Loss Expectancy (SLE) is at $10,000. To understand the detailed procedures at why the SLE is at $10,000, what information should the IT department present?

    A. The qualitative value of the asset and what cost consideration is required to maintain critical data.

    B. Qualitative value of the risk management program and cost-benefit for the SLE.

    C. The exposure factor and asset cost consideration.

    D. The impact of the Annualized Loss Expectancy (ALE) and its quantitative value after a risk assessment.

37. After a risk assessment has been completed, an organization decides to uninstall the chat service from its network. Based on the decision, what risk decision was considered by the organization?

    A. Passed the risk onto another entity for management.

    B. Eliminated the risk through software uninstall.

    C. Based on chat service as a low priority, the risk was accepted.

    D. Avoided risk implications through removing chat service.

38. A company policy states that the business owners must take responsibility for risk and implement changes as required. During a security assessment, a business owner was notified that a critical risk was found within its data handling procedures. As the business owner, what would be the first step in investigating the issue?

    A. Investigate all shared responsibilities and assign the responsibility to appropriate business units.

    B. Notify the CIO and take appropriate action by meeting with the data custodian.

    C. Discipline the data custodian and update policies to reflect responsibilities.

    D. Considering this was an operative risk, the CIO should take full responsibility despite what the policy states, and the business owner should assist with any matters.

39. The process of selecting countermeasures should consider what security methodology?

    A. Control selection that reduces risks without audits.

    B. Has the potential to reduce risk costs associated with changing budgets.

    C. Align to security and risk vision for the governance team.

    D. Derived from a trusted source and protects the availability of assets.

40. When controls are implemented, the overall selection for the controls should consider what component within the security architect?

    A. The security framework and what steps support the implementation details.

    B. Auditing standards and accountability for the control implementation.

    C. What risks will need to be avoided by removing applications?

    D. Change Management and version control for software updates and policy configurations.

41. When new Security personnel enters the datacenter, he notices a warning sign that displays "no information sharing outside the organization boundary." What control procedure has been implemented?

    A. Deterrent Control

    B. Preventative Control

    C. Administrative awareness control

    D. Directive Control

42. **The implementation of an anti-virus solution will support what control type?**

    A. Technical and Administrative

    B. Detective

    C. Compensation

    D. Technical as it relates to Preventive and Corrective controls.

43. **Which statement best supports the overall objective for a security control assessment?**

    A. Performing an assessment may not require the tailoring of controls.

    B. Management, Operational, and Technical controls are omitted for an assessment.

    C. Organizations have flexibility in determining which and how many controls are assessed.

    D. Selecting security controls should be the responsibility of the assessor.

44. **Which one of the following statements describes the difference between a vulnerability assessment and a penetration test?**

    A. Vulnerability assessments are cost-related, and penetration tests are not.

    B. Risks for vulnerabilities are best suited for transfer, while penetration tests remove vulnerabilities.

    C. Vulnerability assessments are aimed at finding vulnerabilities, often without regard to exploitation. Penetration testing usually goes more profound, with its goal of exploiting the vulnerability.

    D. A penetration test requires acceptance, and a vulnerability test requires application access.

45. **To determine the risk valuation for a particular asset, an organization must determine what significant concept?**

    A. The market analysis for the security product being evaluated.

    B. Whether the asset is considered tangible or intangible to an organization.

    C. Whether the impact causes corporately loss.

    D. The actual value for copyrights and trademarks and their risk association.

46. **When comparing security control implementation to a continuous improvement methodology, the fundamental definition can be defined as which answer?**

    A. Planning for change controls requires sound decisions.

    B. Security checks should be implemented to avoid and differences.

    C. If the change was successful, a control assessor could make additional recommendations.

    D. All change controls should be implemented in incremental steps through the "Do" step of continuous improvement.

47. **What is the best description of an enterprise risk management framework?**

   A. Provides a disciplined and structured process that integrates information security and risk management activities.

   B. Provides an emphasis on the selection, implementation, assessment, and reference monitoring of security control.

   C. Links risk management processes at the information system level to risk management processes at other system levels.

   D. The early integration of information security requirements into the system development life cycle is the most cost-effective and efficient method for ensuring that control strategy is implemented.

48. **To accurately develop a threat model, an organization must consider what factors?**

   A. The overall software landscape and any potential risks for high-value programs.

   B. The security architect and the SDLC compliance activities are used to evaluate risk.

   C. A process by which potential threats, such as structural vulnerabilities, can be identified, enumerated, and prioritized.

   D. Attack scenarios and the current state of the security posture.

49. **During a threat assessment, a Security Engineer has discovered an attack method where a hacker can send a fake website to gain information about the corporate security posture. What level of attack should be included with the Threat Model?**

   A. Website attack where propriety information is shared.

   B. Social engineering attack that provides data about the company to employees.

   C. A phishing attack that may use social patterns to determine security access points.

   D. Threat attack that uses new vulnerabilities.

50. **To reduce threat exploitation, an enterprise may resort to what security control method?**

   A. Change the system configuration periodically.

   B. Mandate security and risk management as a single source of protection needs.

   C. Implement controls by assessing new standards.

   D. Implement regulatory control standards that continuously access employee activities and establish a framework of trust with vendors.

51. **As a Security Engineer, you have been tasked to use new technologies to help reduce risks associated with network traffic. Which of the following would you select as a tool of choice to minimize the risks?**

   A. New detection systems that screen traffic and block unauthorized system access.

   B. An intrusion detection system (IDS) provides system alerts and a packet filtering device to read traffic.

   C. An intrusive system with open firewall traffic.

D. Implement a Virtual Private Network (VPN), Virtual Land Area Network (VLAN), and Open Access to Port 23 for traffic analysis.

52. **When an organization decides to acquire shared services from a third-party source, what risks must be addressed before the acquisition becomes approved?**

    A. The current state of its baseline and auditing results for potential risks.

    B. What level of training has been completed by employees that manage their systems.

    C. Auditing standards used for the system.

    D. What level of accountability has been imposed on the users who use the system and its services.

53. **When SEMAIS decides to assess a third-party vendor, what outcome will usually be achieved?**

    A. Assurance that the organization meets SEMAIS security standards.

    B. Shared information can be gained about future risks.

    C. Service-provided solutions can be readily assessed.

    D. Privacy areas are covered for compliance.

54. **After SEMAIS has implemented new security standards, the company discovers that the security team did not address residual risks. To prevent the issue from reoccurring, what should SEMAIS consider?**

    A. Whether key objectives align with its architect.

    B. What design constraints are essential.

    C. Implementing controls to address requirement analysis.

    D. Minimum security and service level changes.

55. **The time required to respond to an incident can be best agreed upon by implementing what requirement?**

    A. Service Level Report about incident stages

    B. Service Level Agreement

    C. Service Level Incident Plan

    D. Incident Report

56. **To determine the need requirements for a security awareness program, an organization can use what resources?**

    A. Previous security violations and employee feedback on risks were discovered.

    B. CIO risk policy and employee vision for upcoming changes.

    C. Knowledge required to build an awareness program.

    D. Security incident responses received.

57. **You receive a report that states, "control "AT-1" for awareness training need to be evaluated." To comply with the requirement, what can you do as a Security Manager?**

    A. Perform a control assessment on management strategies.

    B. Develop new controls and update AT-1 to AT-2.

    C. Inspect user's training to verify what should be completed.

    D. Conduct a periodic review of the previous audit and assess AT-1 control implementation for weakness.

7. Domain 1: Security and Risk Management - Answers and Explanations

1. **B.** The CIA triad addresses confidentiality, modification of data to prevent unauthorized changes, and availability to ensure data is available when required. When users and groups need to make changes, integrity must ensure well-formed transactions occur for segregated groups (separation of duties).

2. **B.** All aspects of system design must consider the impact of Security and controls. Each control is addressed based on its confidentiality, integrity, and availability principle, affecting trade-offs and design factors.

3. **A.** Within the governance strategy, the overall objective is to view the enterprise requirements. This consists of long-range plans and functions to support the organization's risk policies and initiatives. The rest of the answers are a subset of lower tasks derived from the enterprise risk strategy.

4. **D.** Security management is designed to identify and mitigate risks for an organization. This is achieved by assessing the current environment, monitoring, training, and implementing policies. These principles ensure that risks are discovered and necessary controls are implemented for a risk management program.

5. **C.** When an organization encounters changes or events for security-related issues, they must address priorities because a data breach is a serious concern. The overall objective for this scenario is to address the data breach and implement controls to prevent it from happening in the future. Controls can be of Policy or technical changes to a system.

6. **A.** The ISO has full responsibility for implementing policies and procedures for new system changes. Any weakness can be classified as a vulnerability. His overall function is to address the organization's security needs through Policy, procedures, standards, and guidelines.

7. **A.** The data classification is done by business owners, and data backups are the responsibility of the data custodian. Data custodians are accountable for the technical control of data, including Security, scalability, configuration management, availability, accuracy, consistency, audit trail, backup and restore, technical standards, policies, and business rule implementation. Data stewards (business or data owners) are accountable for business controls, data content, and metadata management related to a set of data assets. They work with stakeholders that are impacted by data to develop definitions, standards, and data controls. Information and data owner are the same, and administrators and auditors are not governance-related roles.

8. **D.** A control framework should be consistent, measurable, standardized, comprehensive, and modular. Under consistency, organizations rely on how Security and privacy are applied. Measurable supports goals and standards and allows organizations to develop comparable solutions that are meaningful, comprehensive in addressing extensible requirements, and modular where changes can be accepted.

9. **B.** Due diligence is the action to ensure that your security policy is being enforced using procedures and standards. This is something that every good security professional should do. Due care, due concern, and due practice are not correct terms to refer to what the question is trying to define; the correct term is "due diligence." Please do not forget this for the exam. Due diligence= due detect; due care = due correct.

10. **D.** Due diligence is the action to ensure that your security policy is being enforced using procedures and standards. Due care is a corrective action imposed to correct security issues for an organization. Due diligence= due detect; due care = due correct.

11. **A.** The implementation of risk management can aid in reducing risks and maintaining compliance. Compliance relies on laws, policies, and regulations to achieve its goal. When these factors are successfully followed, the risk is minimized, and compliance is achieved.

12. **B.** Safe Harbor is a legal provision to reduce or eliminate liability as long as good faith is demonstrated. If it is met, an organization is protected from new laws.

13. **D.** Personal identifiable information poses personal challenges to security professionals (Need to Know). The assessor would violate a privacy policy using personal information for financial gain. Trademarks and Copyrights reflect proprietary information for companies. Data Diddling means data was changed. A data breach is an unauthorized movement or disclosure of sensitive information to a party, usually outside the organization, that is not authorized to have or see the information.

14. **D.** Personal identifiable information poses personal challenges to security professionals (Need to Know). The assessor would violate a privacy policy using personal information for financial gain. Trademarks and Copyrights reflect proprietary information for companies. Data Diddling means data was changed.

15. **C.** The Data Protection Directive (officially Directive 95/46/EC on the protection of individuals regarding the processing of personal data and the free movement of such data) is a European Union directive adopted in 1995, which regulates the processing of personal data within the European Union.

16. **B.** Ransomware is a type of malware that restricts access to the computer system that it infects and demands a ransom paid to the creator(s) of the malware for the restriction to be removed. Scareware is a tactic frequently used by criminals involves convincing users that a virus has infected their computer; then suggesting that they download (and pay for) fake antivirus software to remove it.

17. **A.** It is unlawful to use another person's artistic work for personal gain without a formal agreement. Any occurrence outside of this law is considered a violation of intellectual property.

18. **C.** The International Traffic in Arms Regulations (ITAR) and the Export Administration Regulations (EAR) are two important United States export control laws that affect the manufacturing, sales, and distribution of technology. The WA was designed to prevent destabilizing accumulations of arms and dual-use goods and technologies. The arrangement encourages transparency, consultation; where appropriate, national policies of restraint. Trans-border promotes transparency.

19. **A.** Privacy is defined as the rights and obligations of individuals and organizations to protect personal data. A data breach is an incident that deals with the exposure of data. When we address the misuse of personal data, privacy laws are considered—ethics and confidentiality address access control principles.

20. **D.** A data breach is the intentional or unintentional release of secure information to an untrusted environment. Privacy is defined as the rights and obligations of individuals and organizations to protect personal data. When we address the misuse of personal data, privacy laws are considered—ethics and confidentiality address access control principles. A data breach has occurred based on the scenario, and confidential (need to know) information was disclosed.

21. **A.** Trans-border data flow addresses the transmittal of data between foreign locations and applicable laws between both nations.

22. **C.** This is not one of the statements of the (ISC)² Code of Ethics. (ISC)² certified people are free to be in association with any person and any party they want. (ISC)² thinks that their certified people must have the liberty of choice in their associations. However, (ISC)² asks the certified professionals to promote the certification and understand and accept security measures; they also ask the certified people to provide competent services and be proud of their exclusive (ISC)² certified professional status.

23. **B.** Every organization must establish its code of ethics for employees to follow. An employee that on-board a company can find most of the information in the employee handbook, which should be available and disseminated to employees. The code of ethics should cover regulatory compliance for HIPPA and GLBA. Regulatory policies will change despite having a new CIO. Every ethical practice is equally essential for compliance.

24. **A.** Standards, procedures, baselines, and guidelines make up policies. Regulatory Policy is used to ensure that the organization complies with local, state, and federal laws. An example regulatory policy might state: "Because of recent changes to Texas State law, the company will now retain records of employee inventions and patents for 10 years; all email messages and any backup of such email associated with patents and inventions will be stored for one

year." Standards are much more specific than policies. Standards are tactical documents because they lay out specific steps or processes required to meet a particular requirement. As an example, a standard might set a mandatory requirement that all email communication be encrypted. Although it does specify a certain standard, it does not spell out how it is done. That is left for the procedure. Baselines are a minimum level of Security that a system, network, or device must adhere to. Baselines are usually mapped to industry standards. Guideline points to a statement in a policy or procedure by which to determine a course of action. It is a recommendation or suggestion of how things should be done. It is meant to be flexible so that it can be customized for individual situations.

25. **D.** A top-down approach is required to implement Security. Senior Management hast to buy into the security policy for an organization to be effective in managing safety. Regulatory Policy is used to ensure that the organization complies with local, state, and federal laws. An example regulatory policy might state: "Because of recent changes to Texas State law, the company will now retain records of employee inventions and patents for 10 years; all email messages and any backup of such email associated with patents and inventions will be stored for one year." Standards are much more specific than policies. Standards are tactical documents because they lay out specific steps or processes required to meet a particular requirement. As an example, a standard might set a mandatory requirement that all email communication be encrypted. Although it does specify a certain standard, it does not spell out how it is done. That is left for the procedure. Baselines are a minimum level of Security that a system, network, or device must adhere to. Baselines are usually mapped to industry standards. Guidelines point to a statement in a policy or procedure by which to determine a course of action. It is a recommendation or suggestion of how things should be done. It is meant to be flexible so it can be customized for individual situations.

26. **C.** It is not a requirement for the BCP coordinator to move forward with the plan. This is the function of senior management in which they provide the support to move forward with the project.

27. **A.** A business impact analysis (BIA) predicts the consequences of disrupting a business function and process and gathers information needed to develop recovery strategies. If a change has occurred concerning critical devices, the BIA must be reevaluated for changes.

28. **C.** The time required to repair an asset should be of short duration. The time between failures should be a much longer duration. The Mean Time to Repair (MTTR) should be more concise than a Mean Time Between Failure (MTBF). Example: A server that fails every 10 minutes or 10 hours, and the repair time is 10 minutes or 10 hours. The best combination: MTBF 10 hours and MTTR 10 Minutes.

29. **C.** Employee screening is designed to investigate a potential employee's background for credit, education, social security number (SSN), prior employment, and drug offenses. To correct the issue requires a formal policy that screens all employees before onboarding. Screening one employee will not fix the problem.

30. **A.** Explaining to the employee that separation of duties and least privileges are enforced to minimize security risks. Under normal circumstances, the minor rights that a person has reduced risks. By separating user accounts and privileges, an organization can control conflict of interest, wrongdoings and enforce ethics among employees.

31. **D.** When an employee has been terminated, an organization needs to review their account and disable the account access. This procedure ensures that proprietary information and any wrongdoings are viewed for criminal action. Deleting the account once notified removes all evidence. Collection and policy reviews are administrative actions. Disable and deleting accounts is technical action.

32. **C.** For an effective relationship with external partners, agreements need to be established on how their employees will perform tasks, and access to background data should also be discussed. Background data consist of employee identification, work agreements, and period of performance.

33. **B.** To achieve compliance within personnel security, an organization must consider whether policies are designed to address background checks and investigations. The policies are intended to standardize practices for maintaining compliance.

34. A. An organization's privacy can exist beyond regular working hours if information sharing has been used. A company privacy objective should be well developed and addressed within its Policy and procedures.

35. D. As a good practice through Information Risk Management, it is best to access threats and vulnerabilities for potential issues. Based on this scenario, the assessment report must address vulnerabilities and threat exploitation for proper reporting. The process of vulnerability scans is not required since the assessment is within its reporting stage. Vulnerability scans are conducted during the evaluation. All human considerations and impacts are considered within the threat analysis.

36. C. Part of Risk Analysis is to determine Qualitative (Value) and Quantitative (Cost) for a risk-based decision. The SLE is derived by examining the EF (Exposure Factor) and AV (Asset Value). The CIO only needs the calculation for the SLE. The ALE is derived later in the risk analysis process (SLE * ARO = ALE)

37. D. When a risk determination has to be made, an organization can transfer (buy insurance), mitigate (decrease or reduce the risk exposure), accept (a risk that is low in impact does not cause much harm), or avoid (remove the activity that is causing the risk).

38. B. The CIO dictates through policies on risk responsibility. Some organizations have a shared responsibility, and it is outlined within the Policy and procedures.

39. D. Countermeasure should always support the CIA triad. The CIA triad should be audited and derived from a trusted source such as the NIST 800-53 control selection.

40. D. The implementation of controls requires sound knowledge of how the changes will affect the network environment. The changes will require new policy updates and configuration changes that may cause the security architect to change. A security framework is established before any control implementation. Auditing standards are not a significant factor unless an audit is performed, but audit ability is an essential factor determining whether the control can be tested.

41. A. Deterrent control is intended to discourage a potential attacker. A directive control is a mandatory control that has been placed due to regulations. A deterrent control is anything designed to warn a would-be attacker that they should not attack. This could be a posted warning that they will fully be prosecuted of the law, locks on doors, barricades, lighting, or anything that can delay or discourage an attack. Preventive control is to stop something from happening. These can include locked doors that keep intruders out, user training on potential harm (to keep them vigilant and alert), or even biometric devices and guards that deny access until authentication has occurred. The purpose of a detective control is to uncover a violation.

42. D. A preventive control is to stop something from happening. These can include locked doors that keep intruders out, user training on potential harm (to keep them vigilant and alert), or even biometric devices and guards that deny access until authentication has occurred. The purpose of a detective control is to uncover a violation. Anti-virus programs are technical controls that prevent (blocking) and correct (remove).

43. C. Security control assessments provide a line of defense in knowing the strengths and weaknesses of an organization's information system. Security controls assessment determines whether security controls in an information system are operating as intended.

44. C. Securities assessments and vulnerabilities reviews aim to find vulnerabilities, often without exploiting them and getting in. Thus, penetration testing usually goes more profound, seeking to take over systems, use and steal data. At the same time, security and vulnerability assessments are broader, involving looking for security flaws. These assessments involve policy and procedure reviews, which are usually not included in penetration testing.

45. B. A tangible asset is anything that can be seen and has a physical presence, such as cash, property, plant, and machinery or investments. On the other hand, intangible assets cannot be seen, such as the goodwill of a company, trademark, and intellectual property rights.

46. **C.** The Plan–Do–Check–Act (PDCA) cycle is a four-step model for implementing change. Just as a circle has no end, the PDCA cycle should be repeated for continuous improvement. The "Do" stage requires small incremental changes, so risks will not occur. Plan–Do–Check–Act Procedure: "Plan" recognizes an opportunity and plans a difference for security controls. "Do" test the change and carry out a small-scale for control implementation. "Check" reviews the test, analyzes the results, and identifies what you have learned. "Act" based on what you learned in the study step. If the change did not work, go through the cycle again with a different plan. If you were successful, incorporate what you learned from the test into more sweeping changes. Use what you learned to plan new improvements; begin the cycle again.

47. **A.** A Risk Management Framework provides a disciplined and structured process that integrates information security and risk management activities through design, implementation, and continuous monitoring for improvement. For risk management to succeed at all levels of the organization, the organization must have a consistent and practical approach to risk management applied to all risk management processes and procedures - which is the goal of a risk management framework. http://csrc.nist.gov/publications/nistpubs/800-37-rev1/sp800-37-rev1-final.pdf

48. **C.** Security threat modeling, or threat modeling, is a process of assessing and documenting a system's security risks. Security threat modeling enables you to understand a system's threat profile by examining it through the eyes of your potential foes. With techniques such as entry point identification, privilege boundaries, and threat trees, you can identify strategies to mitigate potential threats to your system. Your security threat modeling efforts also enable your team to justify security features within a system or security practices for using the system to protect your corporate asset.

49. **C.** Phishing is a form of social engineering. Phishing attacks use email or malicious websites to solicit personal information by posing as a trustworthy organization. For example, an attacker may send an email seemingly from a reputable credit card company or financial institution that requests account information, often suggesting a problem. When users respond with the requested information, attackers can use it to gain access to the accounts.

50. **D.** To reduce a threat's ability to exploit a system, an organization must ensure controls are implemented and regularly access employees, systems, and operations for weaknesses. Making system changes can induce threats, especially after the system has been tuned and evaluated for weaknesses. New standards are sometimes not the best solution.

51. **B.** Any technology used should screen traffic, block unwanted traffic, and offer increased Security for system access. An intrusion detection system will generate alerts but will not block traffic like an intrusion prevention system. Opening firewall and ports are much more of a security risk.

52. **A.** Before acquiring shared service, it is essential to understand the state of an organization's system audits and baseline status. Risks and security issues can affect your organization as well. Human and personnel security issues are evaluated through audits.

53. **A.** Evaluating a third-party service can be best achieved through an assessment, review, or inspection.

54. **C.** During the system design, SEMAIS must address all security requirements by providing information about its system environment. The Security Architect can gather this information to ensure that the security and protection needs are addressed.

55. **B.** A Service Level Agreement is an important document used to define the level of a service between a service provider and their customer. The agreement is generally expressed in simple language so that the customer can clearly understand it. The document may also include more technical terms for defining the service. The Service Level Agreement is often part of a more comprehensive service contract.

56. **A.** Protection for security training should mirror employee risks such as violations and incidents. The assessment should also focus on the organization's vision. An employee vision does not support awareness training.

57. **D.** Periodic reviews are conducted for security training for needs and training improvement. Any control that addresses the requirement must be assessed.

8. Domain 2: Asset Security - Questions

1. **Within a security control framework, a Security Engineer has developed a minimum set of controls to deploy among all assets. What would be the description for this control implementation?**

   A. A fundamental security baseline for compliance.

   B. Tailored Security to situational needs.

   C. Security standards that support configuration controls.

   D. Data and asset security standards.

2. **Which of the following would least likely support management's baseline security standard?**

   A. Which enterprise component can be protected?

   B. SLA that addresses a vendor's risk profile.

   C. What security level should be applied?

   D. Should the same baseline be deployed enterprise-wide?

3. **Which one of the following would serve as the best reference for developing a security baseline?**

   A. Multiple control frameworks.

   B. A tailored framework designed to assess data security.

   C. Organization security checklist.

   D. ISO 27002 standard.

4. **Baseline deployments are designed to support what specific resources?**

   A. Audit and accountability standards.

   B. Configuration reports that discuss change specifications.

   C. Needs protection and resources for compliance.

   D. Those are designed within the safeguard requirements that align with the system.

5. **When reviewing the data profile for information saved to a company shared location, the user notices that every document has the following label: "This critical information is mandated by law (HIPAA, GLBA) or required by private contract." What would be the best description for this marking?**

   A. A compliance standard that outlines risk and protection of data.

   B. A security term that describes the protection need for the information.

   C. The need for protection as it relates to availability.

   D. Loss of the confidentiality or integrity of the information could cause harm to individuals.

6. When data is described based on its impact on business operations, it can best describe what term?

    A. Reputation Risk: Loss of data will cause significant damage.

    B. Data confidentiality is required by law, Policy, or contractual obligation.

    C. Classifying Data According to Protection Needs.

    D. Classifying Data According to Availability Needs.

7. What specific guidance can be used to describe the limitations for personal data collection?

    A. (ISC)² Code of Ethics

    B. HIPAA

    C. OECD Privacy Principles

    D. European Union (EU) Safe Harbor Act

8. As a Privacy Officer, you want to integrate security controls that support the collection of personal data. After reviewing several references, you decide to use the OECD Privacy Principle. Which principle below supports your decision?

    A. Data Quality Principle

    B. Purpose Specification Principle

    C. Use Limitation Principle

    D. Collection Limitation Principle

9. When collecting private data, why must organizations inform the user of such action?

    A. As an act of Policy in following the Use Limitation principle.

    B. To develop a general policy of openness.

    C. As a method to maintain data quality.

    D. To gain consent for approval and use of distribution.

10. The privacy officer has just instituted a new policy that data must be deleted after use. An employee within the Human Resource department violates the Policy a week after the CEO approved the Policy. The corporate guidelines did not address the appropriate action for violating the Policy. What would be an excellent follow-up action for the company to consider?

    A. Remove and transparency from the current policies.

    B. Mandate the enforcement of the Organization for Economic Cooperation and Development (OECD) Policy and procedures.

    C. Have the organization complete enterprise-wide training on privacy and counsel the employee.

    D. Research new data protection strategies for the organization.

11. A Security Engineer has developed a control to support data in transit over a secured communication path. The protocols selected require confidentiality for user's message data routed between gateways and host devices. What technology has the Security Engineered used?

   A. End-user tunneling over unencrypted communication paths.

   B. Link Encryption.

   C. End-to-End encryption.

   D. Cryptography and packet transfer.

12. A Senior manager has expressed concerns over technical security controls and privacy for data in transit. The security engineer decided to produce a report to demonstrate how the issue may affect the company's reputation; and solution standards that the organization can deploy. To make the communication paths more secure, which of the following aligns with a solution standard that the security engineer could deploy.

   A. Encryption of data.

   B. Transparent routing of technical data.

   C. Traffic confidentiality and availability.

   D. End security for data breaches.

13. When employing security controls based on end-to-end encryption, what should be considered?

   A. Whether a link session will terminate.

   B. What data controls should be implemented to support Security.

   C. Whether the data in transit can remain confidential.

   D. New attacks could occur.

14. When developing countermeasures to deploy against data mining, what should an organization consider?

   A. The protection needs and how to link encryption mirrors end-to-end traffic.

   B. Transparent routing of data.

   C. Whether inference attacks will occur.

   D. Whether a link session will terminate.

15. When data has been classified with privacy controls, what role is responsible for ensuring the updated rules?

   A. Privacy Officer

   B. Data Owner

   C. Security Assessor

   D. Data Custodian

16. **What is the fundamental relationship between a privacy officer and a data owner?**

    A. They ensure that all private data at rest can be protected with the same classification scheme.

    B. To ensure the disclosure or alteration of data remains protected.

    C. Removable media can be stored properly.

    D. To determine how much data will be collected.

17. **A data owner has opted to change the security controls for all health information. The control will specify transfer methods and classification scheme changes. As it relates to privacy, what should the organization consider for the change?**

    A. The protection needs and how to link encryption mirrors end-to-end traffic.

    B. How much will data be collected during the process?

    C. Testing methods used to test the data and privacy standards the data owner considered.

    D. OECD guidelines and policies.

18. **When privacy and information collection are addressed for an organization, what would be considered a principle to follow?**

    A. Public Health data should be disclosed in a manner that supports risk-based decisions.

    B. Restrictions should mirror privacy laws that are aligned with the user's responsibility.

    C. The type and information collected should set limitations for the owner of the personal data.

    D. Health information collected should align to reasonable, acceptable use.

19. **The human resource department has emailed all employees concerning record updates and data recall based on race, sex, and home address. As it relates to privacy, what has HR collected?**

    A. Privacy information that supports the collection of data.

    B. Personal Identifiable Information (PII).

    C. Standard employee profile information.

    D. Disclosure information for employee tracking.

20. **The human resource department has emailed all employees concerning records updates and data recall based on race, sex, and home address. The email specified that each employee's data would not be shared with outside vendors. Which answer is the best fundamental privacy rule that has been applied?**

    A. Collection of information based on reasonable intentions.

    B. Personal limitations.

    C. Disclosure of personal data with limitations.

    D. Employee data collection standards.

21. **What is the fundamental rule for information collection of personal data?**

    A. Protect the disclosure and limit owners to information dissemination.

    B. Transfer the data with security control.

    C. Allow controls to become auditable.

    D. Explain how the information will be used and for what specific purpose.

22. **A Privacy Officer has decided to draft a policy that would address residual data after purging or clearing files. What term describes this policy action?**

    A. Storage Allocation

    B. Data Diddling

    C. Data Remanence

    D. Media Destruction

23. **An organization has developed a privacy control that requires technicians to erase by overwriting data by zero writing. What action has been performed?**

    A. New control implementation for data destruction.

    B. The technician has cleared the information to protect privacy.

    C. Data disposal.

    D. Rendered the media unusable.

24. **A system has been configured with controls that require data to be degaussed. What other specific term could describe this concept?**

    A. Purging of data records.

    B. Overwriting zero data.

    C. Write function.

    D. Destroying physical evidence.

25. **What three countermeasures are used to address data remanence?**

    A. Zero write, overwrite data as unusable, and destruction.

    B. Clearing, Destroying, and write execution.

    C. Disposal, Destruction, and disk save.

    D. Disposal, Zero Write, and recovery.

26. **Which of the following is the best example to describe data ownership of assets?**

    A. Maintain data set Security.

    B. A clearly defined role.

    C. Understand the information cost and what impact it has on the organization.

    D. Instill data accountability.

27. **A new employee has joined an organization and has been reading through the privacy regulations to determine how his role supports the organization when securing and transmitting data. The best example of this process can be described as what specific action?**

    A. Maintaining data set Security.

    B. Privacy control and implementation for use.

    C. Employee roles.

    D. Understanding data management policies.

28. **What is the benefit of encrypting data on end-user devices (EUDs)?**

    A. To ensure encrypted data can be read from the drive.

    B. To protect the user from performing acts of misuse, violations of disclosure, or alteration.

    C. To operate with a Data Rest Environment.

    D. Assure compliant practices are developed.

29. **Which role supports the proper use for media removal?**

    A. Store the media in a disclosed location to prevent tampering.

    B. Utility file encryption software to protect the data.

    C. Integrate a password management strategy that requires complex character assignments.

    D. Upgrade to self-encrypting universal serial bus (USB) devices.

30. **SEMAIS has installed a shared server for its clients. Some of the clients are complaining that sensitive documents need to be guarded. The security team has decided to address the issue by integrating new technologies. Which technology would be most appropriate?**

    A. A geographical software program that encrypts files for all the users on the same shared source.

    B. Utilize Link and End-to-End technology.

    C. Assess various baseline standards to see which supports the business goal.

    D. Upgrade to Advanced Encryption Standard (AES) as a standard file encryption software resource.

31. **How does an application authenticate a user with a password hash?**

    A. By utilizing compliant encrypting tools.

    B. Incorporating a secure software management tool.

    C. By encrypting the one-way function through secure links.

    D. By performing the hashing operation on the password and compares the resulting hashed value with the password, the hash is stored.

32. **To build an effective data retention policy, an organization should consider what process?**

    A. Describe data and its overuse based on security practices.

    B. Data destruction and records management.

    C. Continuous monitoring based on access control standards.

    D. Compliance and vulnerabilities.

33. **John has discovered that his organization's data retention policy does not include handling data on USB drives. As a security steward, what action should he consider?**

    A. The disposal and spillage control may occur due to negligence or breaches.

    B. Whether the record retention policy address storage of information external to computers.

    C. Crucial documentation of record changes.

    D. USB encryption and its policy to store classified data.

34. **The Chief Information Security Officer (CISO) has designated you to develop a data retention policy supporting data storage for financial reports. What should you least consider about the procedure?**

    A. Whether the storage capability imposes risk on the organization.

    B. What business needs to impact the capability of drafting the policy.

    C. Whether information sharing has been addressed with the storage of information.

    D. The cost analysis for data loss and prevention of data breaches during transporting data.

35. **What is a realistic retention period for data?**

    A. 90 days from the initial storage period.

    B. Length of an organization's legal requirements.

    C. Five years from the first breach.

    D. Length of organization business operations and compliance laws.

36. When an organization's data retention policy addresses safe handling of classified information, what areas of risk should be analyzed to determine impact?

   A.   The risks associated with data loss and its value.

   B.   The cost of destruction and its impact.

   C.   Disposal of critical data and its impact on policy development.

   D.   The estimated benefit of data loss.

37. An organization has implemented shared services to store federal tax information for all its clients. The shared location has been encrypted to prevent data spillage and breaches. In terms of privacy, what are some of the safeguards the company has integrated?

   A.   Described the purpose(s) for which PII is collected, used, maintained, and shared in its privacy notices.

   B.   Established linkage and relationship between privacy and security controls for purposes of enforcing respective privacy and security requirements.

   C.   Developed policies and procedures that minimize the use of PII.

   D.   Developed a strategic organizational privacy plan for implementing applicable privacy policies and procedures.

38. Which of the following represents a formal protection requirement for personal information?

   A.   The process of destroying data after it's used for legal reasons.

   B.   Having data accessible to different CISOs.

   C.   Focus on the European Union (EU) policy for trans-border regulations.

   D.   Following the OECD guidelines for PII.

39. Which of the following addresses the protection of privacy for personal information?

   A.   Kept available until legal errors occur.

   B.   Passing of information through Safe Harbor without legal restrictions.

   C.   Establishing contacts between exporters and importers in the same nation.

   D.   Accurate and updated information that is securely protected within computer boundaries.

40. The Data Protection Directive (officially Directive 95/46/EC) on the protection of individuals with regards to the processing of personal data and the free movement of such data) is a European Union directive. Although it is a European directive, which of the following could be adopted for United States standards?

   A.   Data may be processed when processing is necessary for compliance with a legal obligation.

   B.   Security efforts must be made not to prevent the loss of collected information that the U.S. owns.

   C.   Individuals must have the option to opt-out of the collection and forward transfer of the data to no parties.

   D.   Individuals must be informed that their data is being collected and about how it will be used.

41. **What is the best definition of the EU Safe Harbor Act?**

    A. It protects the US from legal issues abroad when data privacy has been addressed.

    B. It is a policy that governs the EU privacy standards.

    C. US-EU Safe Harbor is a streamlined process for US companies to comply with the EU Directive 95/46/EC to protect personal data.

    D. The Safe Harbor Principles are designed to control US accidental information disclosure or data loss.

42. **When data privacy contains legal practices that restrict data sharing, a security assessor must consider what fundamental standard?**

    A. Some user information is not shareable, so the controls for privacy may be tailored to meet the control framework for the organization.

    B. Resources may be limited for the testing.

    C. Private data may be classified as Top Secret.

    D. Information systems are in a shared location that poses threats.

43. **An assessor has decided to tailor privacy controls for all assets that reside in a protected boundary. After reviewing the current control standards, the assessor determines that the tailoring for the controls needs to change. What effect does this have on the security assessment for the assets?**

    A. The assessment for assets may change, and the privacy controls will require adjustments.

    B. The privacy regulations will need a review.

    C. The assessment will cost more to complete.

    D. The period for the assessment will probably change.

44. **As a Security Consultant, you are tasked with assessing a federal system for your organization. Which of answer would provide measurements and standards for a federal Information Security program?**

    A. NIST 800 Series and its Computer Security Division standards

    B. ISO 2700 Series

    C. Risk Management Framework (RMF)

    D. National Checklist Program (NCP)

45. **Which is the best definition for Critical Infrastructure Cybersecurity?**

    A. The Framework is a living document and cannot be changed due to regulatory standards.

    B. The Framework focuses on using business drivers to guide cybersecurity activities and considering cybersecurity risks as part of the organization's risk management processes.

    C. It protects nuclear plants from a disaster and focuses more efforts on risk management.

    D. It is mandated by congressional approval for nuclear facilities and power plants.

9. Domain 2: Asset Security - Answers and Explanations

1. **A.** A baseline security provides the minimum level of security requirements for an asset. The security level depends on the organization's control framework and security guidelines.

2. **B.** A baseline security standard should address the following: Enterprise assets to be protected by the baseline, deployment of one or more baselines, security level of baseline, and control determination for the baseline.

3. **C.** An organization's internal policies and checklists are the best resources for developing a baseline. ISO 27002 can be used, but there are some flexibility requirements.

4. **D.** The deployment of baselines is designed to meet safeguard requirements for a system-relevant control.

5. **A.** Compliance Risk: Protection of data is mandated by law HIPAA or required by private contract (e.g., non-disclosure agreements). Reputation Risk: Loss of confidentiality or integrity will cause significant damage to SEMAIS reputation. For example, loss of social security numbers or defacement of the SEMAIS website would likely be a news item in the media.

6. **C.** Data can be classified either in terms of its need for protection (e.g., Sensitive Data) or its need for availability (e.g., Critical Data). The protection need is determined by evaluating the impact of confidentiality, integrity, and availability. Each area requires administrative, technical, or operational reviews to finalize the effect; the protection standard is determined for the organization. A Data Classification Program is a significant first step to building a secure organization. Data may be classified as public, internal, confidential (or highly confidential), restricted, regulatory, or Top Secret.

7. **C.** Internationally, the OECD Privacy Principles provide the most commonly used privacy framework. They are reflected in existing and emerging privacy and data protection laws; serve as the basis for creating leading practice privacy programs and different principles.

8. **D.** With the Collection Limitation Principle, there should be limits to collecting personal data; any such data should be obtained by lawful and fair means, where appropriate, with the knowledge or consent of the data subject. http://oecdprivacy.org/#collection

9. **D.** The data subject must have proper and legal knowledge of personal data and its use. http://oecdprivacy.org/#collection

10. **C.** The appropriate action is to have training for all employees and counsel the employee to violate the privacy regulations. Since no action was stipulated about employee disciplining for a privacy violation, the company can counsel the employee. Using OECD would not support the issue since OECD is guidance and not an internal policy for the organization.

11. **C.** Users use end-to-end encryption, but only the data payload is encrypted. End-to-end encryption is the most secure way to communicate privately and securely online. By encrypting messages at both ends of a conversation, end-to-end encryption prevents anyone in the middle from reading private communications. Service providers use link encryption, and it provides encryption to headers, trailers, addresses, and routing data. The communication path is encrypted (confidentiality), and packets are transferred for both link and end-to-end encryption.

12. **A.** The transfer of confidential information through routing channels requires encryption. This is a technical security control, so the technology is focused on a technical relationship for confidentiality. Confidentiality refers to protecting information from being accessed by unauthorized parties. A failure to maintain confidentiality means that someone who should not have data access (privacy) has obtained a permit through intentional behavior or accident. Such a failure of confidentiality, commonly known as a breach, typically cannot be remedied.

13. **C.** Data in transit should remain in a stable state. When the data is encrypted, it should stay in the same format until decrypted.

14. C. Traffic confidentiality hides addressing information when transmitting data, which prevents an inference attack. An inference attack is a data mining technique performed by analyzing data to gain knowledge about a subject or database illegitimately.

15. B. The data owner has full responsibility for updating controls. The privacy officer's role is to enforce the policies and procedures for privacy. Data custodians are accountable for the technical control of data, including security, scalability, configuration management, availability, accuracy, consistency, audit trail, backup and restore, technical standards, policies, and business rule implementation. A security assessor's role is to evaluate security controls.

16. A. A data owner and privacy officer ensures that sensitive data is collected and managed for a system with specific controls.

17. C. When data controls are changed, the data owner must ensure the changes are transparent and do not affect operations.

18. D. Individually identifiable health information should be collected, used, and disclosed only to the extent necessary to accomplish a specified purpose(s) and never to discriminate inappropriately. Reasonable use of data provides a guide to good data service as with governing laws such as HIPPA.

19. B. Personal information is defined as recorded information about an identifiable individual including, but not limited to the individual's name, home or business address or home or business telephone number, the individual's race, national or ethnic origin, color, or religious or political beliefs or associations the individual's age, sex, marital status or family status, an identifying number, symbol or other particular assigned to the individual.

20. C. Disclose means to release, transmit, reveal, expose, show, provide copies of, tell the contents of, or intentionally or unintentionally give personal information to someone by any means. Disclose includes the oral transmission of information by telephone or in-person, provision of personal information on paper, facsimile copy, or any other format and electronic communication through electronic mail, data transfer, or the Internet.

21. D. When personal information is collected about an individual, employees must tell the individual the reason(s) the personal data is needed, how their personal information will be used, their options regarding the provision of the personal information, consequences of not providing it, including any limitations on services that may result, and contact information of a person who can answer their questions about the collection of their knowledge.

22. C. Data remanence is used to describe the remnants of data left on a machine such as a computer after the data has been deleted or erased. Not all data erasure methods will permanently delete data. This data will leave traces (i.e., the data remanence) on the machine in question that allows specific software programs to recover.

23. B. Clearing is defined as a level of sanitization that renders media unreadable through normal means. The clearing is typically accomplished through an overwriting process that replaces actual data with zeros or random characters. Clearing prevents data from being recovered using standard disk and file recovery utilities. Disposal is defined as the act of discarding media with no other sanitization considerations. Destroying is defined as rendering media unusable.

24. A. Purging is defined as a more advanced level of sanitization that renders media unreadable even through an advanced laboratory attack.

25. A. Clearing is defined as a level of sanitization that renders media unreadable through normal means. The clearing is typically accomplished through an overwriting process that replaces actual data with zeros or random characters. Clearing prevents data from being recovered using standard disk and file recovery utilities. Disposal is defined as the act of discarding media with no other sanitization considerations. Destroying (Destruction) is defined as rendering media unusable. Purging consists of using specialized utilities that repeatedly overwrite data.

26. C. Data ownership consists of understanding replacement costs and the impact information has on an organization. Maintaining data set security is a data custodianship duty, and accountability is shared for all roles of data responsibilities.

27. **D.** Data Management is an administrative process by which the required data is acquired, validated, stored, protected, and processed. Its accessibility, reliability, and timeliness are ensured to satisfy the needs of the data users. The data management policy contains defined roles and responsibilities.

28. **B.** The purpose of encryption is to ensure confidentiality is achieved. The acts of misuse from unauthorized users can be prevented by encrypting data and disclosing sensitive data.

29. **C.** The use of a complex password increases the difficulty and guessing for the character assignments. The complexity should be a minimum of 8 characters.

30. **A.** The purpose of encrypting files is to create a safe transfer of data among the users. The use of a file encryption software program will help to save the data within a geographical location.

31. **D.** When the application receives a username and password from a user, it performs the hashing operation on the password. It compares the resulting hashed value with the password hash stored in the database for the user. If the two hashes are an exact match, the user provided a valid username and password. The benefit of hashing is that the application never needs to store the clear text password. It holds only the hashed value.

32. **B.** A data retention policy should address destruction methods and schedules. The policy should consider model business strategies and procedures to address the proper destruction of records.

33. **A.** A data retention policy should address hardware, software, and media devices. A USB drive that retains sensitive data should be handled with care to avoid data breaches.

34. **D.** The least important aspect of the data retention policy is cost analysis. The impact of cost analysis is concerned with a risk assessment. The focus of the policy is to ensure all the functional areas such as storage, influence, and sharing capability has been addressed.

35. **B.** The retention of data can serve as a legal artifact in court. Organizations should establish a period to ensure legal responsibilities are covered.

36. **A.** The value of the data loss poses affects a risk assessment. When an organization performs a risk assessment, it must consider quantitative and qualitative analysis. There is no benefit to data loss; **it's** more of qualitative loss to an organization. The cost of destruction and impact toward policy development is a non-factor for risk assessment.

37. **B.** The purpose of encrypting a shared location is to establish a link between security controls and privacy requirements. The concept of policy development addresses answers A, C, and D. The creation of those policies sets administrative standards. Creating a PII framework along with security controls are technical aspects of controlling spillage and breaches.

38. **A.** All organizations enforce privacy safeguards based on destroying the data after its purpose and use. The EU and OECD apply as a guideline to follow, and organizations must follow destruction policies to become legally sound in privacy laws.

39. **D.** To protect privacy, an organization must secure the data within all its computer boundaries. This prevents spillage and breaches from occurring. The practice of exporting and importing affects areas worldwide. Answers A and B do not protect the privacy of information.

40. **B.** The data subject has the right to be informed when his data is being processed. The controller must provide his name and address, the purpose of processing, the recipients of the data, and all other information required to ensure the processing is fair. 1) Notice that individuals must be informed that their data is being collected and how it will be used. 2) Choice - individuals must have the option to opt-out of the collection and forward transfer of the data to third parties. 3) Onward Transfer - transfer of data to third parties may only occur to other organizations that follow adequate data protection principles. 4) Security - reasonable efforts must be made to prevent the loss of collected information. 5) Integrity - data must be relevant and reliable for the purpose it was collected for. 6) Access - individuals must access information about them and correct or delete it if inaccurate. 7) Enforcement - there must be effective means of enforcing these rules.

41. **C.** The data subject has the right to be informed when his data is being processed. The controller must provide his name and address, the purpose of processing, the recipients of the data, and all other information required to ensure the processing is fair. The data subject has the right to be informed when his data is being processed. The controller must provide his name and address, the purpose of processing, the recipients of the data, and all other information required to ensure the processing is fair. 1) Notice that individuals must be informed that their data is being collected and how it will be used. 2) Choice - individuals must have the option to opt-out of the collection and forward transfer of the data to third parties. 3) Onward Transfer - transfer of data to third parties may only occur to other organizations that follow adequate data protection principles. 4) Security - reasonable efforts must be made to prevent the loss of collected information. 5) Integrity - data must be relevant and reliable for the purpose it was collected for. 6) Access - individuals must access information about them and correct or delete it if inaccurate. 7) Enforcement - there must be effective means of enforcing these rules.

42. **C.** Tailoring of controls is needed because the baseline assignments include some assumptions that may limit the applicability or effectiveness of rules, as follows: Information systems are located in physical facilities, user information is relatively persistent, information systems are multi-user, some user information is not shareable, information systems exist in networked environments, systems are general-purpose, resources exist to implement controls.

43. **A.** The effect of changing the assessment means that specific controls will have to be assessed while others will not require an evaluation. The cost and time associated with the review are non-factor. The overall objective is to determine what controls should be tested and the procedures to complete the evaluation.

44. **A.** The Computer Security Division (CSD), a component of NIST's Information Technology Laboratory (ITL), provides standards and technology to protect information systems against threats to the confidentiality, integrity, and availability of information and services. The RMF is a component of the NIST 800 series.

45. **B.** The Framework focuses on using business drivers to guide cybersecurity activities and considering cybersecurity risks as part of the organization's risk management processes. The Framework consists of three parts: The Framework Core, the Framework Profile, and the Framework Implementation Tiers.

10. Domain 3: Security Architecture and Engineering - Questions

1. When describing the specification requirements for a non-(public key infrastructure) PKI key management system, which of the following should Senior Management consider?

    A. Creation and Validated

    B. Handled and Monitoring

    C. Expiration and Non-use

    D. Authorization and PKI

2. Which of the following is considered a management function?

    A. Key usage

    B. Recovery Planning

    C. Recovery Failures

    D. Key Creation

3. What is a model for cryptanalysis which assumes that the attacker can choose random plaintexts to be encrypted and obtain the corresponding ciphertexts?

    A. Ciphertext-only attack

    B. Known-plaintext attack

    C. Chosen-plaintext attack

    D. Chosen-ciphertext attack

4. Understanding the foundational security concepts, principles, and best practices and how those concepts, regulations, and techniques can be seamlessly applied to and integrated within a comprehensive system engineering effort is essential for organizations desiring to fundamentally increase the trustworthiness and resiliency of the systems they deploy in support of mission/business operations. What area of security would support this statement?

    A. System security implementation based on risk frameworks and custom design principles.

    B. Control security assessment and implementation for security.

    C. Engineering of a security lifecycle and identifying vulnerabilities in a system operating environment.

    D. Not assessing susceptibility to threats in the project.

5. Based on the principles for Security Engineering, which would demonstrate the development and acquisition for system development?

    A. Establish a security policy that supports the engineering lifecycle.

    B. Provide assurance practices that reduce vulnerabilities.

C. Integrate security with network structure in mind.

D. Review most minor privilege requirements for all applications and infrastructure change management strategies.

6. **During the system development process, a Security Engineer has decided to examine the detailed design plan based on the requirements. After reviewing the detailed design, the Security Engineer has discovered significant flaws that will cause the project to fail. Which would least likely occur based on the design flaw?**

   A. The requirements will be re-evaluated to determine whether the initial plan was correct.

   B. The information system security engineer will analyze design constraints.

   C. The information system security engineer will trace system security requirements.

   D. The final detailed security design will examine interface specifications that provide enough information for acquisition.

7. **As a Security Engineer, you may be tasked to support audits and continuous monitoring for security-related functions. Which answer best describes this fundamental task for a Security Engineer?**

   A. Transform security requirements into specifications.

   B. Generate an impact assessment for activities via initializing a plan of action.

   C. Perform certification and accreditation for the system security posture.

   D. Maintain operations through inspections and audits.

8. **When a security engineer performs a security validation of a system, which of the following would define the task achieved by the Security Engineer?**

   A. Conducting a security validation to determine whether the system protections conform to stakeholder security requirements.

   B. Reduced risk to an acceptable level.

   C. Implement least privileged access to the environment.

   D. Disposal of IT lifecycle requirements.

9. **When designing memory protection for malware, an organization should consider what common practice?**

   A. Address specification and user virtual memory allocation for resources.

   B. Functional access control policies can block unwanted programs from attacking critical resources.

   C. Common approach used by OWASP that stipulates memory protection.

   D. Virtual and Secondary memory allocation.

10. **A Security Consultant has identified a need to redesign a current security approach due to risks being identified. A common approach to improving the current security for the organization would require which methodology?**

    A. A service strategy that implements ITIL through service transition.

B. The Zachman framework.

C. A management system and architecture that addresses service design.

D. The Open Group Architecture Framework (TOGAF)

11. When setting a security policy, a Security Analyst has noticed that the event logs are triggered during the system boot-up sequence. The logs further show that normal system status was achieved after all the boot sequence events, and indicators show each process state to maintain security. Which security model supports this concept?

A. Multi-level models exist through various changes.

B. A transition that state machine models guide.

C. Non-interference models that address the separation of duties between upper and lower security changes.

D. Information flow control model.

12. A software program that operates at a top-secret level cannot involve information from a lower security level during events. This is developed to ensure no conflict for critical process control within the system's memory during data exchange, and information sharing is restricted between security boundaries. Based on the information provided, which best describes this security concept?

A. The concept of interference between two separate groups of processes.

B. Biba security model for integrity.

C. Separation of duties.

D. Clark Wilson Model.

13. An organization has decided to use multiple security standards for its operations. Within each system, numerous classification schemes operate within different security levels. What model represents this concept?

A. Bell-LaPadula.

B. Biba when selecting mandatory access standards.

C. Multi-level security modes of integrity.

D. Covert Channel Analysis.

14. A Security consultant has decided to examine the clearances and classification scheme used for an organization's privilege. He notices that several user's classification access and clearances are expiring within 90 days after reviewing the data. To address this issue to the CIO, what methodology should the Security Engineer discuss?

A. Multi-level security modes of integrity.

B. Multi-level Security Policy.

C. Separation of duties.

D. The concept of interference between two separate groups of processes.

15. One of the most effective access control mechanisms is to restrict users from using information. Which of the following best supports this concept?

    A. Biba labeling for integrity.

    B. Clark Wilson separation of duties.

    C. Imposing sensitivity labels.

    D. Data Hiding.

16. When a computer or network component fails, and the computer or the network continues to function, it is called a fault-tolerant system. For fault tolerance to operate, the system must be capable of detecting that a fault has occurred and not enter an insecure state of operation. This concept best describes what security principle?

    A. Information Flow Model

    B. Trusted Recovery

    C. Fail-Safe Operation

    D. Fail Secure State

17. During a power outage, ten critical servers shut down and recover without any errors. What security concept supports this process?

    A. Fail secure concept for servers.

    B. Boot sequence mirroring.

    C. A fault-tolerant system with fail-safe mechanisms.

    D. Multi-level security modes of integrity.

18. During a power outage, process termination occurs for a significant software application; non-critical servers remain online and operational through virtual interfaces. After the system comes back online, manual checks identify the system as fully functional, and events trigger the servers to remember an occurring power outage. What security principles apply to this situation?

    A. Fail secure concept for servers.

    B. Fault Tolerance.

    C. A fault-tolerant system with fail secure mechanisms.

    D. Boundary controls to reduce threats.

19. User A has a secret clearance, and User B has top-secret clearance. User B attempts to change data based on User A profile settings. User B receives an error that states: "You do not have rights to change this data." What security model addresses this error?

    A. Biba Security Model

    B. Trusted Recovery

    C. Separation of duties.

D. Bell-LaPadula outlines mandatory Access Control principles.

20. **What states that reading information by a subject at a lower level from an object at a higher level is not permitted (no read up)?**

    A. The concept of interference between two separate groups of processes.

    B. Simple Security Property (SSP).

    C. Separation of duties.

    D. State Machine Model.

21. **A Security Consultant has been hired to access the current environment for organization security. The CIO has directed the consultant to use the organization control framework to view the applications, systems, and strategic business goals for identifying design flaws, implantation failures, and alignment practices for security engineering. What fundamental methodology has the CIO issued for the consultant?**

    A. Strategic allocation of Enterprise Security Engineering to reduce risks.

    B. Principles and practices for the Enterprise Architecture as it relates to Security Engineering.

    C. Boundary controls to reduce threats.

    D. Standard security controls for different security measures.

22. **To determine whether the security requirements for a system have been achieved annually, which of the following processes could be utilized? Select the best answer.**

    A. Implementation of the SDLC through identifying and controlling risks and product evaluation models.

    B. Performance of certification and accreditation for baseline security checks to compare against current security architects.

    C. Identifying trusted computer base and its alignment to the enterprise security architect standards.

    D. The implementation of Information Technology Security Evaluation Criteria (ITSEC) and Trusted Computer System Evaluation Criteria (TCSEC) for C2 ratings.

23. **Company ABC has decided to use the contingency plan information to check a system trusted recovery process. Which of the following identifies the trusted recovery evaluation method being used?**

    A. B3 rating that identifies trusted recovery of systems during emergency operations.

    B. C2 rating that includes Label Security methods during the system transition and contingency operation.

    C. Assurance levels that utilize control resources for defining system integrity.

    D. The B1 rating for Trusted System recovery.

24. **Which of the following describes a protection ring for an operating system (OS) kernel?**

    A. A ring 0 cannot directly access ring 3, but functions in ring 3 can directly access processes in ring 0.

    B. A process in ring 0 cannot directly access a process in ring 3.

C. Ring 0 controls the core functions, while Ring 3 controls user applications.

D. Processes in ring 3 can directly access functions in ring 0.

25. **A Security expert is working on a new project to virtualize several critical servers. The Statement of Work has an entry that requires separate guest and host environments and data hiding capabilities. Which of the following does not describe the functions associated with the design?**

A. Virtualization allows a single host environment to execute multiple functions.

B. A virtual machine is commonly referred to as a guest that is executed in the host environment

C. Basic virtualization enables single hardware equipment to run multiple operating system environments simultaneously, greatly enhancing processing power utilization, among other benefits.

D. Abstraction level between the guest and host environments control storage devices.

26. **During the conclusion of a BIA, an organization has noticed that the loss of Server B2 in the cloud will disrupt the entire network. Further analysis revealed that the dependencies for the main operation and system fault tolerance failed as well. Which of the following describes the general issue for the organization?**

A. The organization's availability will be affected by a single source of failure, which will cause a fail state to exist.

B. The level of redundancy and system availability was not determined.

C. Multiple points of operation can perform through failed states.

D. The system availability and trusted recovery for applications will not operate under failed states.

27. **Why would a security architect consider a client's machine when designing an architect?**

A. Because the single point of access for vulnerabilities is client-based machines.

B. Due to the policies and privileges of clients to be outside the baseline.

C. To protect the security measures and to ensure the loss and exposure of critical resources are protected.

D. Due to applets and Java coding errors are expanding to the desktop.

28. **To protect mobile client-based systems, which of the following should be integrated? Pick the best answer.**

A. Helpdesk resources to execute technical support.

B. Procedures that prevent jailbreak access for the root directories.

C. Security for downloading third-party unapproved apps.

D. Prevention of whole device encryption.

29. **After an audit has been completed, an organization discovers the following vulnerabilities for its datacenter servers: Credentials or authentication tickets passed in clear text: Weak password policies, passwords stored insecurely, and ineffective or lacking password complexity check. What after-action procedures should the organization consider?**

A. Switching from protocols that do not protect passwords to protocols that do.

B. Create a password policy for all users.

C. Develop an Identity Management System to allow Single Sign-On technologies to operate.

D. Implement strong authentication through something you know and have in possession.

30. **A security engineer performs operational checks on a critical server and notices that all users can access and complete work through remote access. According to the corporate policy, the Executive Committee is the only authorized group to have remote access. Also, the Security Engineer notices that critical backups are being completed by Remote User B23. What step should the Security Engineer take to resolve the issue?**

A. Produce a detailed report for the security issue and report the information to management.

B. Develop a separation of duties policy and enforce the change through the system.

C. Delete all VPN access and make reports to management on the status.

D. Implement firewall filtering for remote authentication that is not allowed.

31. **What countermeasures are appropriate for data aggregation?**

A. Restrict content-dependent access control.

B. Perform privilege isolation by not allowing users access to sensitive information.

C. Restrict context-dependent access control.

D. Develop a change procedure to restrict data integrity changes to occur based on the OS and security domain.

32. **A hacker has gained access to the network and deduces information gathered from two security levels within the database tables. What attack has occurred?**

A. An aggregation attack has occurred because of content-dependent access control policies.

B. Separation of duties attacks based on privileges.

C. Polyinstantiation through interactively producing more detailed versions of objects.

D. The hacker has executed an inference attack to derive information via two sources.

33. **Organization ABC has decided to upgrade its Database Management System (DBMS) to support 500 terabytes of data transactions. The upgrade requirements require embedded processes to query large amounts of data at a high rate. What DBMS is appropriate for the organization?**

A. The organization needs a Centralized DBMS where the centralized storage capacity gathers and receives data based on Online Transaction Protocol (OLTP).

B. The organization needs a Client/server DBMS where the data applications are separated into Trust and Identify in Education and Research (TIER) structures.

C. The organization needs a Parallel DBMS that processes multiple transactions.

D. The organization needs a Distributed DBMS where logically interrelated collection of shared data is physically distributed over a computer network.

34. Organization ABC is concerned about upscaling its Database Management System (DBMS) based on recent reports from the System Engineer. The report provides essential data that the shared resources will cause latency from new transactions being processed from Shared Storage 1 and Shared Storage 1A. The organization would like an architecture that will support a shared location for various locations to resolve the issue. What current architecture is being used, and what architecture can fix the problem?

   A. The current architect is using a Distributed DBMS, and the organization should transition to a Parallel DBMS.

   B. The current architect is using a Parallel DBMS, and the organization should transition to a Distributed DBMS.

   C. The current architect is using a Centralized DBMS, and the organization should transition to a Parallel DBMS.

   D. The current architect is using a Distributed DBMS, and the organization should transition to a Centralized DBMS.

35. A cryptographic system has been updated to support new integrity requirements based on recent attacks. The outcome for each episode presented evidence that the mathematical operation for each transmission did not have the appropriate strength to protect message communication. As a Security Engineer, which one of the following solutions would you implement to secure the system?

   A. Implement a Secure Hash Algorithm (SHA) 3-384 version for secure hashing and use SHA-2 as a backup.

   B. Implement a secure hashing system that uses SHA-1 at 160 bits to offset an integrity error.

   C. Implement a message digest (MD) 5 version for secure hashing and use SHA-1 as a backup.

   D. Implement a triple data encryption standard (3DES) version for secure hashing and use SHA-3 as a backup.

36. Which of the following are known vulnerabilities for cryptographic systems when keys are not randomized for message transmission?

   A. Keys are not encrypted during storage or transmission, which defines disclosure.

   B. Keys expire, which causes the critical age to extend past the regular use or cycle.

   C. Keys are too strong for application use, and the vulnerability allows random numbers to be long in length.

   D. Keys are weak, and the vulnerability allows random numbers to be short in length.

37. A security assessment has been conducted for a Supervisory Control and Data Acquisition (SCADA) system. The delivered reports conclude that the system has a flawed security design. The control framework has a controlled labeled PP-1 that addresses continuous policy updates for documentation. As a security assessor, what may you consider as a mitigation step to eliminating the risk?

   A. No specific or documented security procedures were developed from the security policy for the industrial control system (ICS).

   B. Vulnerabilities are often introduced into ICS because of incomplete, inappropriate, or nonexistent security documentation.

   C. Lack of ICS-specific configuration change management for the system exists.

   D. OS and vendor software patches may not be developed until significantly after security vulnerabilities are found.

38. The critical infrastructure for Region 1 has been defined as a vital power source for over 14,000 homes. A cyber-attack has also been defined as a significant consideration to many failed infrastructure devices based on risk assessments. The attack crossed several security boundaries. Which of the following best describes the result of a cyber-attack?

    A. Electric power is often thought to be one of the most prevalent sources of disruptions of interdependent critical infrastructures.

    B. SCADA systems and DCS are often networked together. This is the case for electric power control centers and electric power generation facilities.

    C. For an ICS, human safety and fault tolerance prevent loss of life or endangerment of public health or confidence, regulatory compliance, failure of equipment, loss of intellectual property, or lost or damaged products are the primary concerns.

    D. An incident in one infrastructure can, directly and indirectly, affect other infrastructures through cascading and escalating failures.

39. A web developer has finished updating the code for a new web application that stores user's private information. The application uses a database to store the data, and each user must provide credentials to access the database. On Monday, the security team conducts a web application scan and notices that users can access the application web page and insert 10,000 characters to a web form at block 3 for the date. What vulnerability has been detected?

    A. The application is susceptible to input validation vulnerabilities and buffers under flow conditions.

    B. The application is susceptible to buffer overflow and validation input vulnerabilities.

    C. The application is at risk of having a session management vulnerability.

    D. Query injection on structured query language (SQL) command vulnerability.

40. SEMAIS has updated all mobile devices to a new platform. After the update, SEMAIS notices that confidential information is openly accessible to unauthorized users of the devices. What mitigation strategy is appropriate for the vulnerability?

    A. Encrypt the device passwords with data encryption standard (DES) technology.

    B. Install applications that ask for passwords and authentication data.

    C. Encrypt the device with a 128-bit pin code.

    D. Encrypt the electronic serial number (ESN) for the mobile device.

41. A Security Architect must develop best practices to mitigate buffer overflow vulnerabilities associated with standard embedded systems. Which of the following will support the Security Architect to complete the task?

    A. The Security Architect should examine the web-based application platform for embedded systems.

    B. The Security Architect should consult with the developers for programming errors have been identified.

    C. The Security Architect should address external and internal code changes for the firmware within the embedded systems.

    D. Mobile phones within the organization should be evaluated for Internet of Things (IoT) Technology.

42. **A hacker has changed the input form for a shopping cart from $65.00 to $.65. What mitigation is appropriate for this issue?**

   A. Perform adequate pre-validation and post validation for form fields to ensure common currency is transmitted.

   B. Create defenses for cross-site scripting vulnerabilities.

   C. Perform post validation to ensure $.65 is valid and release the transaction for sound currency.

   D. Verify the format for the data and change the pre-validation parameters to match $.65.

43. **Which of the following is a mitigation step for web session management vulnerabilities?**

   A. Change hypertext transfer protocol secure (HTTPS) traffic to hypertext transfer protocol (HTTP) only for web-based sessions.

   B. Validate session input and session IDs for every request.

   C. Configure HTTPS to communicate traffic for port 443 and port 80.

   D. Configure the web application to restrict clear text communication.

44. **Which of the following represents mitigation of insufficient programming errors and its outcome for a web-based application?**

   A. A web developer documents input string errors and develop a root cause analysis for its vulnerabilities.

   B. A web developer validates input string errors and develops a root cause analysis for its vulnerabilities.

   C. Assign a separate development team to perform a source code analysis to reduce exploits.

   D. A developer decides to perform a source code analysis before finding any vulnerabilities, reducing the production cost.

45. **A Security Engineer has failed to make global changes to all application servers to allow cookies to be deleted before closing a browser. Additionally, the input information from a user has been directed to an attack server for gaining access by use of a malicious injection. What attaches has been executed?**

   A. Server cross-site scripting (XSS) where trusted user-supplied data is included in a hypertext markup language (HTML) response generated by the server.

   B. XSS attacks where a type of injection has used malicious codes of the script.

   C. Reflected XSS where user input is stored on the target server.

   D. Code injection of stored data vulnerability.

46. **SEMAIS creates web roles and certificate distribution to all web applications hosted in its cloud environment for subscribed clients. Before the process occurs, an actual inventory was executed, and the results indicate several keys are expiring. As a result of the discovery, what can be concluded about the tickets?**

   A. The cloud will use separate key streams due to the configuration.

   B. The critical repository has been changed to support cloud services that hold vital expiration.

C. The Expiration phase of key management represents the deprecation period for the key.

D. The Expiration phase of key management represents the beginning of the essential lifecycle.

47. **How does the inclusion of data and critical management relate?**

A. Archival of expired, decommissioned keys should be based on whether data still exists.

B. Data can be exchanged with archived keys.

C. Key archival is based on service level agreement (SLA).

D. Key archival is based key management agreements.

48. **Bob and Alice wish to exchange information via a cloud service environment. The organization has outsourced key management to the service provider. PKI has been developed and implemented. After a review, the organization notices that key management and certificates are not handled correctly for the cloud environment. The CIO asks for a brief statement describing the environment. What response would support the CIO's request?**

A. All the certificates are enabled via a service provider.

B. All the certificates are enabled via a service provider, and public keys are integrated for public cryptographic communication.

C. Service certificates are attached to cloud services and enable secure communication to and from the service, and PKI integration uses two keys in the cloud called public and private.

D. Service symmetric certificates are attached to cloud services and enable secure communication to and from the service, and PKI integration uses one key in the cloud called public.

49. **Which of the following separates symmetric and asymmetric key definitions?**

A. Secret Key Cryptography (SKC) uses multiple keys for both encryption and decryption.

B. Secret Key Cryptography (SKC): uses a single key for both encryption and decryption.

C. Asymmetric keys use the sender's public key via encryption and the receiver's public key via decryption.

D. Asymmetric keys use the sender's private key via encryption and the receiver's public key via a hashing algorithm.

50. **Alice has been issued a new authentication method that requires X.509 technology. She has been issued a new certificate, but it does not function for her during secure socket layer (SSL) connections to semais.train.us1. As a simple troubleshooting method, what action should Alice consider?**

A. Contacting the person that initiates the certificate process to confirm the validity of the certificate.

B. Attempt to perform a new registration process through self-service access.

C. Make a new request to the Certification Authority (CA) that her certificate needs re-registering.

D. Change the X.509 technology to a more comparable key management solution.

51. **Alice and Bob wish to exchange data using Public Key cryptography. Bob has been notified that Alice sent an encrypted message to his email account. If Bob wants to open the message and send an email back to Alice, what must occur?**

A. Use Alice's Private Key to decrypt the message and use the same key to encrypt a message to Alice.

B. Use a Symmetric Key to decrypt the message and his public key to encrypt the message.

C. Bob must decrypt the message with Alice's Public Key and encrypt the reply with her public key.

D. Install pretty good privacy (PGP) to allow even key exchange.

52. **Which one of the following defines good key management practices?**

A. Key lifetime should be extended for high usage.

B. The key length should be long enough to provide the necessary level of protection.

C. Keys should be highly random, and the algorithm should use the full spectrum of the key space.

D. Destruction of keys should happen midway between lifecycles to avoid management issues.

53. **A hardware cryptographic device has been installed, and the security team starts to implement security controls for the device. After doing the first three steps, the team notices that unauthorized users can easily interpret data traffic. What is a possible solution to resolve the issue?**

A. Rebuild the key infrastructure for normal authentication.

B. Increase the randomization for the algorithm used.

C. Develop a cleartext communication check to determine where the data transmit and delete the data path.

D. Verify that the remaining controls address encrypted data and the removal of cleartext communication.

54. **During a security control assessment, an assessor determines that the keys used for the organization have lifecycle revocation issues and private keys are accessible to unauthorized users. Which of the following supports a unified procedure to mitigate the issue for the organization?**

A. Key management infrastructure

B. Key management

C. Key Management Practices Statement (KMPS)

D. Key revocation

55. **As part of key management strategies, an organization must ensure the algorithm and keys match secure operation. Which of the following statements supports this security measure?**

A. Key pairs reduce the burden for the transformation of plaintext data into ciphertext data.

B. A secure key algorithm can be used so an entity with knowledge of the key can reproduce or reverse the operation.

C. Secure operation requires dual key pairs that are defined as symmetric encryption.

D. A cryptographic key can be used in conjunction with an algorithm so an entity with knowledge of the key can reproduce or reverse the operation.

56. **Alice has just completed typing an important email that is regarded to be highly sensitive. The organization's rules require addressing integrity and confidentiality. Based on the policy requirements, which one of the following steps should she execute?**

A. Alice should provide a digital signature and encrypt the message to satisfy the organization's requirements.

B. Alice should perform a one-way hash and use a digital signature for the message.

C. Alice should authenticate the message and digitally sign the message as well.

D. Alice should encrypt the message using a digital signature, which will provide integrity as well.

57. **Which of the following addresses digital signature technology and hashing algorithms for message integrity?**

A. Implementation of a one-way hash function takes a variable-length string (a message) and produces a variable-length value called a hash value.

B. The implementation of a one-way hash function should not be computed in the opposite direction.

C. Designing a one-way function that is easier to compute in one direction and the opposite direction as well.

D. The implementation of a two-way hash function should not be computed in the opposite direction.

58. **A System Administrator has downloaded a new application and its license, which is valid for one year. After 12-months, the organization notices that they need to update the license key for the application. After several attempts of using a free license, the application locks out and sends this notice "You must purchase a new license key before access is granted." What technology has been addressed for the license key issue?**

A. A security policy has blocked access to the file by using access restriction technologies.

B. License key retrieval and digital protection of data have been implemented as a technology.

C. The concept of Digital Rights Management (DRM) has been addressed to protect the program and its license.

D. Key management technologies have been used to restrict access.

59. **When an email is sent from User A to User B, what technology helps ensure non-repudiation occurs due to the message exchange?**

A. The use of a secure key distribution and hashing values that are protected.

B. The use of digital signatures and certificate which provides proof of origin.

C. The use of a key management solution that is bind to a user's profile.

D. A one-way hash takes a variable-length string (a message) and produces a variable-length value called a hash value.

60. **An outside intruder has just hacked company ABC. After conducting their forensic analysis, the company discovers that User A has previously sent an email to the hacker. To prove that the email was valid and sent from User A, the company decides to verify whether User A. can dispute the argument Which of the following provides valid proof that User A sent the email?**

A. A digital signature that correlates to the hacker's User ID from a remote host.

B. A digital certificate owned by the hacker is saved by User A.

C. User A profile settings changed after the incident occurs.

D. The email audit logs have a valid timestamp that correlates to User A sending an email to the hacker.

61. Which of the following represents the proper use of a hash value?

A. You can sign a hash value with checksum errors and message codes that use asymmetric key codes.

B. Hash values can be used for providing confidentiality of messages.

C. You can sign a hash value with checksum errors and message codes that use asymmetric key codes.

D. A hash value (message digest) uses digital signature technology for private key encryption.

62. When using HMAC-SHA, what is added to the hash function to generate the variable bits of 256 or 512k bits? Select the correct answer.

A. The value mixes one round of secret keys to the message code.

B. The function mixes two rounds of secret keys to the message data.

C. The function mixes X.509 public-key encryption scheme with the message data.

D. The function mixes two rounds of hash-based message authentication codes and one round of secret keys.

63. Which of the following does not represent message integrity technologies for hashing values?

A. Message Authentication codes and digital signatures.

B. Digital Certificates and private keys.

C. DES, hash-based message authentication code (HMAC), cipher block chaining-message authentication code (CBC-MAC), and cipher-based message authentication code (CMAC).

D. Nonrepudiation and digital signatures.

64. If the algorithm does produce the same value for two distinctly different messages, what attack can occur based on the two values?

A. Eavesdropping of message data.

B. Dictionary attack.

C. Dictionary and birthday attack.

D. Collision as well as a birthday attack.

65. What is a countermeasure for replay attacks as a result of failed cryptographic algorithms?

A. Adjusting the timestamps and sequence numbers based on available threshold settings.

B. Configure the message codes and traffic to bypass specific settings.

C. Tune an Intrusion Detection System (IDS) to identify replay attacks.

D. Limit the amount of encrypted data that is generated from a network source.

66. An attacker has decided to use a new alternative to determine the crypto algorithm for a transport layer security (TLS)/SSL. During the process, the attacker finds out that the various computations take a certain period to execute. If the hacker decides to explore the data gathered, what possible attack could he or she perform?

    A. The attacker can generate a differential fault analysis in which secrets are discovered by introducing faults in a computation.

    B. The attacker can execute a timing side-channel attack to to see timing sequences and also execute calculations.

    C. A data remanence side-channel attack in which sensitive data is read after supposedly having been deleted.

    D. A brute-force attack to decrypt any encrypted data.

67. A new datacenter has been built along the path of a busy intersection. The initial design did not include any factors that deter violence and prevent traffic stops. Upon a review, the company decides that the initial process must be reviewed for the amount of violence. What fundamental methodology should have been employed from the initial design of the building?

    A. The initial assessment should have followed Crime Prevention Through Environment Design (CPTED).

    B. The organization should have used natural surveillance to detect violence in the area.

    C. The organization should have implemented sidewalks and grassy areas to guide vehicle traffic to only enter and exit through specific locations.

    D. The organization should have used a secure zone methodology to deter crime on the street.

68. When a datacenter has been constructed using an in-depth defense model that restricts unauthorized access, what fundamental conclusion can be drawn from the design?

    A. The organization is employing controls to restrict fire damage within the datacenter.

    B. The design has employed security zones to restrict access and entry points to the datacenter.

    C. The organization has employed restricted zones for fire code safety.

    D. The organization is employing design factors that compensate for physical controls.

69. What is the fundamental goal for a physical risk assessment in a large enterprise?

    A. Minimize the GRC issues associated with CPTED.

    B. Align a risk analysis approach that will deter crime through layered defense activities.

    C. Help identify risks based on threat and vulnerability pairing.

    D. Reduce the vulnerabilities and design steps for the buildings.

70. Across the hall from that datacenter is an office where employees sit daily, accessing valuable information from their desktop personal computers (PCs), laptops, and handheld devices over various networks. Adjacent to the location is the local area network (LAN) Closet 1. The additional closets are in a restricted zone that requires specialized access. The company budget has been restricted for any physical upgrades until after the audit. As a security measure in protecting the closets, what should the organization pursue?

A. Move closet 1 to a secure zone that requires access.

B. Request that the audit ceases and move the closets to a safer zone.

C. Employ security features such as cameras in closet 1.

D. Lock access to closet 1 and assign a security officer at the entry to the restricted zones.

71. **Bob has attempted to enter Datacenter 1 with his badge and receives an error that his access has been denied. The previous day he was able to access the datacenter. What control method has been deployed to restrict Bob's access?**

A. A technical control has been implemented.

B. An operational control has been deployed, and it restricts physical rights to the datacenter.

C. Physical control has been implemented that uses a "something you are" technology.

D. A physical control restriction has been deployed using "something you are" technology.

72. **To protect media from accidental loss, what concept should an organization use?**

A. The organization should employ natural surveillance.

B. The organization should use a lock or a cabinet that has a locking mechanism.

C. Label the data within the cabinet.

D. Label the data within the cabinet and deter employees from using the data.

73. **Which one of the following provides proof that criminal data has not been removed from a physical location?**

A. The court documents have pictures of the evidence.

B. The shelving system identifies evidence by serial numbers.

C. Evidence storage for criminal filings has been following rules of behavior policy.

D. Evidence storage for criminal filings has been following a chain of custody policy.

74. **When building a government Sensitive Compartmented Information Facility (SCIF), what fundamental requirement must be followed?**

A. The company must follow a security level agreement (SLA) based on government standards.

B. Door frames must follow a commercial standard.

C. All doors must be of the National Security Agency (NSA) approval and specifications.

D. The restriction of date leaks, ambient noise, and visual access to space is restricted.

75. **When entering a datacenter, a user must swipe their badge and insert a pin within the keypad. What has access control rule been applied? Select the best answer.**

A. A something you know and have technology rule.

B. A something you are technology rule.

C. A biometric principle to access the datacenter.

D. A datacenter security and access control policy.

76. **Which of the following principles support heating, ventilation, and air conditioning (HVAC) use and technology?**

A. The HVAC system should maintain the appropriate temperature and humidity levels and provide open-loop recirculating air-conditioning.

B. Positive pressurization and ventilation should also be implemented to control contamination.

C. Air flow should be restricted to close loop systems for saving power.

D. An open-loop recirculating air-conditioning system should be installed to maintain air quality.

77. **An organization is installing a pipe system for water sprinklers. The design statement has concluded that the average weather is -10 below zero for 9 months in a year. What pipe system is appropriate for the design?**

A. A dry pipe system always contains water in the pipes and is usually discharged by temperature–control–level sensors.

B. A wet pipe system always contains water in the pipes and is usually discharged by temperature–control–level sensors.

C. A dry pipe system is appropriate since the pipes do not freeze.

D. A wet pipe system is appropriate since the pipes do not freeze.

78. **Once a fire has started, what is an initial step or response concerning the HVAC?**

A. Ensure that alternative airflow is cooling the datacenter.

B. Ensure that all the backup power has been switched to emergency mode.

C. Ensure that all the backup power has been switched to a stand-by mode.

D. The HVAC should be turned off, so smoke will not spread throughout the building.

11. Domain 3: Security Architecture and Engineering - Answers and Explanations

1. **A.** The Key Management Specification (KMS) should address how access to the cryptographic device components and functions is authorized, controlled, and validated to request, generate, handle, distribute, store, and use keying material. Any use of passwords and personal identification numbers (PINs) should be included. For PKI cryptographic applications, role and identity-based were privileged, and the use of any tokens should be described.

2. **B.** Planning for recovery from system failures is an essential management function. Interruptions of critical infrastructure services should be anticipated, and planning for maintaining the continuity of operations supporting an organization's primary mission requirements should be done.

3. **B.** During ciphertext-only attacks, the attacker has access to several encrypted messages. The attacker has no idea what the plaintext data or the secret key value. A known-plaintext attack is where the attacker has access to corresponding plaintext and ciphertext. Chosen-plaintext attack is where the attacker can choose arbitrary plaintexts to be encrypted and obtain the corresponding ciphertexts. A chosen-ciphertext attack is where the attacker chooses a ciphertext and obtains its decryption under an unknown key.

4. **C.** Systems security engineering is a specialty engineering discipline of systems engineering. The discipline applies scientific, mathematical, engineering, and measurement concepts, principles, and methods to deliver, consistent with defined constraints and necessary trade-offs, a trustworthy asset protection capability that satisfies stakeholder requirements, presents a residual risk that is deemed acceptable and manageable to stakeholders, as part of a comprehensive systems engineering effort that identifies and assesses vulnerabilities in a system and its operating environment.

5. **C.** When a security engineer has to design a system with the network in mind, the structure aligns to the SDLC Development and Acquisition phase. Under the Security Foundation: Develop policies, and Increased Resilience: Reduce Vulnerabilities.

6. **A.** The information systems security engineer analyzes design constraints, examines trade-offs, does complex system and security design, and considers life-cycle support. The information systems security engineer traces all the system security requirements to the elements until all are addressed. The final detailed security design results in component and interface specifications that provide sufficient information for acquisition when the system is implemented. Answer A would least occur because it is part of the project initiation phase. Answers B, C, and D define the development and acquisition for security for the SDLC and Develop Detailed Security Design for the Security Engineering phases. Reference NIST 800-160 Security Engineering and The Information Systems Security Engineering Process IATF Release 3.1—September 2002.

7. **D.** During this phase, the system performs its work. Typically, the system is also being modified by hardware and software and by numerous other events. Activities include security operations and administration, operational assurance, and audits and monitoring Initiation: During the initiation phase, the need for a system is expressed, and the system's purpose is documented. Activities include conducting an impact assessment per Federal Information Processing Standards (FIPS)-199 http://csrc.nist.gov/publications/fips/fips199/FIPS-PUB-199-final.pdf). Development/Acquisition: During this phase, the system is designed, purchased, programmed, developed, or otherwise constructed. This phase often consists of other defined cycles, such as the system development and acquisition cycles. Activities include determining security requirements, incorporating security requirements into specifications, and obtaining the system. Implementation: During implementation, the system is tested and installed or fielded. Activities include installing/turning on controls, security testing, certification, and accreditation. Operation/Maintenance: During this phase, the system performs its work. Typically, the system is also being modified by installing hardware and software and numerous other events. Activities include security operations and administration, operational assurance, and audits and monitoring. Disposal: The disposal phase of the IT system lifecycle involves the disposition of information, hardware, and software. Activities include moving, archiving, discarding, or destroying information and sanitizing the media.

8. **A.** A Security Engineer validates a system to determine whether the design conforms to requirements and stakeholders' concerns. Reducing risk and implementation of least privilege are technical steps to mitigate security risks. Lifecycle Disposal happens after a system is no longer serviced or required to be operational.

9. **B.** The primary purpose of memory protection is to prevent a process from accessing memory that has not been allocated. This prevents a bug or malware from affecting other operations or the operating system itself.

10. **C.** Service Design identifies service requirements and devises new service offerings and changes and improvements to existing ones. Service Transition will translate designs into operational services after the service design has been achieved. Zachman and TOGAF are standards to address Enterprise Architect requirements.

11. **B.** This model captures the state of systems. A state can change only at discrete points in time, i.e., triggered by a clock or input event. How to use state machine models?
   • Define the state set so that it captures "security."
   • Check that all state transitions starting in a "secure" state yield a "secure state."
   • Check that the initial state of the system is "secure."
   • A state transition is secure if it goes from a secure state to a secure state.

12. **A.** This model is related to the information flow model with restrictions on the information flow. The basic principle of this model is that a group of users (A), who are using the commands (C), do not interfere with the user group (B) who are using the commands (D). In this scenario, Top Secret information is restricted to lower security areas. This concept prevents data leakage and covert channels from existing. Due to the separation of the security level, interference and conflicts for data exchange will never exist.
   http://www.computer.org/csdl/proceedings/csfw/2001/1146/00/11460237.pdf

13. **A.** Multi-level Security Policy-Systems with multi-level security policy must have sensitivity labels for both subjects and objects and must use mandatory access control. The Bell-Lapadula model defines a secure state through 3 multilevel properties. The first 2 properties implement mandatory access control, and the third one permits discretionary access control: 1. SSP states that reading information by a subject at a lower sensitivity level from an object at a higher sensitivity level is not permitted (no read up). **2.** Security Property (star*) states that writing of info by a subject at a higher level of sensitivity to an object at a lower level of sensitivity is not permitted (no write down). 3. Discretionary Security Property (DSP) uses an access matrix to specify discretionary access control (DAC).

14. **B.** Multi-level Security Policy-Systems with multi-level security policy must have both sensitivity labels for both subjects and objects and must use mandatory access control. Classification and clearances represent multiple layers of security.

15. **C.** A security label is assigned to a resource to denote a type of classification or designation. This label can then indicate special security handling, or it can be used for access control. Once labels are assigned, they usually cannot be altered and are an effective access control mechanism.

16. **B.** Trusted recovery refers to mechanisms and procedures necessary to ensure that failures and discontinuities of operation do not compromise a system's secure process. Whenever a hardware or software component of a trusted system fails, the loss mustn't compromise the security policy requirements of that system. Also, the recovery procedures should not provide an opportunity for violation of the systems security policy.

17. **C.** When a computer or network component fails, and the computer or the network continues to function, it is called a fault-tolerant system. For fault tolerance to operate, the system must be capable of detecting that a fault has occurred, and the system must then correct the flaw or maneuver around it. In a fail-safe system, program execution is terminated, and the system is protected from being compromised when a hardware or software failure occurs and is detected.

18. **B.** When a computer or network component fails, and the computer or the network continues to function, it is called a fault-tolerant system. For fault tolerance to operate, the system must be capable of detecting that a fault has occurred, and the system must then correct the defect or operate around it. In a fail-safe system, program execution is terminated, and the system is protected from being compromised when a hardware or software failure occurs and is detected.

19. **D.** The Bell-LaPadula (BLP) model is built on the state machine concepts. BLP focuses on Confidentiality. This concept defines a set of allowable states in a system. Transition functions define the transition from one state to another upon receipt of an input. The objective of this model is to ensure that the initial state is secure and that the transitions always result in a secure state. BLP defines a secure state through 3 multi-level properties: 1) SSP – states that reading of information by a subject at a lower level from an object at a higher level is not permitted (no read up). 2) Security Property (Star) – states that writing of information by a subject at a higher level to an object at a lower level is not permitted (no write down). 3) Discretionary Security Property (DSP) – uses an access matrix to specify discretionary access controls. The model prevents users and processes from reading above their security level. Also, it prevents processes with any given classification from writing data associated with a lower classification. The "no write down" prevents placing data that is not sensitive but contained in a sensitive document into less sensitive files.

20. **B.** The Bell-LaPadula (BLP) model is built on the state machine concepts. BLP focuses on Confidentiality. This concept defines a set of allowable states in a system. Transition functions define the transition from one state to another upon receipt of an input. The objective of this model is to ensure that the initial state is secure and that the transitions always result in a secure state. BLP defines a secure state through 3 multilevel properties: 1) SSP – states that reading of information by a subject at a lower level from an object at a higher level is not permitted (no read up). 2) Security Property (Star) – states that writing of information by a subject at a higher level to an object at a lower level is not permitted (no write down). 3) Discretionary Security Property (DSP) – uses an access matrix to specify discretionary access controls. The model prevents users and processes from reading above their security level. Also, it prevents processes with any given classification from writing data associated with a lower classification. The "no write down" prevents placing data that is not sensitive but contained in a sensitive document into less sensitive files.

21. **B.** Enterprise security architecture (EISA) is the practice of applying a comprehensive and rigorous method for describing a current and future structure and behavior for an organization's security processes, information security systems, personnel, and organizational sub-units so that they align with the organization's core goals and strategic direction.

22. **B.** Certification is a technical review that assesses the security mechanisms and evaluates their effectiveness. Accreditation is management's official acceptance of the information in the certification process findings. The process utilizes baseline checks to derive and find any deviations from the baseline standard, which indicates a risk. The end state ensures the baseline is implemented and compliant through annual reviews. Answer A, C, and D deal with product evaluation models, not annual certifying requirements.

23. **A.** The trusted recovery process is a B3 rating for systems. A system must be able to recover from failures without its security level being compromised. When the system starts up and loads its operating system and components, it must be done in an initial secure state to ensure that any system's weakness cannot be taken advantage of in this slice of time. B1 and C2 do not apply.

24. **C.** These protection rings provide an intermediate layer between processes and are used for access control when one method tries to access another approach or interact with system resources. The ring number determines the access level a process has—the lower the ring number, the greater the amount of privilege given to the process running within that ring. A ring 3 cannot directly access ring 1, but ring 1 can directly access processes in ring 3.

25. **D.** The hypervisor is the central program that controls the execution of the various guest operating systems and provides the abstraction level between the guest and host environment.

26. **A.** Redundancy and High-availability clusters are the key factors to avoid Single Point of Failures (SPOFs). Both logical redundancy and physical redundancy are needed to be achieved. High availability clusters minimize the outages (99.99% availability) of the system components included in the cloud. A failed state can exist for an organization if the failed condition disrupts all services and operations via a single source.

27. **C.** Architects must consider that every asset has risks. During the design of a system, the risks employed for the assets must be included within the design to enforce security and ensure resource protection exists.

28. B. Client-based devices such as mobile devices should be configured to prevent root directory entry and allow full encryption to protect the device. Organizations should prevent unapproved apps from being downloaded.

29. D. Enforce strong password policies. Enforce password complexity requirement by requiring a long password with a combination of upper case, lower case, numeric and special characters. This helps mitigate the threat posed by dictionary attacks. If possible, also enforce automatic password expiry. The use of multi-factor authentication is the best choice for password protection.

30. A. The Security Engineer should report the information to management. Making any changes to the system would affect backups and any other tasks that are being executed.

31. B. To prevent aggregation, the subject and any application or process acting on the subject's behalf must be prevented from gaining access to the whole collection, including the independent components.

32. D. The inference problem happens when a subject deduces the full story from the pieces he learned through aggregation. This is seen when data at a lower security level indirectly portrays data at a higher level. The inference is the intended result of aggregation. Polyinstantiation involves interactively producing more detailed versions of objects by populating variables with different values or other variables. It is often used to prevent inference attacks. Content-dependent access control is based on the sensitivity of the data.

33. C. The architecture should be structured for a Parallel DBMS. The Parallel database system architecture consists of multiple Central Processing Units (CPUs) and data storage disks in parallel. Hence, they improve processing and Input/Output (I/O) speeds. Parallel database systems are used to query extensive databases or process a vast number of transactions per second.

34. B. Disadvantage for a Parallel DBMS is that the process was often executing access shared resources. A slowdown may result from interference of each new process as it completes existing operations for commonly held resources, such as shared data storage disks, system bus, and so on. The transition to a Distributed DBMS supports a single database (on the server) that can be shared across several distinct client (application) systems. The use of a distributed database architecture provides greater efficiency and better performance.

35. A. In cryptography, SHA-1 (Secure Hash Algorithm 1) is a cryptographic hash function designed by the United States National Security Agency and is a U.S. Federal Information Processing Standard published by the United States. SHA-1 produces a 160-bit (20-byte) hash value known as a message digest. An SHA-1 hash value is typically rendered as a hexadecimal number, 40 digits long. SHA-1 is no longer considered secure against well-funded opponents. The SHA-3 standard was released by NIST on 5th August 2015. SHA-3 uses the Keccak cryptographic hash designed by Guido Bertoni, Joan Daemen, Michaël Peeters and Gilles Van Assche. SHA-3 was developed as a backup to SHA-2, rather than a replacement if any unexpected security weaknesses are found in SHA-2. Use algorithms proved flawed or weak (DES, 3DES, MD5, Sha1, AES, Blowfish, Diffie Hellman).

36. D. Too short or not random enough. Use human chosen passwords as cryptographic keys. 1) Key disclosure - Keys are not encrypted during storage or transmission; keys are not cleaned appropriately after use; keys are hard-coded in the code or stored in configuration files. 2) Key updates - Allow keys to age. https://www.owasp.org/index.php/Category:Cryptographic_Vulnerability

37. B. Vulnerabilities are often introduced into ICS because of incomplete, inappropriate, or nonexistent security documentation, including policy and implementation guides (procedures). Security documentation, along with management support, is the cornerstone of any security program. Corporate security policy can reduce vulnerabilities by mandating conduct such as password usage and maintenance or requirements for connecting modems to ICS.

38. D. Vulnerabilities in ICS may occur from flaws, misconfigurations, or poor administration of ICS networks and connections with other networks. These vulnerabilities can be eliminated or mitigated through various security controls, such as defense-in-depth network design, encrypting network communications, restricting network traffic flows, and providing physical access control for network components. Critical infrastructures are highly interconnected and mutually dependent in complex ways, both physically and through a host of information and communications technologies. An incident in one infrastructure can, directly and indirectly, affect other infrastructures through cascading and escalating failures.

39. **B.** The vulnerability exposed is based on input validation. When a user can input 10,000 characters into a website input form, this results from the validation errors. This can also cause buffer overflow attacks to occur. SQL injection vulnerabilities allow data to be changed. Session management causes authentication vulnerabilities.

40. **C.** One of the configuration practices for mobile phones is to encrypt the passwords. Encryption of other sources is used to protect those sources as not the pin. The minimum encryption should be set to 128-bit.

41. **B.** An embedded system is a system built into a more extensive system designed for dedicated functions. It consists of a combination of hardware, software, and optionally mechanical parts. Many vulnerabilities for embedded systems stem from programming errors, leading to control flow attacks (e.g., input parsing vulnerabilities leading to buffer overflow problems and memory management problems such as using pointers referring to memory locations freed).

42. **A.** Pre-validation Input controls verifying data are in the appropriate format and compliant with application specifications before submission to the application. An example of this would be form field validation, where web forms do not allow letters in a field expecting to receive a number (currency) value. 1) Post-validation: Ensuring an application's output is consistent with expectations (that is, within predetermined constraints of reasonableness). 2) Client-side validation: Input validation is done at the client before it is even sent back to the server to process. 3) Cross-site scripting (XSS): An attack where a vulnerability is found on a website that allows an attacker to inject malicious code into a web application. 4) Parameter validation: The values that are being received by the application are validated to be within defined limits before the server application processes them within the system.

43. **D.** The aspect of session management requires consideration before delivering applications via the Web. Commonly, the most used method of managing client sessions is by assigning unique session IDs to every connection. A session ID is a value sent by the client to the server with every request that uniquely identifies the client to the server or application. If an attacker could acquire or even guess an authenticated client's session ID and render it to the server as its session ID, the server would be fooled, and the attacker would have access to the session. The proper mitigation is to encrypt the session to include cookies.

44. **C.** The first pillar of implementing security principles is analyzing the website architecture. The clearer and simpler a website are, the easier it is to explore its various security aspects. Once a website has been strategically analyzed, the user-generated input into the website must be critically scrutinized. As a rule, all input must be considered unsafe or rogue and sanitized before being processed. Likewise, all output generated by the system should also be filtered to ensure private or sensitive data is not disclosed.

45. **B.** Cross-Site Scripting (XSS) attacks are a type of injection in which malicious scripts are injected into otherwise benign and trusted websites. XSS attacks occur when an attacker uses a web application to send malicious code, generally in the form of a browser side script, to a different end-user. Flaws that allow these attacks to succeed are quite widespread and occur anywhere a web application uses input from a user within the output it generates without validating or encoding it. https://www.owasp.org/index.php/Types_of_Cross-Site_Scripting

46. **C.** The Expiration phase of key management represents the beginning of the deprecation period for the key. Key rotation should be completed before expiration, with all data encrypted with that key converted to the new key. The objective is to have the key replaced within the production system (but not removed) before it expires. In a sense, expiration represents a gating factor for planning, as much as it is a discrete phase in the lifecycle.

47. **A.** The absolute last thing that you want to do when managing crypto systems is to destroy a key that still has data associated with it. Therefore, the second-to-last phase in the lifecycle is included, with a potentially open-ended mandate to not proceed to the final phase. Archival of expired, decommissioned keys should be based on

determining whether data still exists somewhere in the data ecosystem that may be encrypted with the archived key. The data ecosystem extends beyond "live" data in production to backups that may exist in disaster recovery sites, as well as to all offline backups. If there is a requirement for data to be recoverable, the keys must be archived parallel to that data.

48. **C.** In PKC, one of the keys is designated the public key and may be advertised as widely as the owner wants. The other key is set as the private key and is never revealed to another party. It is straightforward to send messages under this scheme. Suppose Alice wants to send Bob a message. Alice encrypts some information using Bob's public key; Bob decrypts the ciphertext using his private key. This method could also be used to prove who sent a message; Alice, for example, could encrypt some plaintext with her private key; when Bob decrypts using Alice's public key, he knows that Alice sent the message (authentication) and Alice cannot deny having sent the message (non-repudiation). Service certificates are attached to cloud services and enable secure communication to and from the service. For example, you would want to supply a certificate to authenticate an exposed HTTPS endpoint if you deployed a web role. Service certificates, defined in your service definition, are automatically deployed to the virtual machine running an instance of your role.

49. **B.** Uses a single key for both encryption and decryption, also called symmetric encryption. They are primarily used for privacy and confidentiality. Public Key Cryptography (PKC) uses encryption, and another for decryption also called asymmetric encryption. They are mainly used for authentication, non-repudiation, and key exchange. Hash Functions uses a mathematical transformation to irreversibly "encrypt" information, providing a digital fingerprint. They are primarily used for message integrity.

50. **A.** The registration authority (RA) performs the certification registration duties. The RA establishes and confirms an individual's identity, initiates the certification process with a CA on behalf of an end-user, and performs certificate life-cycle management functions. The RA cannot issue certificates but can act as a broker between the user and the CA. When users need new certificates, they make requests to the RA, and the RA verifies all necessary identification information before allowing a request to go to the CA.

51. **C.** If Alice encrypts data with her private key, Bob must copy Alice's public key to decrypt it. Bob can decrypt Alice's message and decide to reply to Alice in an encrypted form. All he needs to do is encrypt his reply with Alice's public key, and then Alice can decrypt the message with her private key. It is impossible to encrypt and decrypt using the same key when using an asymmetric key encryption technology because, although mathematically related, the two keys are not the same key as they are in symmetric cryptography. Alice can encrypt data with her private key, and Bob can then decrypt it with Alice's public key. Bob can be sure the message came from Alice by decrypting the message with Alice's public key. A message could be decrypted with a public key only if the message was encrypted with the corresponding private key.

52. **B.** Key management is critical for proper protection. The following are responsibilities that fall under the key management umbrella:
   * The key length should be long enough to provide the necessary level of
   * protection.
   * Keys should be stored and transmitted by secure means.
   * Keys should be highly random, and the algorithm should use the full
   * spectrum of the key space.
   * **The key's lifetime should correspond with the sensitivity of the data it is.**
   * **protecting. (Less secure data may allow for a longer key lifetime, whereas more)**
   * Sensitive data might require a shorter key lifetime.
   * The more the key is used, the shorter its lifetime should be.
   * Keys should be backed up or escrowed in case of emergencies.
   * Keys should be destroyed appropriately when their lifetime comes to an end.

53. **D.** Keys should not be in cleartext outside the cryptography device. Many cryptography algorithms are known publicly, which puts more stress on protecting the secrecy of the key. If attackers know how the actual algorithm works, in many cases, all they need to figure out is the key to compromise a system. Therefore, keys should not be available in cleartext—the key is what brings secrecy to encryption.

54. C. Key management is the activities involving the handling of cryptographic keys and other related security parameters (e.g., initialization vectors (IVs) and passwords) during the entire lifecycle of the keys, including their generation, storage, establishment, entry and output, and destruction. Key management infrastructure is the framework and services that provide for the generation, production, distribution, control, accounting, and destruction of all cryptographic material, including symmetric keys, as well as public keys and public key certificates. It includes all elements (hardware, software, other equipment, and documentation); facilities; personnel. Key revocation is a stage in the lifecycle of keying material, a process whereby notice is made available to affected entities that keying material should be removed from operational use before the end of the established crypto period keying material. The Key Management Practices Statement (KMPS) shows a trusted root and specifies how key management procedures and techniques are used to enforce the KMPS. For example, a KMPS might state that secret and private keys shall be protected from unauthorized disclosure. The corresponding KMPS might then state that secret and private keys shall be either encrypted or physically protected. It is the responsibility of the network systems administrator to ensure that the keys are adequately safeguarded.

55. C. A parameter is used in conjunction with a cryptographic algorithm that determines its operation so that an entity with knowledge of the key can reproduce or reverse the procedure, while an entity without knowledge of the ticket cannot. Examples include: 1) the transformation of plaintext data into, 2) ciphertext data, 3) the transformation of ciphertext data into plaintext data, 4) the computation of a digital signature from data, 5) the verification of a digital signature, 6) the computation of an authentication code from data, and 7) the computation of a shared secret that is used to derive keying material. The use of symmetric key pairs uses a single key for both communication paths.

56. A. A message can be encrypted, which provides confidentiality. A message can be hashed, which provides integrity. A message can be digitally signed, which provides authentication, nonrepudiation, and integrity. A message can be encrypted and digitally signed, which provides confidentiality, authentication, nonrepudiation, and integrity. A digital signature scheme typically consists of three algorithms: 1) A key generation algorithm selects a private key uniformly from a set of possible private keys. The algorithm outputs the private key and a corresponding public key. 2) A signing algorithm that, given a message and a private key, produces a signature. 3) A signature verifying algorithm that, given the message, public key, and signature, either accepts or rejects the message's claim to authenticity.

57. B. A one-way function is a mathematical function that is easier to compute in one direction than in the opposite direction. A one-way hash is a function that takes a variable-length string (a message) and produces a fixed-length value called a hash value.

58. C. DRM can be viewed as an attempt to provide "remote control" of digital content. The required level of protection goes beyond simply delivering the digital content. Restriction on the use of the content must be maintained after it has been delivered. In other words, DRM requires "persistent protection," i.e., protection that stays with the contents. Requiring users to have a valid key before using software is an example of DRM.

59. B. There are three main practical uses for digital certificates: 1) to prove identity for purposes of electronic commerce, 2) to prove identity for purposes of access control, and 3) to prove identity to prevent spoofing. Certificates are issued by a Certification Authority (CA). In their simplest form, they could just contain a public key and a name. To be of any practical use, the certificate will also include an expiration date, the name of the CA that issued the certificate, a serial number, and probably additional information. It should contain the digital signature of the certificate issuer. A one-way hash is a function that takes a variable-length string (a message) and produces a fixed-length value called a hash value. When a user provides a digital signature, they issue proof of origin that cannot be repudiated.

60. D. Nonrepudiation can be obtained through 1) Digital Signatures-- function as a unique identifier for an individual, much like a written signature. 2) Confirmation Services -- the message transfer agent can create digital receipts to indicated that messages were sent and received. 3) Timestamps - contain the date and time a document was composed and prove that a document existed at a specific time.

61. D. A hash value is a numeric value of a fixed length that uniquely identifies data. Hash values represent large amounts of data as much smaller numeric values, so they are used with digital signatures. You can sign a hash value more efficiently than signing the more significant value. Hash values are also helpful in verifying the integrity of data sent through insecure channels. The hash value of received data can be compared to the hash value of data as it was sent to determine whether the data was altered. A MAC function is an authentication scheme derived by applying a secret key to a message in some form. Encryption provides confidentiality, while hashing provides integrity via private keys.

62. **B.** HMAC-SHA is a type of keyed hash algorithm constructed from the SHA hash function and used as an HMAC or hash-based message authentication code. The HMAC process mixes a secret key with the message data, hashes the result with the hash function, mixes that hash value with the secret key again, and then applies the hash function a second time. The output hash is 256 or 512 bits in length.

63. **C.** A MAC function is an authentication scheme derived by applying a secret key to a message in some form. This does not mean the symmetric key is used to encrypt the message, however. There are three primary MACs: a hash MAC (HMAC), CBC-MAC, and CMAC. Encryption provides confidentiality, while hashing provides integrity via private keys. A digital signature and certificate will produce the integrity required for nonrepudiation.

64. **D.** A robust hashing algorithm does not produce the same hash value for two different messages. If the algorithm does produce the same value for two distinctly different messages, this is called a collision. An attacker can attempt to force a collision, which is referred to as a birthday attack.

65. **A.** Timestamps and sequence numbers are two countermeasures to replay attacks. Packets can contain sequence numbers so that each machine will expect a specific number on each receiving packet. If a packet has a sequence number that has been previously used, this is an indication of a replay attack. Packets can also be timestamped. A threshold can be set on each computer only to accept packets within a certain timeframe. If a packet is received that is past this threshold, it can help identify a replay attack.

66. **B.** In cryptography, a side-channel attack is any attack based on information gained from the physical implementation of a cryptosystem, rather than brute force or theoretical weaknesses in the algorithms (compare cryptanalysis). For example, timing information, power consumption, electromagnetic leaks, or even sound can provide an additional source of information, which can be exploited to break the system.

67. **A.** Crime Prevention Through Environmental Design (CPTED) is a discipline that outlines how the proper design of a physical environment can reduce crime by directly affecting human behavior. It guides loss and crime prevention through good facility construction and environmental components and procedures. Any activity, design factors, or crime beyond the building's premises is not within the company's control.

68. **B.** An environment's space should be divided into zones with different security levels, depending upon who needs to be in that zone and the associated risk. The zones can be labeled as controlled, restricted, public, or sensitive.

69. **C.** The physical security team needs to carry out a risk analysis, identifying the organization's vulnerabilities, threats, and business impacts. The team should present these findings to management and work with them to define an acceptable risk level for the physical security program.

70. **D.** The most secure method is to lock the closet. There is no budget to relocate the closet, and it is not beneficial to stop the audit.

71. **A.** The something you are is a biometric standard. Since Bob has a badge, then biometric was not used for entry. A technical control prevented his entry into the datacenter through an entry point system. Operational controls and administrative rights do not relate to the scenario.

72. **B.** It is best to store media in a fire-rated locker that is locked. Having surveillance does not support the spillage of information. It just provides proof of the activity.

73. **C.** The proper chain of custody must be employed when storing evidence. The evidence must have serial numbers or other forms of data to distinguish its name. The removal of the evidence from storage should follow evidence removal and storage policies. Following the rules of behavior, a policy does not provide proof of removal.

74. **D.** Sensitive Compartmented Information Facility (pronounced "skiff"), a U.S. Department of Defense term for a secure room, can be a secure room or datacenter that guards against electronic surveillance suppresses data leakage of sensitive security and military information. SCIFs are used to deny unauthorized personnel, such as foreign intelligence services or corporate spies, the opportunity for undetected entry into facilities for the exploitation of sensitive activities.

75. **A.** Access control consists of something you know, have, and are. A User ID and password are something you know; a swipe badge is something you have, and a biometric represents something you are. A security and access control policy is not a rule.

76. **B.** The HVAC system should maintain the appropriate temperature and humidity levels and provide closed-loop recirculating air-conditioning and positive pressurization and ventilation. Closed-loop means the air within the building is reused after properly filtered instead of bringing outside air in. Positive pressurization and ventilation should also be implemented to control contamination. Positive pressurization means that when an employee opens a door, the air goes out, and outside air does not come in.

77. **C.** Wet pipe systems always contain water in the pipes and are usually discharged by temperature-control–level sensors. One disadvantage of wet pipe systems is that the water in the pipes may freeze in colder climates. Also, if there is a nozzle or pipe break, it can cause extensive water damage. These types of systems are also called closed head systems. In dry pipe systems, the water is not held in the pipes. The water is contained in a "holding tank" until it is released. The pipes hold pressurized air, which is reduced when a fire or smoke alarm is activated, allowing the water valve to be opened by the water pressure. Water is not allowed into the pipes that feed the sprinklers until an actual fire is detected. First, a heat or smoke sensor is activated; then, the water fills the pipes leading to the sprinkler heads, the fire alarm sounds, the electric power supply is disconnected, and finally water can flow from the sprinklers. These pipes are best used in colder climates because the pipes will not freeze.

78. **D.** The HVAC system should be turned off before activating a fire suppressant to ensure it stays in the needed area and that smoke is not distributed to different areas of the facility.

12. Domain 4: Communication and Network Security - Questions

1. A security manager has just received a threat report for source spoofing attacks. He notices that filtering and mitigation techniques are not adequately implemented for unauthorized IP Addresses after reviewing the information. As a security manager, which of the following would be the most appropriate countermeasure to deploy?

    A. Determine whether filters are configured to block external IP Addresses that are not within the network boundary.

    B. Gathering data on what protocol and block requests are needed for internal IP addresses that are not recognized.

    C. Gathering access control list (ACL) rule requests and analyzing the implementation steps.

    D. Staying informed of platform patches to fix Transmission Control Protocol/Internet Protocol (TCP/IP) vulnerabilities, such as predictable packet sequences.

2. A Security Operational Center (SOC) Analyst has reviewed the threat logs for network traffic and notices several hosts have experienced above regular traffic activity. Host 1 shows about 2,000 echo replies within 30 seconds, and Host 2 has been experiencing 2,000 failed echo requests within the same time. What must configuration change be implemented?

    A. Configure Host 1 to block internet control message protocol (ICMP) outgoing traffic and configure Host 2 to block ICMP incoming traffic.

    B. Configure individual Host1 to not respond to ICMP requests or broadcasts, and adjust the audit logs to backup audit data for a specific threshold.

    C. Configure Host 1 to block IDS outgoing traffic and configure Host 2 to block IDS incoming traffic.

    D. Configure individual Host1 and Host2 to respond to ICMP requests or broadcasts.

3. Which of the following represents secure communication during a remote management session?

    A. A system that restricts SSH and Telecommunications Network (TELNET).

    B. A system that is configured with VPN protocols and SSHv2.

    C. A configured system using HTTP-SSL and port 23 for tunneling traffic.

    D. A configured system that restricts port 23 and HTTP-SSL.

4. Corporate executives for a major corporation are required to travel extensively for work outside their local regions. Feedback from the remote teams indicates that none of the locations have secure LAN connections. The security engineering team has been tasked to support the change and report their recommendations to the CEO and provide technologies that would help the difference for the organization. Which of the following would provide the best solution for the CEOs to access the corporate network?

    A. Establish a telecommuting program that would require Remote Desktop Services.

    B. Integrate a local LAN at each site and configure access through wireless infrastructure.

    C. Reconfigure the LAN at the primary site to extend its architecture and communication to remote regions.

    D. Establish a telecommuting program that would require VPN and wireless access.

5. Which of the following represents a secure method to protecting modems from being hacked?

   A. A security engineer has restricted the call for the modem to four rings.

   B. Modems that are not in use are configured for standby communications.

   C. Voice and fax communication is restricted for the modem.

   D. Remote users are restricted to using fax lines.

6. Organization ABC wants to increase its network protection by implementing zone security measures. One of the security measures requires every IP address to be examined and filtered before entering the network. Which security device is appropriate for this service?

   A. A firewall that restricts outbound IP addresses.

   B. The use of a router that examines and restricts via ingress filtering.

   C. The use of a router that examines and restricts outgoing traffic.

   D. The use of a switch that filters IP address schemes.

7. SEMAIS has installed a dual-homed firewall at its premises; there are reports of firewall bypassing errors. As the information security consultant, what will you recommend to SEMAIS?

   A. Disable packet forwarding or routing at OS.

   B. Enable packet forwarding or routing at OS.

   C. Change the firewall architecture.

   D. Use a firewall in conjunction with IDS.

8. SEMAIS is undergoing an IT security audit; SEMAIS traffic is routed to undisclosed locations during the audit. SEMAIS is susceptible to which of the next attack?

   A. Distributed DOS

   B. ARP poisoning

   C. Smurf

   D. Tear Drop

9. An Information Security Engineer at SEMAIS has strong suspicion about web-based programs being accessed at Layer 7. Which of the following strategy will he adopt for managing the suspicious behavior of these programs?

   A. Circuit Proxy

   B. Stateful firewall

   C. Application firewall

   D. IDS

10. SEMAIS has a hosted mail server for its employees and business correspondence. Most employees and business contacts are receiving spam through the SEMAIS mail server. The mail server is susceptible to which of the following attack?

    A. Open Relay

    B. Denial of Service (DoS)

    C. Malware Infected

    D. Fraggle

11. Information Security Engineers at SEMAIS reported to top management that of Bluejacking attack; what this attack stands for?

    A. An unsolicited message was sent.

    B. A cell phone was cloned.

    C. An infrastructure management (IM) channel introduced a worm.

    D. Traffic was analyzed.

12. Internet Protocol Security (IPSec) protocol used to function at which open systems interconnection (OSI) model layer?

    A. Data Link

    B. Transport

    C. Session

    D. Network

13. Which of the following is not a benefit of Network Address Translation (NAT)?

    A. Hiding the internal IP addressing scheme.

    B. Sharing a few public internet addresses with many internal clients.

    C. Using the private IP addresses from request for comment (RFC) 1918 on an internal network.

    D. Filtering network traffic to prevent brute-force attacks.

14. When you are designing a security system for Internet-delivered email, which of the following is least important?

    A. Nonrepudiation

    B. Availability

    C. Message integrity

    D. Access restriction

15. What is it called when email itself is used as an attack mechanism?

    A. Masquerading

    B. Mail-bombing

    C. Spoofing

    D. Smurf attack

16. Why is spam challenging to stop?

    A. Filters are ineffective at blocking inbound messages.

    B. The source address is usually spoofed.

    C. It is an attack requiring little expertise.

    D. Spam can cause denial-of-service attacks.

17. Which of the following is a connection that can be described as a logical circuit that always exists and is waiting for the customer to send data?

    A. Integrated Services for Digital Network (ISDN)

    B. Permanent Virtual Circuit (PVC)

    C. Virtual Private Network (VPN)

    D. Switched Virtual Circuit (SVC)

18. In addition to maintaining an updated system and controlling physical access, which of the following is the most effective countermeasure against Private Branch Exchange (PBX) fraud and abuse?

    A. Encrypting communications.

    B. Changing default passwords.

    C. Using transmission logs.

    D. Taping and archiving all conversations.

19. An attacker is trying to attack the admin interface of SEMAIS hosted web service; the attacker is trying every possible password. What type of attack is the attacker launching to gain access?

    A. Brute-force attacks

    B. Denial of service

    C. Social engineering

    D. Port scanning

20. **Which of the following is not a denial of service (DoS) attack?**

    A. Exploiting a flaw in a program to consume 100 percent of the CPU.

    B. Sending malformed packets to a system, causing it to freeze.

    C. Performing a brute-force attack against a known user account.

    D. Sending thousands of emails to a single address.

21. **What authentication protocol offers no encryption or protection for log-in credentials?**

    A. Password Authentication Protocol (PAP)

    B. Challenge Handshake Authentication Protocol (CHAP)

    C. Secure Socket Layer (SSL)

    D. Remote Authentication Dial-in User Service (RADIUS)

22. **Alice recently received an electronic mail message from Bob. What cryptographic goal would need to be met to convince Alice that Bob was the message's sender?**

    A. Nonrepudiation

    B. Confidentiality

    C. Availability

    D. Integrity

23. **SEMAIS has hired you as a network architect for safeguarding its private network and publicly hosted services. What will be your ideal choice for protecting SEMAIS IT infrastructure?**

    A. Circuit Proxy

    B. Virtual Land Area Network (VLAN)

    C. Demilitarized Zone (DMZ)

    D. Router

24. **You are working as a network administrator at SEMAIS. By monitoring the log of hosted web server, you come to know about half-open transmission control protocol (TCP) connections. SEMAIS is a victim of which type of attack?**

    A. Fraggle

    B. Simulation and Modeling Underlying Radio Frequencies (SMURF)

    C. Tear drop

    D. Denial of Service (DoS)

25. The CEO of SEMAIS is receiving emails from illegitimate senders that are luring him to different incentives and vacation packages through email links. The CEO is a victim of which attack?

    A. Social engineering

    B. Whaling

    C. Email Bomb

    D. Distributed DoS

26. Which one of the following cannot be achieved through a secret key cryptosystem?

    A. Nonrepudiation

    B. Confidentiality

    C. Availability

    D. Key distribution

27. Which of the following cryptosystem, if appropriately implemented, cannot be broken by a cryptanalyst?

    A. Data Encryption Standard (DES)

    B. One Time Pad

    C. Cesar Cipher

    D. Substitution cipher

28. What is the minimum number of cryptographic keys required for secure two-way communications in symmetric key cryptography?

    A. Three

    B. Four

    C. No Key

    D. One

29. Rivest-Shamir-Adleman (RSA) is a widely used asymmetric cryptographic algorithm; RSA is based on which mathematical problem?

    A. Addition

    B. Multiplication

    C. Integer Factorization

    D. Discrete logarithm problem

30. **Cryptographic Hash functions are used to provide which of the following properties?**

    A. Confidentiality

    B. Availability

    C. Integrity

    D. Nonrepudiation

31. **Senior management has created a policy that governs that all digital signatures must follow a unique standard. Upon reviewing the change, a security engineer decides to evaluate the results. The findings indicate that digital fingerprints were used. What other security relationship describes the results?**

    A. A hash converts variable-sized input into fixed output.

    B. A message converts invariable-sized input into fixed output.

    C. A key converts variable-sized input into variable output.

    D. A hash converts invariable-sized input into invariable output.

32. **SEMAIS has hired you as a Cybersecurity Consultant to detect and prevent cyber-attacks on its IT infrastructure border. What tool would support the SEMAIS initiative?**

    A. IDS

    B. Firewall

    C. Router

    D. IPS

33. **SEMAIS has hired you as a network administrator to segregate its private network. What can be implemented to segregate the network?**

    A. LAN

    B. VLAN

    C. Firewall

    D. Switch

34. **A network administrator at SEMAIS must integrate independents LANs. Which device below would best support their efforts?**

    A. Router

    B. Bridge

    C. Switch

    D. Hub

35. In tunnel mode, the _____ is protected (encrypted, authenticated, or both). The IPsec headers and trailers then encapsulate the packet. Finally, a new IP header is prefixed to the packet, specifying the IPsec endpoints as the source and destination.

   A. Entire IP packet

   B. IP header

   C. IP payload

   D. IP Flags

36. Systems built on the OSI framework are considered open systems. What does this standard indicate?

   A. They do not have authentication mechanisms configured by default.

   B. They have interoperability issues.

   C. They are built with internationally accepted protocols and standards, so they can easily communicate with other systems.

   D. They are built with international protocols and standards to choose what types of systems they will communicate with.

37. Which of the following protocols work in the following layers: application, data link, network, and transport?

   A. FTP, ARP, TCP, and UDP

   B. FTP, ICMP, IP, and UDP

   C. TFTP, ARP, IP, and UDP

   D. TFTP, Reverse Address Resolution Protocol (RARP), IP, and ICMP

38. A telephonic network is a typical example of which of the following?

   A. Packet-switched

   B. Circuit-switched

   C. Frame Relay

   D. SONET

39. A particular interest group has manipulated over 10,000 victim devices on the SEMAIS network through a dummy system. The CEO requests that all perimeter devices be evaluated for log activity and data breaches. What specific infection has occurred?

   A. Internet

   B. Botnet

   C. Telnet

   D. Zombie

40. **Secure shell (SSH) network protocol is used for which of the following?**

   A. Secure data communication

   B. Remote command-line login

   C. Remote command execution

   D. All the mentioned options.

41. **Which of the following protocol is specific to public key certificate generation?**

   A. X.25

   B. X.509

   C. X.400

   D. X.500

42. **Which of the following attack is considered most effective against Virtual Private Network (VPN) solutions?**

   A. Brute Force

   B. Replay

   C. Man in the Middle

   D. Tear Drop

43. **A system log file shows that over 34,000 events are executed every 2 minutes. Upon investigating the logs, it is discovered that an attack has occurred which disrupts network traffic. Additionally, a second attack occurred simultaneously that did depend on large packet sizes to affect the network. Which answer would describe the second attack?**

   A. Ping of Death

   B. Email Bomb

   C. Synchronize Flood

   D. Virus

44. **Being an Information Security Engineer at SEMAIS, you must propose a cryptographic system solution based on either symmetric key system or an asymmetric key (Public key) system. By considering performance-related issues, what will be your ideal choice?**

   A. Symmetric key

   B. Public Key

   C. Split knowledge

   D. Hash

45. Which of the following protocols is used for a Wi-Fi network?

    A. User Diagram Protocol (UDP)

    B. Wi-Fi Protected Access (WPA)2

    C. Secure Socket Layer (SSL)

    D. Transport Layer Security (TLS)

46. SEMAIS has a wireless fidelity (Wi-Fi) network on its premises that has been infiltrated from outside using various methods except for the benefit of phone numbers. What specific technique wir been used by the hacker?

    A. War dialing

    B. AP hijack

    C. War driving

    D. None of the mentioned options.

47. An attacker has discovered various IP addresses of a critical subnet. The hacker penetrates the subnet and discovers that each database file has empty tables and image files that "state you have been caught." The hacker believes he was monitored a lured down a monitored path. What defensive scheme did the organization install to attract the hacker?

    A. Hub

    B. Honeypot

    C. Zombie

    D. Intrusion Detection System (IDS)

48. A Wide Area Network (WAN) technology is used to transmit data in fixed cells and high data rate?

    A. Asynchronous Transfer Mode (ATM)

    B. Synchronous Optical Networking (SONET)

    C. Frame Relay

    D. Integrated Services for Digital Network (ISDN)

49. Which one of the following signaling protocols are used for voice over internet protocol (VoIP) communication?

    A. User Diagram Protocol (UDP)

    B. Session Initiation Protocol (SIP)

    C. Internet Message Protocol (ICMP)

    D. Transmission Control Protocol (TCP)

50. Smurf attack uses which one of the following protocols as its attack vector?

    A. Internet Message Protocol (ICMP)

    B. Secured Socket Layer (SSL)

    C. User Diagram Protocol (UDP)

    D. X.25

51. Which one of the services are not offered by the cloud computing model?

    A. Infrastructure as a Service (IaaS)

    B. Software as a Service (SaaS)

    C. Platform as a Service (PaaS)

    D. Storage Area Network (SAN)

52. Fourth generation of GSM is employing which of the following multiple access technique?

    A. Frequency division multiple access (FDMA)

    B. Orthogonal frequency division multiple access (OFDMA)

    C. Time-division multiple access (TDMA)

    D. Code division multiple access (CDMA)

53. Which one of the following keys is used to generate a certificate?

    A. The receiver's private key

    B. The sender's public key

    C. The sender's private key

    D. The receiver's public key

54. Which transmission media has the highest transmission speed in a network?

    A. Coaxial cable

    B. Twisted pair cable

    C. Optical fiber

    D. Electrical cable

55. **Devices that provide the connectivity to a World Interoperability for Microwave Access (WiMAX) network are known as:**

    A. Subscriber stations

    B. Base stations

    C. Gateway

    D. None of the mentioned options.

56. **The size of the internet protocol (IP) address in IPv6 is one of the following?**

    A. 64bits

    B. 128bits

    C. 92 bits

    D. 48bits

57. **In which of the following topology has a central controller or hub?**

    A. Star

    B. Mesh

    C. Ring

    D. Bus

13. Domain 4: Communication and Network Security - Answers and Explanations

1. **A.** Spoofing is a means to hide one's identity on the network. To create a spoofed identity, an attacker uses a fake source address that does not represent the actual address of the packet. Spoofing may be used to hide the source of an attack or to work around network access control lists (ACLs) that are in place to limit host access based on source address rules. Although carefully crafted spoofed packets may never be tracked to the original sender, a combination of filtering rules prevents spoofed packets from originating from your network, allowing you to block spoofed packets. Countermeasures to prevent spoofing include: 1) Filter incoming packets that appear to come from an internal IP address at your perimeter; and 2) Filter outgoing packets originating from an invalid local IP address.

2. **B.** ICMP is also used as the core protocol for a network tool called Traceroute. Traceroute is used to diagnose network connections, but since it gathers many vital network statistics, attackers use the tool to map out a victim's network. This is similar to a burglar "casing the joint," meaning that the more the attacker learns about the environment, the easier it can be for her to exploit some critical targets. While the Traceroute tool is a good networking program, a security administrator might configure the IDS sensors to monitor for extensive use of this tool because it could indicate an attacker attempting to map out the network's architecture. The countermeasures to these attacks are to use firewall rules that only allow the necessary ICMP packets into the network and IDS or IPS to watch for suspicious activities. Host-based protection (host firewalls and host IDS) can also be installed and configured to identify this type of suspicious behavior. ICMP ECHO REQUESTS should be disabled for incoming traffic. Adjusting the audit logs is appropriate to capture data for failed attempts. Setting the threshold will prevent the overloading of audit information.

3. **C.** Remote Desktop Services (RDS), known as Terminal Services, uses various ports to communicate during a session. RDP is mainly used to access another host for maintenance. This is a service most helpdesk has to troubleshoot a user's computer. Two of the ports used are SSH (Port 22) and Telnet (Port 23) through HTTP-SSL (HTTPS). Telnet is used for remote management and sometimes for the initial setup for some devices, especially network hardware like switches, access points, etc.

4. **D.** The best solution is to provide VPN access to the corporate network. Since the local LAN is not functional, the organization will need wireless access for an internet connection.
    https://en.wikipedia.org/wiki/Virtual_private_network

5. **A.** Modems should be configured to answer after a predetermined number of rings to counter war dialers. Disable or remove modems if not in use. All modems should be consolidated into one location and managed centrally if possible.

6. **B.** IP Address filtering occurs at layer 3 of the OSI model. This layer filters via a firewall and router. Filtering inbound traffic is known as ingress filtering. Outgoing traffic can also be filtered using a process referred to as egress filtering.

7. **A.** Dual-homed firewalls can be bypassed if the operating system does not have packet forwarding or routing disabled.

8. **B.** Altering an address resolution protocol (ARP) table so an IP address is mapped to a different mandatory access control (MAC) address is called ARP poisoning and can redirect traffic to an attacker's computer or an unattended system. A denial of service (DoS) attack is a malicious attempt to make a server or a network resource unavailable to users, usually by temporarily interrupting or suspending the services of a host connected to the Internet. ARP spoofing is a type of attack in which a malicious actor sends falsified ARP messages over a local area network. This results in linking an attacker's MAC address with the IP address of a legitimate computer or server on the web. The Smurf Attack is a distributed denial-of-service attack in which large numbers of Internet Control Message Protocol (ICMP) packets with the intended victim's spoofed source IP are broadcast to a computer network using an IP Broadcast address. A teardrop attack is a denial-of-service (DoS) attack that involves sending fragmented packets to a target machine. Since the machine receiving such packets cannot reassemble them due to a bug in TCP/IP fragmentation reassembly, they overlap, crashing the target network device.

9. **C.** An Application-Level Firewall or Web Application Firewall (WAF) is a firewall where one application-level (i.e., not kernel) process is used to forward each session that an internal user makes to a network resource on the public network. Application proxy firewalls provide high security and have full application-layer awareness about suspicious applications. A circuit-level gateway is a type of firewall that works at the session layer of the OSI model or as a "shim-layer" between the application layer and the transport layer of the TCP/IP stack. They monitor TCP handshaking between packets to determine whether a requested session is legitimate. In computing, a stateful firewall (any firewall that performs stateful packet inspection (SPI) or stateful inspection) is a firewall that keeps track of the state of network connections (such as TCP streams, UDP communication) traveling across it. An IDS is a device or software application that monitors a network or systems for malicious activity or policy violations.

10. **A.** An open mail relay is an SMTP server configured to allow anyone on the Internet to send e-mail through it, not just mail destined to or originating from known users. A denial of service (DoS) attack is a malicious attempt to make a server or a network resource unavailable to users, usually by temporarily interrupting or suspending the services of a host connected to the Internet. Malware, short for malicious software, is any software used to disrupt computer operations, gather sensitive information, gain access to private computer systems, or display unwanted advertising. A Fraggle Attack is a denial-of-service (DoS) attack that involves sending a large amount of spoofed UDP traffic to a router's broadcast address within a network. It is similar to a Smurf Attack, which uses spoofed ICMP traffic rather than UDP traffic to achieve the same goal.

11. **A.** Bluejacking occurs when someone sends an unsolicited message to a device that is Bluetooth enabled. Bluejackets look for a receiving device, i.e., phone, PDA, tablet PC, laptop, etc., then send a message to it.

12. **D.** The network layer is the third level of the Open Systems Interconnection Model (OSI) Model and the layer that provides data routing paths for network communication. Data is transferred in packets via logical network paths ordered format controlled by the network layer. IPSec protocol is used to function at the network layer of the OSI model. The data link layer or layer 2 is the second layer of the seven-layer OSI model of computer networking. This layer is the protocol layer that transfers data between adjacent network nodes in a vast area network (WAN) or between nodes on the same local area network (LAN) segment. The transport layer is the layer in the open system interconnection (OSI) model responsible for end-to-end communication over a network. It provides logical communication between application processes running on different hosts within a layered architecture of protocols and other network components. In the seven-layer OSI model of computer networking, the session layer is layer 5. The session layer provides the mechanism for opening, closing, and managing a session between end-user application processes, i.e., a semi-permanent dialogue.

13. **D.** Network address translation (NAT) is a method of remapping one IP address space into another by modifying network address information in Internet Protocol (IP) datagram packet headers while they are in transit across a traffic routing device. NAT does not protect against or prevent brute-force attacks.

14. **B.** Cryptography used to maintain communication security: In reliability theory and reliability engineering, the term availability has the following meanings: The degree to which a system, subsystem, or equipment is in a specified operable and committable state at the start of a mission, when the task is called for at an unknown, i.e., a random, time. Although availability is a crucial aspect of security, it is the least important security system aspect for Internet-delivered email. Nonrepudiation is the assurance that someone cannot deny something. Typically, nonrepudiation refers to the ability to ensure that a party to a contract or a communication cannot deny the authenticity of their signature on a document or send a message that they originated. Message integrity is verification that message has not been altered during its transmission. Access restriction is that access is restricted to the mail system.

15. **B.** Email bombing is a form of internet abuse in which massive volumes of identical emails are sent to a specific email address to affect a computer's operating system. When the mailbox gets flooded with countless unwanted emails, its capacity gets exhausted, leading to an inability to receive further emails. This may prevent the victim from receiving or noticing some other important message in their mail. A sluggish system or inability to send or receive emails can be indications of getting email bombed. This happens because the system is already preoccupied with processing countless emails.

16. **B.** It is often difficult to stop spam because the source of the messages is usually spoofed.

CISSP Examination Review Guide V1.0   78

17. B. A permanent virtual circuit (PVC) is a software-defined logical connection in a network such as a frame relay network. A PVC can be described as a logical circuit that always exists and waits for the customer to send data. Integrated Services for Digital Network (ISDN) is a set of communication standards for simultaneous digital transmission of voice, video, data, and other network services over the traditional circuits of the public switched telephone network. A virtual private network, also known as a VPN, is a private network that extends across a public network or internet. It enables users to send and receive data across shared or public networks as if their computing devices were directly connected to the private network. In a network, a switched virtual circuit (SVC) is a temporary virtual circuit established and maintained only for the duration of a data transfer session. A PVC is a continuously dedicated virtual circuit.

18. B. Changing default passwords on PBX systems provide the most effective increase in security.

19. A. Brute force (also known as brute force cracking) is a trial and error method used by application programs to decode encrypted data such as passwords or keys through exhaustive effort (using brute force) rather than employing intellectual strategies. Trying every possible password is a Brute-force attack. A denial of service (DoS) attack is a malicious attempt to make a server or a network resource unavailable to users, usually by temporarily interrupting or suspending the services of a host connected to the Internet. Social engineering is an attack vector that relies heavily on human interaction and often involves tricking people into breaking standard security procedures. A port scanner is an application designed to probe a server or host for open ports. Administrators often use this to verify their networks' security policies and attackers to identify services running on a host and exploit vulnerabilities.

20. C. A brute-force attack is not considered a DoS. Brute force (also known as brute force cracking) is a trial and error method used by application programs to decode encrypted data such as passwords or keys through exhaustive effort (using brute force) rather than employing intellectual strategies.

21. A. Password Authentication Protocol (PAP) is a standardized authentication protocol for PPP. PAP transmits usernames and passwords. It offers no form of encryption. It simply provides a means to transport the logon credentials from the client to the authentication server. In computing, the Challenge-Handshake Authentication Protocol (CHAP) authenticates a user or network host to an authenticating entity. That entity may be, for example, an Internet service provider. The Secure Sockets Layer (SSL) and Transport Layer Security (TLS) is the most widely deployed security protocol used today. It is essentially a protocol that provides a secure channel between two machines operating over the Internet or an internal network. Remote Authentication Dial-In User Service (RADIUS) is a networking protocol that provides centralized Authentication, Authorization, and Accounting (AAA or Triple-A) management for users who connect and use a network service.

22. A. Nonrepudiation prevents the sender of a message from denial sending the message. Nonrepudiation is the assurance that someone cannot deny something. Typically, nonrepudiation refers to the ability to ensure that a party to a contract or a communication cannot deny the authenticity of their signature on a document or send a message that they originated. In reliability theory and reliability engineering, the term availability has the following meanings: The degree to which a system, subsystem, or equipment is in a specified operable and committable state at the start of a mission, when the task is called for at an unknown, i.e., a random, time. Message integrity is verification that message has not been altered during its transmission. confidentiality is a set of rules that limits access to information.

23. B. Demilitarized zone (DMZ) is a physical or logical sub-network that separates an internal local area network (LAN) from other untrusted networks; usually, the Internet. External-facing servers, resources, and services are located in the DMZ, so they are accessible from the Internet, but the rest of the internal LAN remains unreachable. De-Militarized Zone is an ideal choice for safeguarding SEAMIS public and private networks. A circuit-level gateway is a type of firewall. Circuit-level gateways work at the session layer of the OSI model or as a "shim-layer" between the application layer and the transport layer of the TCP/IP stack. They monitor TCP handshaking between packets to determine whether a requested session is legitimate. A VLAN is any broadcast domain partitioned and isolated in a computer network at the data link layer (OSI layer 2). LAN is an abbreviation for local area networks. To subdivide a network into virtual LANs, one configures network equipment. A router is a networking device that forwards data packets between computer networks. Routers perform the traffic directing functions on the Internet. A data packet is typically forwarded from one router to another through the networks that constitute the internetwork until it reaches its destination node.

24. **D.** Denial of Service (DoS) is a type of attack where multiple compromised systems, which are often infected with a Trojan, are used to target a single system causing a denial of service (DoS) attack. An attacker is trying to make half-open TCP connections to SEMAIS web server, which is a manifestation of DoS. A Fraggle Attack is a denial-of-service (DoS) attack that involves sending a large amount of spoofed UDP traffic to a router's broadcast address within a network. It is similar to a Smurf Attack, which uses spoofed ICMP traffic rather than UDP traffic to achieve the same goal. The Smurf Attack is a distributed denial-of-service attack in which large numbers of Internet Control Message Protocol (ICMP) packets with the intended victim's spoofed source IP are broadcast to a computer network using an IP Broadcast address. A teardrop attack is a denial-of-service (DoS) attack that involves sending fragmented packets to a target machine. Since the machine receiving such packets cannot reassemble them due to a bug in TCP/IP fragmentation reassembly, they overlap, crashing the target network device.

25. **B.** Whaling is a type of social engineering in which CEOs and higher officials are targeted. These whaling attacks are a form of personalized phishing, or spear phishing, aimed at senior executives or others in an organization with access to lots of valuable or competitive information. Social engineering is an attack vector that relies heavily on human interaction and often involves tricking people into breaking standard security procedures. An email bomb is a form of net abuse consisting of sending huge volumes of email to an address in an attempt to overflow the mailbox or overwhelm the server where the email address is hosted in a denial-of-service attack. Distributed DoS is a type of DoS attack where multiple compromised systems, often infected with a Trojan, are used to target a single system causing a denial of service (DoS) attack.

26. **A.** Nonrepudiation requires using a public key cryptosystem to prevent users from falsely denying that they originated a message. Nonrepudiation prevents the sender of a message from denial sending the message. Nonrepudiation is the assurance that someone cannot deny something. Typically, nonrepudiation refers to the ability to ensure that a party to a contract or a communication cannot deny the authenticity of their signature on a document or send a message that they originated. In reliability theory and reliability engineering, the term availability has the following meanings: The degree to which a system, subsystem, or equipment is in a specified operable and committable state at the start of a mission, when the task is called for at an unknown, i.e., a random, time. Key distribution is the distribution of keying material to participants.

27. **B.** In cryptography, the one-time pad (OTP) is an encryption technique that cannot be cracked if used correctly. In this technique, a plaintext is paired with a random secret key (also referred to as a one-time pad). A one-time place is the only known cryptosystem that is not vulnerable to attacks. The Data Encryption Standard (DES) is a symmetric-key block cipher published by the National Institute of Standards and Technology (NIST). The Caesar cipher, also known as a shift cipher, is one of the simplest forms of encryption. It is a substitution cipher where each letter in the original message (called the plaintext) is replaced with a letter corresponding to a certain number of letters up or down in the alphabet. In cryptography, a substitution cipher is a method of encoding by which units of plaintext are replaced with ciphertext, according to a fixed system; the "units" may be single letters (the most common), pairs of notes, triplets of letters, mixtures of the above, and so forth.

28. **D.** Symmetric key cryptography uses a shared secret key. All communicating parties utilize the same key for communication in any direction.

29. **C.** Rivest-Shamir-Adleman (RSA) is one of the first practicable public-key cryptosystems and is widely used to secure data transmission. In such a cryptosystem, the encryption key is public and differs from the decryption key, which is kept secret. The essence of RSA is based on "Integer Factorization." In number theory, integer factorization is the decomposition of a composite number into a product of smaller integers. If these integers are further restricted to prime numbers, the process is called prime factorization.

30. **C.** A cryptographic hash function is a particular class of hash functions with specific properties that make it suitable for cryptography. It is a mathematical algorithm that maps data of arbitrary size to a bit string of a fixed

size (a hash function), also designed to be a one-way function, a function that is infeasible to invert. Hash functions are used for the provision of integrity. Nonrepudiation requires using a public key cryptosystem to prevent users from falsely denying that they originated a message. Nonrepudiation prevents the sender of a message from denial sending the message. Nonrepudiation is the assurance that someone cannot deny something. Typically, nonrepudiation refers to the ability to ensure that a party to a contract or a communication cannot deny the authenticity of their signature on a document or send a message that they originated. In reliability theory and reliability engineering, the term availability has the following meanings: The degree to which a system, subsystem, or equipment is in a specified operable and committable state at the start of a mission, when the task is called for at an unknown, i.e., a random, time. Key distribution is the distribution of keying material to participants.

31. **A.** A cryptographic hash function is a particular class of hash functions with specific properties that make it suitable for cryptography. It is a mathematical algorithm that maps data of arbitrary size to a bit string of a fixed size (a hash function), also designed to be a one-way function, a function that is infeasible to invert. Cryptographic hash functions convert variable-sized input into fixed output. Cryptographic hash functions have many information security applications, notably in digital signatures, message authentication codes (MACs), and other forms of authentication. They can also be used as ordinary hash functions, index data in hash tables, fingerprinting, detect duplicate data or uniquely identify files, and checksums to detect accidental data corruption. Indeed, in information security contexts, cryptographic hash values are sometimes called (digital) fingerprints, checksums, or just hash values, even though all these terms stand for functions with somewhat different properties and purposes.

32. **D.** An Intrusion Prevention System (IPS) is a network security/threat prevention technology that examines network traffic flows to detect and prevent vulnerability exploits. IPS is the only option available for detecting and preventing cyber-attacks. An intrusion detection system is a device or software application that monitors a network or systems for malicious activity or policy violations. A firewall is a network security system designed to prevent unauthorized access to or from a private network. Firewalls can be implemented in both hardware and software or a combination of both. A router is a networking device that forwards data packets between computer networks. Routers perform the traffic directing functions on the Internet. A data packet is typically forwarded from one router to another through the networks that constitute the internetwork until it reaches its destination node.

33. **B.** A VLAN is any broadcast domain partitioned and isolated in a computer network at the data link layer (OSI layer 2). To subdivide a network into virtual LANs, one configures network equipment. VLAN can be adopted for the segregation of private networks. A local area network (LAN) is a computer network that interconnects computers within a limited area such as a residence, school, laboratory, university campus, or office building and has its network equipment and interconnects locally managed. A firewall is a network security system designed to prevent unauthorized access to or from a private network. Firewalls can be implemented in both hardware and software or a combination of both. A network switch (also called switching hub, bridging hub, officially MAC bridge) is a computer networking device that connects devices on a computer network using packet switching to receive, process, and forward data to the destination device.

34. **B.** A bridge is a type of computer network device that provides interconnection with other bridge networks that use the same protocol. Bridge devices work at the data link layer of the Open System Interconnect (OSI) model, connecting two different networks and providing communication between them. A bridge is used to bridge independents LANs. A router is a networking device that forwards data packets between computer networks. Routers perform the traffic directing functions on the Internet. A data packet is typically forwarded from one router to another through the networks that constitute the internetwork until it reaches its destination node. A network switch (also called switching hub, bridging hub, officially MAC bridge) is a computer networking device that connects devices on a computer network using packet switching to receive, process, and forward data to the destination device.

35. **A.** Internet Protocol Security (IPsec) is a protocol suite for secure Internet Protocol (IP) communications that works by authenticating and encrypting each IP packet of a communication session. IPSec has two modes, i.e., tunneled mode and transport mode. In tunnel mode, IPsec protects the whole packet.

36. **C.** An open system is a system that has been developed based on standardized protocols and interfaces. Following these standards allows the systems to interoperate more effectively with other systems that follow the same standards.

37. C. Each layer has specific functionality and has several different protocols to live at that layer and carry out that particular functionality. These listed protocols work at these associated layers: Trivial File Transfer Protocol (TFTP) (application), ARP (data link), IP (network), and UDP (transport).

38. A. Packet-switched describes the type of network in which relatively small units of data called packets are routed through a network based on the destination address contained within each packet. Breaking communication down into packets allows the same data path to be shared among many users in the network. Telephonic networks are packet-switched. A type of communication in which a dedicated channel (or circuit) is established for the duration of a transmission. Frame Relay is a standardized comprehensive area network technology that specifies digital telecommunications channels' physical and data link layers using a packet switching methodology. Synchronous Optical Networking (SONET) and Synchronous Digital Hierarchy (SDH) are standardized protocols that transfer multiple digital bit streams synchronously over optical fiber using lasers or highly coherent light from light-emitting diodes (LEDs).

39. B. A botnet (also known as a zombie army) is several Internet computers that, although their owners are unaware of it, have been set up to forward transmissions (including spam or viruses) to other computers on the Internet. Botnets are victim devices controlled and manipulated by the attacker. The Internet is the global system of interconnected computer networks that use the Internet protocol suite (TCP/IP) to link billions of devices worldwide. Telnet is a user command and an underlying TCP/IP protocol for accessing remote computers. Through Telnet, an administrator or another user can access someone else's computer remotely. A zombie is a computer connected to the Internet that has been compromised by a hacker, computer virus, or trojan horse program and can be used to perform malicious tasks of one sort or another under remote direction.

40. D. Secure Shell (SSH), sometimes known as Secure Socket Shell, is a UNIX-based command interface and protocol for securely getting access to a remote computer. network administrators widely use it to control Web and other kinds of servers remotely. SSH is used to provide all the listed options.

41. B. In cryptography, X.509 is an essential standard for a PKI to manage digital certificates and public-key encryption and a key part of the Transport Layer Security protocol used to secure web and email communication. X.509 defines the format for public-key certificate. X.25 is an ITU-T standard protocol suite for packet-switched wide area network (WAN) communication. An X.25 WAN consists of packet-switching exchange (PSE) node hardware leased lines, plain old telephone service connections, or ISDN connections as physical links. X.400 and X.500 are irrelevant options.

42. C. A man-in-the-middle attack (often abbreviated MitM, MiM attack, MitMA, or the same using all capital letters) is an attack where the attacker secretly relays and possibly alters the communication between two parties who believe they are directly communicating with each other. Most active attack against VPN solution is Man in the Middle (MitM) in which attacker place himself between sender and receiver. Brute force (also known as brute force cracking) is a trial and error method used by application programs to decode encrypted data such as passwords or keys through exhaustive effort (using brute force) rather than employing intellectual strategies. A replay attack (also known as a playback attack) is a form of network attack in which valid data transmission is maliciously or fraudulently repeated or delayed. A teardrop attack is a denial-of-service (DoS) attack that involves sending fragmented packets to a target machine. Since the machine receiving such packets cannot reassemble them due to a bug in TCP/IP fragmentation reassembly, they overlap, crashing the target network device.

43. D. First three options are relevant to DoS attack, whereas the virus has no dependence on packet size or large volume of data. A ping of death is a type of attack on a computer system that involves sending a malformed or otherwise malicious ping to a computer. A correctly formed ping packet is typically 56 bytes in size, or 84 bytes when the Internet Protocol header is considered. an email bomb is a form of net abuse consisting of sending huge volumes of email to an address in an attempt to overflow the mailbox or overwhelm the server where the email address is hosted in a denial-of-service attack. A SYN flood is a form of denial-of-service attack in which an attacker sends a succession of SYN requests to a target's system in an attempt to consume enough server resources to make the system unresponsive to legitimate traffic.

44. A. Symmetric key cryptographic algorithms are faster than public-key cryptographic algorithms, so these solutions are preferred in performance constraint environments. Asymmetric encryption is slower than symmetric encryption. It requires far more processing power to both encrypt and decrypt the content of the message.

45. B. WPA2, Short for Wi-Fi Protected Access 2 - Pre-Shared Key, also called WPA or WPA2 Personal, is a method of securing your network using WPA2 with the use of the optional Pre-Shared Key (PSK) authentication, which was designed for home users without an enterprise authentication server. WPA2 is a prevalent protocol for protecting Wi-Fi networks. UDP (User Datagram Protocol) is an alternative communications protocol to Transmission Control Protocol (TCP) to establish low-latency and loss tolerating connections between applications on the Internet. SSL (Secure Sockets Layer) is the standard security technology for establishing an encrypted link between a web server and a browser. This link ensures that all data passed between the web server and browsers remain private and integral. Transport Layer Security (TLS) and its predecessor, Secure Sockets Layer (SSL), both frequently referred to as "SSL," are cryptographic protocols that provide communications security over a computer network.

46. C. War driving is an attack on the Wi-Fi network from outside. War dialing or war dialing is a modem technique to automatically scan a list of telephone numbers, usually dialing every number in a local area code to search for computers, bulletin board systems (computer servers), and fax machines. AP hijacking is a mechanism for the hijacking access point.

47. B. A honeypot is a decoy computer system for trapping hackers or tracking unconventional or new hacking methods. Honeypots are designed to purposely engage and deceive hackers and identify malicious activities performed over the Internet. Multiple honeypots can be set on a network to form a honeynet. Honeypot is a vulnerable system to attract attackers to itself. A hub is a common connection point for devices in a network. Hubs are commonly used to connect segments of a LAN and contain multiple ports. When a packet arrives at one port, it is copied to the other ports so that all segments of the LAN can see all packets. A zombie (also known as a bot) is a computer that a remote attacker has accessed and set up to forward transmissions (including spam and viruses) to other computers on the Internet. The purpose is usually either financial gain or malice. Attackers typically exploit multiple computers to create a botnet, also known as a zombie army. An intrusion detection system (IDS) is a device or software application that monitors a network or system for malicious activity or policy violations.

48. A. ATM is WAN technology used to transmit data in fixed cells and high data rate. ATM provides functionality similar to both circuit switching and packet switching networks: ATM uses asynchronous time-division multiplexing and encodes data into small, fixed-sized packets (ISO-OSI frames) called cells. Synchronous Optical Networking (SONET) and Synchronous Digital Hierarchy (SDH) are standardized protocols that transfer multiple digital bit streams synchronously over optical fiber using lasers or highly coherent light from light-emitting diodes (LEDs). Frame Relay is a standardized wide area network technology that specifies digital telecommunications channels' physical and data link layers using a packet switching methodology. Integrated Services Digital Network (ISDN) is a set of communication standards for simultaneous digital transmission of voice, video, data, and other network services over the traditional circuits of the public switched telephone network.

49. B. The Session Initiation Protocol (SIP) is a communications protocol for signaling and controlling multimedia communication sessions. The most common SIP applications are Internet telephony for voice and video calls and instant messaging over Internet Protocol (IP) networks. SIP (Session Initiation Protocol) is a signaling protocol widely used for VoIP communications sessions. The User Datagram Protocol (UDP) is the most straightforward Transport Layer communication protocol available in the TCP/IP protocol suite. It involves minimum amount of communication mechanisms. UDP is an unreliable transport protocol, but it uses IP services that provide a best-effort delivery mechanism. The Internet Control Message Protocol (ICMP) is one of the main protocols of the internet protocol suite. It is used by network devices, like routers, to send error messages indicating, for example, that a requested service is not available or that a host or router could not be reached. TCP/IP (Transmission Control Protocol/Internet Protocol) is the Internet's basic communication language or protocol. It can also be used as a communications protocol in a private network (either an intranet or an extranet).

50. A. The Smurf Attack is a distributed denial-of-service (DoS) attack in which large numbers of Internet Control Message Protocol (ICMP) packets with the intended victim's spoofed source IP are broadcast to a computer network using an IP Broadcast address. Smurf attack uses ICMP protocol as its attack vector.

51. D. A storage area network (SAN) is a network that provides access to consolidated, block-level data storage. SANs are primarily used to enhance storage devices, such as disk arrays, tape libraries, and optical jukeboxes, accessible to servers so that the devices appear to the operating system as locally attached devices. The Cloud computing model does not offer SAN. Infrastructure as a Service (IaaS) is a form of cloud computing that provides virtualized computing resources over the Internet. Software as a Service is a software licensing and delivery model in which software is licensed on a subscription basis and is centrally hosted. It is sometimes referred to as "on-demand software." SaaS is typically accessed by users using a thin client via a web browser. Platform as a service (PaaS) is a category of cloud computing services that provides a platform allowing customers to develop, run, and manage applications without the complexity of building and maintaining the infrastructure typically associated with developing and launching an app.

52. B. Orthogonal frequency division multiple access (OFDMA) is employed in 4th generation GSM. Frequency division multiple access or FDMA, a channel access method used in multiple-access protocols as a channelization protocol. FDMA gives users an individual allocation of one or several frequency bands or channels. It is particularly commonplace in satellite communication. Time-division multiple access (TDMA) is a channel access method for shared medium networks. It allows several users to share the same frequency channel by dividing the signal into different time slots. The users transmit in rapid succession, one after the other, each using its time slot. Code division multiple access (CDMA) is a channel access method used by various radio communication technologies. CDMA is an example of multiple access, which is where several transmitters can send information simultaneously over a single communication channel.

53. C. A digital signature is a message digest that has been signed with the sender's private key.

54. C. A fiber optic cable consists of a bundle of glass threads capable of transmitting messages modulated onto light waves. Optical fiber has the highest transmission speed in a network. Coaxial cable or coax is a cable type with an inner conductor surrounded by a tubular insulating layer, surrounded by a tubular conducting shield. Many coaxial cables also have an insulating outer sheath or jacket. Twisted pair cabling is a type of wiring in which two conductors of a single circuit are twisted together to cancel out electromagnetic interference (EMI) from external sources; for instance, electromagnetic radiation from unshielded twisted pair (UTP) cables and crosstalk between neighboring pairs. The electrical cable is not relevant here.

55. A. Subscriber stations provide connectivity to a WiMAX network.

56. B. IPv6 is the sixth revision to the Internet Protocol and the successor to IPv4. It functions similarly to IPv4 in that it provides the unique, numerical IP addresses necessary for Internet-enabled devices to communicate. However, it makes sport one significant difference: it utilizes 128-bit addresses.

57. A. A star topology is a topology for a Local Area Network (LAN) in which all nodes are individually connected to a central connection point, like a hub or a switch. A star takes more cable than, e.g., a bus, but the benefit is that only one node will be brought down if a line fails. Star topology has a central controller or hub. A mesh network is a network topology in which each node relays data for the web. All mesh nodes cooperate in the distribution of data in the network. Mesh networks can relay messages using either a flooding technique or a routing technique. A ring network is a network topology in which each node connects to exactly two other nodes, forming a single continuous pathway for signals through each node - a ring. Data travels from node to node, with each node along the way handling every packet. A bus network is a network topology where nodes are directly connected to a standard linear (or branched) half-duplex link called a bus.

14. Domain 5: Identity and Access Management (IaM) - Questions

1. **SEMAIS is developing internal network controls to support user roles and role-based privileges. The mechanism for controlling the users' privileges applies to which of the following authentication methodologies?**

   A. Access to vital resources.

   B. Access control to vital resources.

   C. Allow access to vital resources.

   D. Deny access to vital resources.

2. **SEMAIS has installed a biometric access control for user authentication. The features for the biometric access control require facial recognition. Which one of the following would use this form of authentication? Pick the best answer.**

   A. Access control mechanism enforced by network administrator on critical servers.

   B. Access control for catering entry/exit requirements.

   C. Access control mechanism as defined in SEMAIS security policy.

   D. Rule-based access control.

3. **A subject is an active entity that requests access to an object or the data within an object. A subject can be all except one of the following?**

   A. User accessing an object.

   B. Program accessing peripherals of computer.

   C. Process accessing memory.

   D. Deployed critical servers.

4. **What is the sequence of logical steps for the access control model?**

   A. Identification, Authentication, Authorization, Accountability.

   B. Authentication, Authorization, Accountability, Identification.

   C. Authorization, Authentication, Accountability, Identification.

   D. Accountability, Authorization, Authentication, Identification.

5. **SEMAIS is planning to deploy biometric-based access control across its premises. As a technical manager of SEMAIS, what is your primary consideration in selecting Biometric access controls from different vendors?**

   A. Biometric system with 90% Type 1 error.

   B. Biometric system with 90% Type 2 error.

C. Biometric system with minimum crossover error rate (CER).

D. Biometric system with maximum crossover error rate (CER).

6. **Which one of the following is not a biometric-based access control/authentication mechanism?**

   A. Voice Print

   B. Iris Scan

   C. Fingerprint

   D. Passwords

7. **SEMAIS executes an organization-wide policy for secure passwords; therefore, all users must protect individual and system passwords. There is a suspicion that some users are using a retired password for several applications. The password was retired by the CEO due to security concerns. The CEO knows that the password is "secure101." Which of the following would be the quickest method to determine whether the password has been entirely changed from all users' accounts?**

   A. Brute forcing individual's password.

   B. Trick employees to get their passwords through social engineering.

   C. Dictionary attack to get employees' passwords.

   D. Manually keep track record of all users' passwords.

8. **The prevalent technique for breaking passwords by comparing already calculated hashes in an efficient and timely manner represents which of the following?**

   A. Using a rainbow table with precomputed hash values.

   B. Dictionary made of usernames with probable passwords.

   C. Trying every possible option for retrieving the correct password.

   D. List of all users over the world.

9. **As a network administrator, you must assign rights so subjects can access specific resources. This access control model represents which answer?**

   A. Access rights are assigned by security classification and categorization of the object.

   B. The owner of resources can access rights.

   C. Access rights are assigned based on the employee position.

   D. Access rights are assigned based on the accessor's identity.

10. **SEMAIS must provide IT consultancy services to a commercial enterprise having thousands of employees. As a consultant, which one of the following access control models will be your most ideal choice to minimize the users' management overhead?**

    A. Access rights are assigned based on the employee position.

    B. Owner of resources assigns the rights of access.

C. Access rights are assigned to security classification and security categorization.

D. Access rights are assigned based on the CEO's decision.

11. SEMAIS must provide IT consultancy services to sensitive resources. The resources are labeled: Confidential but Sensitive information. As a consultant, which one of the following access control models will be your most ideal choice?

A. Owner of resources assigns the rights of access.

B. Access rights are assigned based on the position of and employee.

C. Access rights are assigned to security classification and security categorization.

D. Access rights are assigned based on the identity of the accessor.

12. Firewall employs one of the following access control models to filter traffic?

A. Owner of resources assigns the rights of access.

B. Access rights are assigned based on the position of and employee.

C. Access rights are assigned to security classification and security categorization.

D. Traffic deny or allow based on rules defined.

13. Which one of the following is not an access control mechanism/technique?

A. Access controls dictated by the enterprise's security policy.

B. Access controls deployed at entry/exit point.

C. Access controls enforced by network administrator.

D. Access control mechanism introduced by individual users against the enterprise security policy.

14. SEMAIS has an internal LAN. There are reports that unauthorized employees of the IT departments are accessing data of the payroll department. As a network administrator, how can you restrict inter-departmental access?

A. Divide LAN into VLANs

B. Employee Firewall within LAN

C. Employee IDS within LAN

D. Employee Host-based Firewall within LAN

15. There are various methodologies used to separate a network into security zones. As a security engineer, which would not be a routine task for executing the statement?

A. Ensure physical security of networking equipment.

B. Deploy employee encryption across SEMAIS LAN.

C. Restrict access to the network.

D. Deploy closed-circuit television (CCTV) cameras across SEMAIS.

16. **SEMAIS has installed a security information and event management (SIEM) system. There are strong indicators that SEMAIS is being attacked, and there are no active indicators. It is believed that the attacker is deleting log entries. This incident proves which of the following?**

    A. Scrubbing is occurring.

    B. The IDS deployed sensor is not placed at its proper network position.

    C. The Security Information and Event Management (SIEM) is misconfigured.

    D. Indications of SEMAIS being attacked are false.

17. **SEMAIS has been hired to consult on a new datacenter design. The organization wants to protect spurious emissions outside the datacenter. As a consultant, which one of the following will you not recommend?**

    A. Use white noise to be mixed with electrical signals.

    B. Establish Faraday cage across sensitive servers of the datacenter.

    C. Datacenter concrete walls are sufficient to protect spurious emissions.

    D. Implement an employee control zone across the datacenter.

18. **What would be a great choice to strengthen security for an intrusion detection system (IDS) as an ethical hacker?**

    A. Unfilter a Denial-of-service attack.

    B. Send alerts when the IDS has incorrect data patterns.

    C. Both options A & B.

    D. Options A & B are not viable for the IDS.

19. **Sensors are an integral component for SEMAIS IDSs and attacks. As a network administrator of SEMAIS, what will be your least consideration for the IDS sensors?**

    A. Place a sensor outside of the firewall.

    B. Place a sensor inside the firewall (in the perimeter network) to detect actual intrusions.

    C. Place a sensor within DMZ.

    D. Place a sensor within the internal LAN.

20. **You are in the process of purchasing an IDS for SEMAIS; what will be your most important consideration in selecting the IDS?**

    A. Choosing an IDS vendor with an excellent customer report.

    B. The IDS system's threshold for processing network traffic.

C. IDS with a large signature pattern

D. Whether an IDS is already installed at an alternate site.

21. **SEMAIS is configured in a switched environment. You have to install a network-based IDS for SEMAIS. What will be your most important consideration in installing and configuration the Network Intrusion Detection System (NIDS)?**

   A. Configure a spanning port where the IDS sensor is located.

   B. Use a bridge instead of a switch.

   C. Use a hub instead of a switch.

   D. Use a router instead of a switch.

22. **Which one of the following is a social engineering attack that affects access control techniques?**

   A. Trying every possible option.

   B. Pre-computed hash calculated for addressing overhead.

   C. UDP-based denial of service attack at the broadcast address.

   D. Email received with an embedded link from a trustworthy source.

23. **Which access control system discourages the violation of security processes, policies, and procedures?**

   A. Access control for incident detection after the occurrence.

   B. Access control is intended to prevent an incident from occurring.

   C. Access control to bring the environment into regular operations.

   D. Access control to deter an attacker.

24. **What type of access control system is deployed to deter unauthorized access physically?**

   A. Access control is intended to prevent incidents from occurring.

   B. Access control methodologies that detect potential attackers.

   C. Access control to bring the environment back to regular operations.

   D. Access control to provide an alternative measure of control.

25. **Which of the following does not reflect the protected elements under an access control methodology?**

   A. The system remains intact as required.

   B. The system can be extended and updated.

   C. A person accessing the system is liable for individual actions.

   D. The system is enforcing all confidential measures.

26. **Which one of the following represents hardware, software, or procedures that define administrative access and restriction rights?**

    A. Logical control

    B. Technical control

    C. Access control

    D. Answer A and B

27. **To adequately protect an IT infrastructure against dictionary and other password attacks, which of the following should not be considered?**

    A. Passwords to be sent to the authentication server in cleartext.

    B. Use hard-to-guess passwords.

    C. Change passwords frequently.

    D. Protect password files.

28. **To prevent SEMAIS employees from pharming attack, which one of the following would not be recommended?**

    A. Be skeptical of e-mails indicating password change.

    B. Review the address bar to see if the domain name is correct.

    C. Do not click an HTML link within an e-mail. Type the URL out manually instead.

    D. Have an alphanumeric password with a minimum of 10 characters in length.

29. **Which one of the following principles is not a great choice at restricting users' access?**

    A. Only allow those access rights which are relevant to employees' duties.

    B. Only share information with employees which is duty-specific.

    C. Network administrator activities should be audited frequently.

    D. Allow all access to all employees for maximum efficiency and meeting goals.

30. **Which one of the following languages are used to enforce access control and implement security policies?**

    A. Extensible Access Control Markup Language (XACML)

    B. Service Provisioning Markup Language (SPML)

    C. Extensible Markup Language (XML)

    D. C++

31. SEMAIS has discovered that an attack has occurred on its enterprise. The final report states the attack involved capturing access control information, and its subsequent retransmission and unauthorized access were granted. What attack has been described in the report?

    A. Rainbow table

    B. Dictionary Attack

    C. Brute force Attack

    D. Replay attack

32. SEMAIS has selected smart cards as a new authentication method across its enterprise. During the risk assessment, the security team decides to list attack scenarios based on threats and vulnerabilities associated with smart cards. In the final risk report, what threats should the team reference?

    A. Replay attack

    B. Side-channel attack

    C. Dictionary attack

    D. Brute force attack

33. An IT Security officer is suggesting that developers implement challenge-response protocols across SEMAIS IT infrastructure. What is a challenge-response protocol? Choose the best answer.

    A. An Advanced Encryption Standard (AES).

    B. An authentication service generates a challenge, and the smart token generates a challenge response.

    C. The token challenges for using VPNs.

    D. The token challenges the user's password against a database of stored credentials.

34. Which of the following is the widely used and cheapest access control mechanism?

    A. Password-based access control mechanism.

    B. Smart card for the sake of user authentication.

    C. USB Tokens for validation and authentications at enterprise's critical servers.

    D. Fingerprint scanning before access.

35. Which could be considered a single point of failure within a single sign-on (SSO) implementation?

    A. An authentication server that's deployed for entertaining users' requests.

    B. User's workstation for making authentication requests.

    C. Login credentials traversed to a server after encryption.

    D. Login credentials traversed to a server after encryption and hashing.

36. **What is the relationship between fingerprint biometric and an access control mechanism?**

    A. Identification for the sake of access control.

    B. Authentication access controls, subsequently for authorization and accountability.

    C. Authorization of users and designated objects when performing duties.

    D. Accountability in case of any mishap.

37. **SEMAIS wants to implement a solution that allows its employees to remember one password across different systems and platforms. In which of the following SEMAIS should be interested?**

    A. Password generation for all platforms at the central location.

    B. Password dictionaries maintained by SEMAIS network administrator.

    C. Password rainbow tables.

    D. Password synchronization.

38. **Which of the following types of access control seeks to discover evidence of unwanted, unauthorized, or illicit behavior or activity?**
    A. Access control to stop an incident from occurring.

    B. Access control to discourage a potential attacker.

    C. Access control to identify incidents.

    D. Access control to fix items after the incident occurrence.

39. **Which of the following is not a valid password criteria?**

    A. Difficult to guess or unpredictable.

    B. Meet threshold length requirements.

    C. Meet specific complexity requirements.

    D. Password should have encrypted parts of the username.

40. **What is the best data source to utilize when recreating the history of an event, intrusion, or system failure?**

    A. Security policies are implemented at the enterprise level.

    B. Log files being created across controls deployed.

    C. Audit reports of an annual audit.

    D. Implement business continuity planning to help business operations.

41. When performing access review audits, which type of account is the most important to audit?

    A. User accounts

    B. Deleted accounts

    C. Privileged accounts with maximum access rights

    D. Management accounts

42. Which of the following aligns with to absence of using due care as a security practice?

    A. Periodic security review audits.

    B. Deployment controls deployed across SEMAIS.

    C. Performance reviews of employees.

    D. No security policy at SEMAIS.

43. A new control has been implemented to monitor uses activity after a successful login. During the authorization stage, a user notices that several notices are generated through email that states: Your access to database 1 has been logged. What specific event has caused the notification to execute?

    A. Authentication of users at the time of identification.

    B. The accountability of user accounts.

    C. Account lockout after a certain period of inactivity.

    D. User entitlement reviews for access rights.

44. Which one of the following is not a technology that uses centralized management as an authentication scheme?

    A. Remote Authentication Dial-In User Service (RADIUS)

    B. Terminal Access Controller Access Control System (TACACS+)

    C. Diameter (an authentication, authorization, and accounting protocol for computer networks)

    D. Peer-to-peer working group

45. Which of the following protocol is used for authentication, authorization, and configuration between network access and authentication servers?

    A. Remote Authentication Dial-In User Service (RADIUS)

    B. Internet Protocol Security (IPsec)

    C. Layer 2 Tunneling Protocol (L2TP)

    D. Point-to-Point Tunneling Protocol (PPTP)

46. **Which one of the following is not an advantage of using passphrases as compared to passwords?**

    A. Difficult to crack by using brute force attack.

    B. Easier to remember.

    C. Longer than passwords.

    D. Passphrases require more typing compared to passwords.

47. **Which one of the following attacks involves actions to mimics one's identity?**

    A. Brute force attack

    B. Spoofing attack

    C. Fraggle attack

    D. Social Engineering Attack

48. **Which one of the following correctly describes Role-Based Access Control (RBAC)?**

    A. It enforces enterprise-specific security policies in a way that maps user profile groups.

    B. It enforces enterprise-specific security policies in a way that maps organization structure.

    C. It enforces enterprise-specific security policies in a way that maps according to the access control list.

    D. It enforces enterprise-specific security policies as per security classification.

49. **Departmental managers have been granted read access to their employee's salaries and restricted access to external departments' employee salaries. A database security mechanism that enforces this policy would be providing which one of the following?**

    A. Content Dependent access control

    B. Context-Dependent access control

    C. Lest privilege access control

    D. Need to know access control

50. **Internet service providers (ISP) employ which of the following protocols for user authentication and authorization?**

    A. Remote Authentication Dial-In User Service (RADIUS)

    B. Terminal Access Controller Access Control System+ (TACACS+)

    C. Diameter (an authentication, authorization, and accounting protocol for computer networks)

    D. Terminal Access Controller Access Control System (TACACS)

51. **Which answer represents the most insecure practice for datacenter design?**

    A. Physically separated datacenter.

    B. Location of datacenter on the ground floor or centralized location.

    C. Biometric-based access control to be deployed at the datacenter.

    D. The datacenter should be in the basement of the building.

15. Domain 5: Identity and Access Management (IaM) - Answers and Explanations

1. **B.** Access control is a broad term covering several different mechanisms that enforce access control features on computer systems, networks, and information. Access control is essential because it is one of the first lines of defense in battling unauthorized access to systems and network resources.

2. **B.** Biometric-based access control is a typical example of physical access control. Logical access controls are technical tools used for identification, authentication, authorization, and accountability. They are software components that enforce access control measures for systems, programs, processes, and information. Mandatory access control is an access control mechanism that restricts subjects' access to objects based on the security clearance of the issue and the classification of the object.

3. **D.** All are the typical examples of subjects as a subject can be a user, program, or process that accesses an object to accomplish a task except deployed critical servers as these critical servers are objects by itself.

4. **A.** The correct sequence of logical steps for any access control model is Identification, Authentication, Authorization, Accountability. Identification describes a method of ensuring that a subject (user, program, or process) is the entity it claims to be. Identification can be provided with the use of a username or account number. Authentication is the process of verifying the subject's identity; it can be a password, passphrase, cryptographic key, personal identification number (PIN), anatomical attribute, or token. Authorization is when a subject provides its credentials and is properly identified and authenticated; the system it is trying to access needs to determine if it has been given the necessary rights and privileges to carry out the requested actions. Accountability is auditing logs and monitoring to track subject activities with objects.

5. **C.** Type I error (false rejection rate) is when a biometric system rejects an authorized individual. Type II error (false acceptance rate) when the system accepts impostors should be dismissed. The goal is to obtain low numbers for each error, but Type II errors are the most dangerous and the most important to avoid. Many other variables are used when comparing different biometric systems, but one of the most important metrics is the crossover error rate (CER). This rating is stated as a percentage and represents the point at which the false rejection rate equals the false acceptance rate. This rating is the most important measurement when determining the system's accuracy. As a general principle, the lower the CER percentage, the more accurate the biometrics system. Also called Equal Error Rate (ERR).

6. **D.** A password is something that the user knows, and it is non-biometric access control. A password is a protected string of characters that is used to authenticate an individual. People's speech sounds and patterns have many subtle distinguishing differences. A programmed biometric system to capture a voice print and compare it to the information held in a reference file can differentiate one individual from another. The iris is the colored portion of the eye that surrounds the pupil. The iris has unique patterns, rifts, colors, rings, coronas, and furrows. The uniqueness of each of these characteristics within the iris is captured by a camera and compared with the information stored. Fingerprints are made up of ridge endings and bifurcations exhibited by friction ridges and other detailed characteristics called minutiae. It is the distinctiveness of these minutiae that gives each individual a unique fingerprint.

7. **C.** A dictionary of password files comprising weak passwords is compared to the user's password until a match is found. A brute force attack is performed by trying all possible character, number, and symbol combinations to uncover a password. In social engineering, an attacker falsely convinces an individual by employing different techniques that he/she has the necessary authorization to access specific resources.

8. **A.** Rainbow table contains all possible passwords already in a hash format. This is a prevalent technique used by attackers to break passwords in an efficient and timely manner. Dictionary is a list of user's passwords. Routers maintain an IP table for routing TCP/IP traffic. The user table is irrelevant in this scenario.

9. **B.** In the DAC access control model, data owners, decide who has access to resources, and ACLs are used to enforce these access decisions. MAC access control model determines access based on security labels. In the RBAC model, access decisions are based on each subject's role and functional position.

10. **A.** The clue in this question is an enterprise with thousands of employees and minimizing the management overhead. RBAC is the ideal choice as the enterprise has limited roles and many employees working under these roles. In the DAC access control model, data owners decide who has access to resources, and ACLs enforce these access decisions. MAC access control model determines access based on security labels.

11. **C.** When the MAC model is employed, every subject and object must have a sensitivity label called a security label. It contains classification and different categories. The classification indicates the sensitivity level, and the categories enforce need-to-know rules. In the DAC access control model, data owners decide who has access to resources, and ACLs enforce these access decisions. In the RBAC model, access decisions are based on each subject's role and functional position. When the MAC model is employed, every subject and object must have a security label's sensitivity label.

12. **D.** Firewalls use rules to determine which types of packets are allowed into a network and rejected. Rule-based access control is a type of compulsory control because the administrator sets the rules, and the users cannot modify these controls. In the DAC access control model, data owners decide who has access to resources, and ACLs enforce these access decisions. In the RBAC model, access decisions are based on each subject's role and functional position.

13. **D.** All the mentioned options are access control mechanisms/techniques employed. Access control consists of three broad categories: administrative, technical, and physical. Each category has different access control mechanisms that can be carried out manually or automatically. All of these access control mechanisms should work in concert to protect infrastructure and its data. Administrative controls are management initiatives and access control policies. Physical controls are physical devices employed across an enterprise. Technical controls are logical controls employed for restricting access to an unauthorized user. Access control mechanisms introduced by individual users against the enterprise security policy are not introduced at an enterprise level.

14. **A.** The most effective solution to prohibit inter-departmental access is to divide the LAN into separate VLANs with access rules enforced. All other options are irrelevant as firewalls and IDS are installed on the gateway to protect LAN from an outsider. A VLAN is a group of devices on one or more LANs configured to communicate as if they were attached to the same wire located on several different LAN segments.

15. **D.** All the mentioned options are necessary to cater network probing, manipulation, network sniffing, making a connection to switch without authorization of network department across, etc., except deploying CCTV cameras across SEMAIS as it is management initiative, not the network administrator.

16. **A.** Deleting specific data within audit logs is called scrubbing. Attackers often delete audit logs that hold this incriminating information. Deleting this information can cause the administrator not to be alerted or aware of the security breach and destroy valuable data. Therefore, audit logs should be protected by strict access control. All other options are irrelevant.

17. **C.** Concrete walls of datacenter are not sufficient to protect spurious emissions. All electronic devices emit electrical signals. These signals can hold important information, and if an attacker buys the right equipment and positions himself in the right place, he could capture this information from the airwaves and access data transmissions as if he had a tap directly on the network wire. All other options are valid for making a Faraday cage or protecting spurious emissions.

18. **B.** It is common for ethical hackers to first identify whether an IDS is present on the network they are preparing to attack. If one is present, that attacker may implement a denial-of-service attack to ascertain its security strength. Another tactic is to send the IDS incorrect data, which will make the IDS send specific alerts indicating a certain attack is under way when in truth, it is not.

19. **D.** Sensor placement is a critical part of configuring an effective IDS. An organization can place a sensor outside of the firewall to detect attacks and place a sensor inside the firewall (in the perimeter network) to detect actual intrusions. Sensors should also be placed in susceptible areas, DMZs, and on extranets. There is no practical usability for placing sensors in protected LAN unless insider threats are considered.

20. **B.** IDS system's threshold for processing network traffic is the most important option to be considered. If the network traffic volume exceeds the IDS system's threshold, attacks may go unnoticed. Each vendor's IDS product has its threshold, and you should know and understand that threshold before you purchase and implement the IDS. In very high-traffic environments, multiple sensors should be in place to ensure all packets are investigated. If necessary, to optimize network bandwidth and speed, different sensors can analyze each packet for different signatures. Therefore, the analysis load can be broken up over different points.

21. **A.** NIDSs have a more challenging time working on a switched network than traditional non-switched environments because data are transferred through independent virtual circuits and not broadcasted, as in non-switched environments. The IDS sensor acts as a sniffer and does not have access to all the traffic in these individual circuits. Therefore, we have to take all the data on each virtual private connection, make a copy of them, and put the copies of the data on one port (spanning port) where the sensor is located. This allows the sensor to access all the data going back and forth on a switched network. All other options are irrelevant.

22. **D.** Phishing is a type of social engineering to obtain personal information, credentials, credit card number, or financial data. The attacker's lure, or fish, for sensitive data through various methods. Brute force (also known as brute force cracking) is a trial and error method used by application programs to recover passwords or keys through exhaustive effort. A rainbow table is a precomputed table for reversing cryptographic hash functions, usually for cracking password hashes. A Fraggle Attack is a denial-of-service (DoS) attack that involves sending a large amount of spoofed UDP traffic to a router's broadcast address within a network. It is similar to a Smurf Attack, which uses spoofed ICMP traffic rather than UDP traffic to achieve the same goal.

23. **D.** Deterrent access control is deployed to discourage violation of security policies. A deterrent control picks up where prevention leaves off. A detective access control is deployed to discover unwanted or unauthorized activity. Often detective controls are after-the-fact controls rather than real-time controls. Preventative access control is deployed to stop unwanted or unauthorized activity from occurring. Corrective access control is deployed to restore systems to normal after an unwanted or unauthorized activity has occurred.

24. **A.** Preventive access control is deployed to stop unwanted or unauthorized activity from occurring. Deterrent access control is deployed to discourage violation of security policies. A deterrent control picks up where prevention leaves off. A detective access control is deployed to discover unwanted or unauthorized activity. Often detective controls are after-the-fact controls rather than real-time controls. A compensation access control is deployed to provide various options to other existing controls to aid in the enforcement and support of a security policy.

25. **B.** Scalability is the irrelevant option. Access control provides security through confidentiality, integrity, and accountability. Integrity is a security principle that makes sure that information and systems are not modified maliciously or accidentally. Accountability is a security principle indicating that individuals must be identifiable and held responsible for their actions.

26. **C.** Access control is any hardware, software, or organizational administrative policy or procedure that grants or restricts access, monitors and records attempts to access, identifies users trying to access, and determines whether access is authorized. Logical controls (also called technical controls) use software and data to monitor and control access to information and computing systems. Examples of logical controls are passwords, network firewalls, access control lists

27. **A.** All options are part of the password security policy except passwords to be sent to the authentication server in cleartext. Passwords should be sent in encrypted form to an authentication server to avoid sniffing.

28. **D.** Password security has nothing to do with pharming attacks. All the mentioned options are necessary to counter pharming attacks. Pharming is a cyber-attack intended to redirect a website's traffic to another fake site. Pharming can be conducted either by changing the hosts' files on a victim's computer or exploiting a vulnerability in DNS server software.

29. D. Allow all access to all employees for maximum efficiency, and meeting goals is irrelevant in this context. The least privilege and need-to-know principles limit users' rights to only what is needed to perform their job tasks. The need-to-know principle is similar to the least-privilege principle. The principle of least privilege is an important concept in computer security, promoting minimal user profile privileges on computers based on users' job necessities. It is based on the concept that individuals should be given access only to their required information to perform their job duties. The network administrator account needs to be audited frequently to detect any malicious activities.

30. A. Extensible Access Control Markup Language (XACML), a declarative access control policy language implemented in XML and a processing model, describes how to interpret security policies. Service Provisioning Markup Language (SPML) is an XML-based framework being developed by OASIS for exchanging user, resource, and service provisioning information between cooperating organizations. Extensible Markup Language (XML) is a set of rules for encoding documents in machine-readable form to allow interoperability between various web-based technologies. C++ is a programming language for software development.

31. D. Replay attack is the most destructive attack as login credentials are traversing in plain. A replay attack is a form of network attack in which valid data transmission is maliciously or fraudulently repeated to obtain unauthorized access. A rainbow table is a precomputed table for reversing cryptographic hash functions, usually for cracking password hashes. A dictionary attack attempts to gain illicit access to a computer system by using many words to generate potential passwords. Brute force is a trial and error method used by application programs to recover passwords through exhaustive effort (using brute force) rather than employing intellectual strategies.

32. B. Smart cards are susceptible to side-channel attacks. A side-channel attack is carried out by gathering data on how something works and using it to attack it or crack it, as in differential power analysis or electromagnetic analysis. A replay attack is a form of network attack in which valid data transmission is maliciously or fraudulently repeated to obtain unauthorized access. A dictionary attack attempts to gain illicit access to a computer system by using many words to generate potential passwords.

33. B. An asynchronous token device is based on challenge/response mechanisms. The authentication service sends the user a challenge value, which the user enters into the token. The token encrypts or hashes this value, and the user uses this as her one-time password. AES is an encryption standard. All other options are not valid.

34. A. Passwords provide the least amount of protection but are the cheapest because they do not require extra readers (as with smart cards and memory cards), do not require devices (as do biometrics), and do not require much overhead in processing (as in cryptography). Passwords are the most common type of authentication method used today.

35. A. In a single sign-on technology, all users are authenticating to one source, i.e., an authentication server. If that server goes down, authentication requests cannot be processed. Login credentials traversed to the server after encryption and hashing are desired features for any single sign-on technology.

36. B. Fingerprint biometric device is primarily used for authentication of the identified user. Authentication is to verify the identity of a subject requesting a system and access to network resources. Authorization is granting access to an object after the issue has been properly identified and authenticated. Accountability is a security principle indicating that individuals must be identifiable and held responsible for their actions. Identification is that a subject provides some type of data to an authentication service. Identification is the first step in the authentication process.

37. D. Password synchronization technologies can allow a user to maintain just one password across multiple systems. The product will synchronize the password to other systems and applications, which happens transparently to the user.

38. C. Detective access controls are used to discover (and document) unwanted or unauthorized activity. A detective access control is deployed to discover unwanted or unauthorized activity. Often detective controls are after-the-fact controls rather than real-time controls. Preventative access control is deployed to stop unwanted or unauthorized activity from occurring. A deterrent access control is deployed to discourage the violation of security policies. A deterrent control picks up where prevention leaves off. Corrective access control is deployed to restore systems to normal after an unwanted or unauthorized activity has occurred.

39. **D.** Strong password choices are difficult to guess, unpredictable, and specified minimum or maximum lengths to ensure that password entries cannot be computationally determined. They may be randomly generated and utilize all the alphabetic, numeric, and punctuation characters. Passwords should never be written down or shared; they should not be stored in publicly accessible or generally readable locations, and they should not be transmitted in the clear. Password should not have part of a username.

40. **B.** Log files provide an audit trail for recreating the history of an event, intrusion, or system failure. An audit trail includes log files and can reconstruct an event, extract information about an incident, and prove or disprove culpability. Security policies are documents that define security requirements for an organization. An audit report includes details gleaned from log files. Business continuity planning occurs before an event in an attempt to reduce the impact.

41. **C.** Privileged accounts (such as administrator accounts) are granted the most access and should be a primary focus in an access review audit. Regular user and auditor accounts do not have as much access as privileged accounts and are not necessary. A deleted account does not exist or has been removed entirely.

42. **A.** Failing to perform periodic security audits can result in the perception that due care is not maintained. Such audits alert personnel that senior management is practicing due diligence in maintaining system security. An organization should not indiscriminately deploy all available controls but choose the most effective ones based on risks. Performance reviews are useful managerial practices but not directly related to do care. Audit reports should not be shared with the public.

43. **B.** Accountability is maintained by monitoring the activities of subjects and objects and core system functions that maintain the operating environment and the security mechanisms. Authentication is required for effective monitoring, but it does not provide accountability by itself. Account lockout prevents login to an account if the wrong password is entered too many times. User entitlement reviews can identify excessive privileges.

44. **D.** Centralized administration access control technologies are RADIUS, TACACS+, and Diameter, whereas decentralized administration example is a peer-to-peer working group. Remote Authentication Dial-In User Service (RADIUS) is a client/server protocol and software that enables remote access servers to communicate with a central server to authenticate dial-in users and authorize their access requested system or service. TACACS (Terminal Access Controller Access Control System) is an older authentication protocol common to UNIX networks that allows a remote access server to forward a user's login password to an authentication server to determine whether access can be permitted a given system. Diameter is an authentication, authorization, and accounting protocol for computer networks. It evolved from and replaced the much less capable RADIUS protocol that preceded it.

45. **A:** Remote Authentication Dial-in-User Service (RADIUS) is a protocol used for authentication, authorization, and configuration between the network access server and authentication server. RADIUS is a client/server protocol and software that enables remote access servers to communicate with a central server to authenticate dial-in users and authorize their access to the requested system or service. Internet Protocol Security (IPsec) is a protocol suite for secure Internet Protocol (IP) communications by authenticating and encrypting each IP packet of a communication session. In computer networking, Layer 2 Tunneling Protocol (L2TP) is a tunneling protocol used to support virtual private networks (VPNs) or the delivery of services by ISPs. It does not provide any encryption or confidentiality by itself. The Point-to-Point Tunneling Protocol (PPTP) is an obsolete method for implementing virtual private networks, with many known security issues. PPTP uses a control channel over TCP and a GRE tunnel operating to encapsulate PPP packets.

46. **D.** The use of a passphrase provides stronger passwords, and they are easier to remember but difficult to crack. Passphrases are next to impossible to crack because most highly efficient password cracking tools break down at around 10 characters. Hence, even the most advanced cracking tool will not be able to guess, brute-force, or pre-compute these passphrases.

47. B. A spoofing attack is when a malicious party impersonates another device or user on a network to launch attacks against network hosts, steal data, spread malware, or bypass access controls. There are several different types of spoofing attacks that malicious parties can use to accomplish this. Brute force is a trial and error method used by application programs to recover passwords through exhaustive effort (using brute force) rather than employing intellectual strategies. A Fraggle Attack is a denial-of-service (DoS) attack that involves sending a large amount of spoofed UDP traffic to a router's broadcast address within a network. It is similar to a Smurf Attack, which uses spoofed ICMP traffic rather than UDP traffic to achieve the same goal. Social engineering is an attack vector that relies heavily on human interaction and often involves tricking people into breaking normal security procedures.

48. B. Role-Based Access Control (RBAC) specify and enforce enterprise-specific security policies in a way that maps organization structure. RBAC is easy to manage in a large enterprise. Using RBAC, you can segregate duties within your team and grant only the amount of access to users that they need to perform their jobs. Instead of giving everybody unrestricted permissions or resources, you can allow only certain actions at a scope.

49. The content determines A. Content-dependent control access (sensitivity) to objects within the object. Context-dependent access control (condition) differs from content-dependent access control in that it makes access decisions based on the context of a collection of information rather than on the sensitivity of the data. Example: Content – Cannot draw more than the account balance. Context – Cannot remove more than $2500 per 24 hours. A system that is using context-dependent access control "reviews the situation" and then makes a decision. Lest privilege access control is based on the security principle that requires each subject to be granted the most restrictive set of privileges needed to perform authorized tasks. Need-to-know access control is based on the code that individuals should be given access only to their required information to perform their job duties.

50. A. RADIUS is the appropriate protocol when simplistic username/password authentication can take place and users only need an Accept or Deny for obtaining access, as in Internet Service Provider (ISP). TACACS+ is the better choice for environments that require more sophisticated authentication steps and tighter control over more complex authorization activities, as in corporate networks. Diameter is a protocol that has been developed to build upon the functionality of RADIUS and overcome many of its limitations. TACACS is an earlier version of TACACS+.

51. D. All the mentioned options are vital for establishing a secure data center. The data center should not be located in a basement building because the basement is more prone to earthquakes and rains.

16. Domain 6: Security Assessment and Testing - Questions

1. SEMAIS has conducted an application security assessment where the code was manually evaluated for bugs and errors. The final report revealed that the application code condition statements were omitted from the code review process, and a new assessment needs to be executed. Based on the scenario, what combination of security testing did SEMAIS execute?

    A. A dynamic, static, and white-box testing strategy.

    B. A static code review combined with white-box testing.

    C. Dynamic testing where white-box testing was included.

    D. System testing where static code analysis and white-box testing were combined.

2. SEMAIS management has the intention to explore hidden risks and loopholes in its IT Infrastructure. Which strategy is appropriate to identify potential risks?

    A. Outsource a security assessment to identify potential risks in collaboration with a third party.

    B. Exploit the identified vulnerabilities to satisfy management.

    C. Train its human resource to tackle cyber threats.

    D. Require the networking team that maintains the infrastructure to conduct a security assessment.

3. SEMAIS is implementing a web service that requires third-party access. The web service is accessing database servers deployed by SEMAIS. What security control should be implemented to minimize risks to the database servers?

    A. Third-party web services have full access to SEMAIS database servers.

    B. Third-party web services have no access restricted to SEMAIS database servers.

    C. Third-party web services have restricted access to SEMAIS database servers.

    D. Third-party web services have restricted access to SEMAIS database servers with only read access option.

4. SEMAIS is developing software for its client. The software is developed per the client's requirements, but the software is prone to errors when deployed at client premises. What can be the probable reason for software errors?

    A. Software is not developed as per the requirements of the client.

    B. Software is developed as per the requirements of the client but tested by developers of the software.

    C. Software is developed as per the client's requirements but not tested by an independent testing team to verify the software's behavior.

    D. Software is used to prone to errors, therefore nothing to worry about this aspect.

5. **What is the most probable reason most software market by industry leaders worldwide lack security features they are supposed to provide?**

   A. Developers have no understanding of prevalent cyber threats.

   B. Due to marketing competition, most companies do not pay full attention to cyber threats.

   C. The vendor does not employ security professionals on their teams.

   D. The vendor does not allocate a budget for security features implementation.

6. **SEMAIS is planning to validate its developed software from a third-party security assessment firm. Which of the following is most important to the security assessment firm while validating the software?**

   A. The output of the software is as required and as per its design.

   B. Look for consistency, completeness, and correctness of the software.

   C. Graphics User Interface (GUI) that is user-friendly.

   D. Software is interacting with all dependent software and services.

7. **As an information security architect at SEMAIS, you decided to deploy encryptions for SEMAIS critical nodes. What will be your best choice concerning the network performance?**

   A. Software-based encryptions being economical.

   B. Both software and hardware encryptions can be deployed on the network as they have no performance issues.

   C. Hardware-based encryptions for maximizing the use of network bandwidth.

   D. Software encryptions have greater performance than hardware encryptions.

8. **The process for generating, transmitting, storing, analyzing, and disposing of computer security data is termed the following?**

   A. Key management

   B. Process management

   C. Human resource management

   D. Log management

9. **SEMAIS has multiple security controls deployed in its DMZ and protected LAN with firewalls, IDS/IPS, antivirus, etc. SEMAIS is collecting log data from the central node. What will be most evident with this log collection?**

   A. Log from all the controls dumped at the central location has no significance until it is filtered.

   B. Increasingly large volumes of log data will facilitate more.

   C. High number of log sources makes the decision easy.

   D. Inconsistent log content from multiple sources.

10. **What should be your first line of action when detecting log anomalies?**

   A. Analyze the log until or unless a threat is materialized or realized.

   B. Inform the management about threat imprints and take corrective measures.

   C. Contact with Security Information and Event Management (SIEM) vendor to find false positives and false negatives.

   D. Upload threat imprints relevant query on cybersecurity forum and asks for help.

11. **SEMAIS has a strong suspicion that an employee has infected the internal network with malware. As an information security consultant, which of the following controls would you suggest as an alternative to monitor the employee?**

   A. Deploy firewall in the protected network.

   B. Deploy IDS in a protected network.

   C. Deploy host-based IDS.

   D. Deploy an antivirus solution.

12. **Which of the following is least important for websites for performing HTTP requests to check availability and measure a web page's performance, website, or web application?**

   A. The website is accessible 24 x 7.

   B. The website is not being defaced.

   C. The web server is not compromised.

   D. Website contents are satisfying users.

13. **SEMAIS is planning to launch a highly sensitive software program. Which testing approach is appropriate before releasing the software program?**

   A. Static Testing of software.

   B. Dynamic Testing of software.

   C. White-Box Testing of software.

   D. Source Code Testing of software.

14. **Which one of the following is most realistic in the perspective of software engineering errors?**

   A. Security requirements are not addressed during the information analysis phase.

   B. Security requirements are addressed during the information analysis phase but not incorporated in the design phase.

   C. Programmers failed to understand the security requirements and cannot code properly.

   D. Testing and quality assurance teams are not testing software properly.

15. **The technique employed for software testing by sending larger chunks of data is known as the following?**

    A. Fuzzing

    B. SQL injection

    C. Cross-site scripting

    D. Behavior analysis

16. **SEMAIS has installed third-party software on its critical servers. To keep security requirements updated, the patches are installed regularly. To ensure the patches are approved and safe, what security measures must be employed?**

    A. Download patch from the vendor's site.

    B. Do not patch the critical servers.

    C. Download patches from the vendor's site and verify the hash tag provided by the vendor.

    D. Download patch from any site.

17. **SEMAIS is running a software engineering setup. The project has been slated to last 6-months. Midway through the project, various employees decide to leave the company. The project manager has a concern that multiple iterations of the software exist due to the turnover. What actions should the project manager implement to remove or prevent any issues?**

    A. Programmers should be given more perks and salaries.

    B. Develop a configuration management system for version management and source code archival.

    C. A Project Manager can self-handle the project.

    D. Employee large number of employees to offset the manpower issues.

18. **Which answer does not support implementing change management?**

    A. Change management should be enforced by policy.

    B. The network administrator can make changes without the approval of management.

    C. Changes made to IT infrastructure should be documented.

    D. Changes should not have a drastic effect on the IT infrastructure.

19. **If a software application is susceptible to buffer overflow attacks, which is a corrective measure from the programmer's perspective for avoiding such attacks?**

    A. Implement a bounds checking mechanism.

    B. Run the software in a sandbox.

    C. Develop software as a standalone program.

    D. Use garbage collector for releasing memory.

20. SEMAIS has developed a software solution for a client. The client's feedback is that the software is utilizing maximum memory resources on the deployed system. What is a probable cause?

    A. The software has many features that utilize maximum memory resources.

    B. The programmer has not used a garbage collector for releasing memory.

    C. Software is performance restricted as compared to dedicated hardware.

    D. The client's feedback is not realistic.

21. One security principle is to isolate all the processes running in a system for diminishing software attack vectors. Which one of the following is not a process isolation technique?

    A. Segmented memory addressing.

    B. Time multiplexing of shared resources.

    C. Naming distinctions and virtual mapping of each process.

    D. Non-encapsulation of objects.

22. SEMAIS is planning to conduct penetration testing on its IT infrastructure. Which one of the following is false when employing a third-party penetration testing firm?

    A. They will charge more to SEMAIS.

    B. The output of the penetration testing will be a detailed report.

    C. A third-party firm can employ hackers for the job, which can benefit from SEMAIS.

    D. A third-party firm cannot share the trade and business secrets of SEMAIS with its competitor.

23. Which state of penetration testing describes the following? A process of extracting usernames, machine names, network resources, and other services from a system. All the gathered information is used to identify the vulnerabilities or weak points in system security.

    A. Enumeration ports and services.

    B. Closing ports and services.

    C. Opening ports and services.

    D. Exploiting ports and services.

24. SEMAIS has conducted penetration testing of its IT infrastructure, the penetration testing reveals that critical servers hosted in the DMZ are having exploitable vulnerabilities. Which is the best recommendation concerning exploiting vulnerabilities on a running system?

    A. Vulnerabilities to be exploited on a running system to confirm claims of the penetration tester.

    B. Vulnerabilities should not be exploited on a running system until a backup of critical servers is available.

    C. SEMAIS can live with identified vulnerabilities.

    D. SEMAIS should mention those vulnerabilities as ask for help on an internet forum.

25. It is common practice that developers have a maintenance hook for maintaining software and future patching and enhancement during software development. Which of the following is the in-built problem with these maintenance hooks?

    A. A maintenance hook makes software upgrades easy.

    B. A maintenance hook can be used for patching software.

    C. The maintenance hook enables software to be maintained in real-time.

    D. Maintenance hook, if discovered by the hackers, can be misused.

26. Due to its cost-effectiveness, the software is being used for cryptographic services like encryption, integrity, authenticity, etc. Which one of the following is the most alarming concern for software-based cryptographic constructs?

    A. Software is cost-effective and having no deficiency in cryptographic constructs.

    B. The software can be used across multiple platforms.

    C. If not handled properly, keying material being used in cryptographic constructs can jeopardize the security of software.

    D. Keying material has no impact on the security of software.

27. Which one of the following is the most effective way to determine how controls function within an application?

    A. Contact with developers of software.

    B. Use help provides by the vendor to explore features of the software.

    C. Review licensing information of software.

    D. Review software control features against all possible options with all input parameters.

28. Which one of the following will differentiate white box testing from black-box testing?

    A. Black box testing has nothing to do with software development.

    B. Black box testing deals with the input and output of software (no internal code structure); white box testing deals with indicated details (internal code structure).

    C. White box testing deals with software.

    D. Black box testing is preferable as compared to white box testing.

29. Which one of the following is not correct for log management?

    A. Monitoring the logging status of all log sources.

    B. Monitoring log rotation and archival processes.

    C. Documenting and reporting anomalies in log settings, configurations, and processes.

    D. Ensuring that each logging host's clock is not synched to a common time source.

30. **Which of the following devices facilitates log management at a centralized location for analysis and threat detection?**

    A. Security Information and Event Management (SIEM) systems

    B. Firewall

    C. Intrusion Detection System

    D. Router

31. **Which of the following is not true about web proxy?**

    A. Web proxies make webpage requests on behalf of users.

    B. Web proxies can also restrict web access and add a layer of protection between web clients and web servers.

    C. Web proxies are non- intermediate hosts through which websites are accessed.

    D. Web proxies keep a record of all URLs accessed through them.

32. **Which one of the following system events requires the most attention for network intrusions?**

    A. Frequent System crashes.

    B. Failed login attempts.

    C. System reboots automatically.

    D. System halts frequently.

33. **SEMAIS has a database that is accessible through a hosted web service. Management of SEMAIS wanted to implement database controls based on transaction and usage. Which one of the following controls would not support the transaction and usage requirement?**

    A. The number of transactions occurring at a specific time.

    B. Size of transactions as per specified criteria.

    C. The number of transactions per user.

    D. Database startup and shutdown.

34. **SEMAIS is collecting log data from various feeds domestically and internationally. There is a concern that the data protection scheme and implemented controls may not provide the security protection requirements for the saved data. What sort of measures should be adopted to protect the log data?**

    A. Encrypt the logs and calculate their hash.

    B. Calculate hash logs for the sake of integrity.

    C. Encrypt logs for the sake of confidentiality.

    D. Attackers are not interested in the log, so there is no need to encrypt the log and calculate its hash.

35. Most of the attacks on software are due to memory manipulation. Which one of the following is not a technique for protecting the memory of software?

    A. Base and limit addressing

    B. Address space layout randomization

    C. Data execution authorization

    D. Data execution prevention

36. As a software tester, what would you recommend for access restriction and minimizing software users' controls?

    A. All instructions to be executed in high privileged mode.

    B. All high-level instructions to be executed in user mode.

    C. All instructions to be executed in user mode.

    D. A mix of balance where low-level instructions to be executed in user mode and high-level instructions in privileged mode.

37. Real User Monitoring (RUM) is an approach to web monitoring that aims to capture and analyze every user, website, or application transaction. Which one of the following is not true about RUM?

    A. RUM is a real user measurement.

    B. RUM is active monitoring.

    C. RUM generates Real-user metrics.

    D. RUM is end-user experience monitoring.

38. Synthetic performance monitoring and testing is an approach to web testing. Which of the following makes synthetic performance monitoring preferable as compare to RUM?

    A. Site availability and network problems are evident in synthetic performance monitoring.

    B. Synthetic performance monitoring executes a known set of steps at regular intervals.

    C. Synthetic performance/output is predictable.

    D. Synthetic performance monitoring does not track real user sessions.

39. SEMAIS has an online store displaying showcased items and a backend database for processing customers' orders. Which of the following is the best method for checking database availability?

    A. Website accessibility ensures database availability.

    B. Real User Monitoring (RUM)

    C. Synthetic performance monitoring

    D. SQL injection

40. **A third-party auditor has submitted an audit report to SEMAIS. Who is responsible for enforcing remedial measures mentioned in the audit report?**

    A. SEMAIS Network Administrator

    B. SEMAIS Data Custodian

    C. SEMAIS Employees

    D. SEMAIS Management

41. **What is the correct phase or order for penetration testing?**

    A. Planning, Vulnerability Discovery, Information gathering, Reporting

    B. Planning, Information gathering, Vulnerability Discovery, Reporting

    C. Reporting, Planning, Vulnerability Discovery, Information gathering

    D. Planning, Reporting, Vulnerability Discovery, Information gathering

42. **Threat modeling is an approach to detect threats and predict advance threats. Which of the following is not specific to threat modeling?**

    A. Identification of threats.

    B. Threat modeling is used to diminish all risks.

    C. Calculation of threat impact potential countermeasures.

    D. Countermeasures for threats to be adopted.

43. **When software is behaving abruptly after installation, what is an ideal option for this software?**

    A. Enter to a protected execution domain.

    B. Enter to a problem state.

    C. Enter to a more secure state.

    D. Release all data held in volatile memory.

44. **What type of attack is taking place when a process writes data into the memory of another program?**

    A. Fuzzing

    B. Buffer Overflow

    C. SQL injection

    D. Cross-site scripting

45. **The most economical way of software testing involves which of the following?**

    A. Software testing by the developer.

    B. Software design should be error-free.

    C. Software testing after deployment.

    D. Software testing during development at each SDLC stage.

46. **SEMAIS has implemented threat protection controls across its critical IT infrastructure with an up-to-date threat profile. Which one of the following measures will be most effective concerning threat protection controls?**

    A. SEMAIS has nothing to worry about.

    B. Developing a comprehensive training program that targets threats and appropriate controls.

    C. Invest more in threat protection.

    D. Hire a third-party cybersecurity firm.

47. **SEMAIS is planning to upgrade its already marketed software, which will be marketed as a new version. Which is the most appropriate testing plan for testing the software by SEMAIS?**

    A. The new version of the software does not require testing.

    B. Only changes made to software should be tested.

    C. A new version should be tested from scratch.

    D. None of the options.

48. **The software can be tested by using positive and negative testing. Which one of the following is false concerning negative testing?**

    A. Negative testing determines that your application works as expected.

    B. Negative testing ensures that your application can gracefully handle invalid input.

    C. Negative testing is to prevent applications from crashing.

    D. Negative testing helps to improve the quality of the application and find its weak points.

49. **Which of the following is not specific to Federal Information Security Management Act (FISMA)?**

    A. FISMA applies to federal organizations/agencies across the U.S

    B. FISMA requires agencies to audit themselves.

    C. FISMA requires an independent auditor to review information security implementation.

    D. FISMA applies to international agencies.

50. **SEMAIS is outsourcing its systems, business processes, and data processing to service providers. How can SEMAIS determine that outsourced business will provide the same functionality as SEMAIS?**

   A. Federal Information Security Management Act (FISMA) will ensure that outsourced activities are functioning correctly.

   B. Statement on Auditing Standards (SAS) will ensure that outsourced activities are functioning correctly.

   C. FIPS 140-2 will ensure that outsourced activities are functioning correctly.

   D. NIST SP 800-30 will ensure that outsourced activities are functioning correctly.

51. **ISO 27000 emphasizes the implementation of the Information System Management System (ISMS) across an organization. What is the correct order of stages involved in the development of ISMS?**

   A. Plan, Do, Act, Check

   B. Act, Plan, Do Check

   C. Plan, Do Check, Act

   D. Check, Plan, Do, Act

52. **As an Information Security Consultant at SEMAIS, what will be your primary consideration for suggesting tools and techniques used during security testing?**

   A. SEMAIS business goals and procedures.

   B. SEMAIS security roles and responsibilities for staff.

   C. Attack surface and supported technologies.

   D. Top tools mentioned on the web.

17. Domain 6: Security Assessment and Testing - Answers and Explanations

1. **B.** This is a systematic review of the software source code without executing the code. It checks the syntax of the code, coding standards, code optimization, etc. This is also termed as white box testing or Static Application Security Testing (SAST). This review can be done at any point during development. White box testing is the testing of the internal workings or code of a software application. In contrast, black box or System Testing is the opposite. It involves the external workings of the software from the user's perspective, and it's done by executing a live program. Dynamic testing is also called Dynamic Application Security Testing (DAST).

2. **A.** Outsourcing a security assessment to a third party will be an ideal option. Hidden risks cannot be exploited until or unless it is discovered. HR of SEMAIS has to be trained, but it can be one aspect of the audit. The network team of SEMAIS manages its IT infrastructure is not a good option as they are working the network and can overlook or hide something suspicious.

3. **D.** Third-party web services have restricted access to the SEMAIS Database server with only read access option. These services have neither full access nor access to modify the database.

4. **C.** Software is developed as per the requirements of the client. That is why it is delivered to the client and installed at its premises. An independent testing team does not test software for verifying the behavior of the software and errors made by the developers. It is recommended that the independent testing and quality assurance team should ascertain and test software.

5. **B.** All the options can be candidate answers for this question in one way or another, but the most probable reason is that marketing competition and having an edge over competitors. Most companies do not pay full attention to cyber threats.

6. **B.** All the options are valid in the perspective of security assessment for validating the software. Still, the most precise statement is that software verification looks for the software's consistency, completeness, and correctness.

7. **C.** Both software and hardware encryptions have their pros and cons. It depends upon the link and network where they have to be deployed. As in this question, performance is a primary criterion; therefore, hardware encryptions are preferable compared to software encryptions, even being economical.

8. **D.** Log management is the process for generating, transmitting, storing, analyzing, and disposing of computer security log data. Log management is essential to ensure that computer security records are kept in sufficient detail for an appropriate period. Key management is providing keying material to encrypting devices/processes. Process management is carried out by the operating system for maximum utilization of the CPU. Whereas HR management is irrelevant in this case.

9. **A.** Log from all the controls dumped at a central location has no significance until or unless it is filtered and categorized for better making attack vector identification instead of extensive log data and inconsistent log data.

10. **B.** Being a network administrator at SEMAIS, if you detect log anomalies with probable threat imprints, you should Inform the top management about threat imprints and take corrective measures.

11. **C.** To detect the malicious employee activities on the protected network, it is recommended to deploy host-based IDS. Deployment of Firewall and IDS on a protected network can stop it from outsider threat. An antivirus solution is not relevant in this context.

12. **D.** Web monitoring aims to capture and analyze every transaction of every user of a website or application. Web-monitoring services continuously observe a system in action, tracking availability, functionality, and responsiveness. Website contents are the least important in the context of web monitoring.

13. **B.** As the software in its launch stage, it will be advisable to test it dynamically instead of other approaches. In dynamic testing, the system under test is executed, and its behavior is observed. In contrast, static testing

14. techniques analyze a system without running the system under test. In black-box testing, the tested system is used as a black box, i.e., no internal details of the system implementation are used. In contrast, white-box testing takes the interior system details (e.g., the source code) into account.

15. **A.** This question is a bit tricky; it encompasses all stages of software engineering and analyzes those in the realm of security engineering. Security requirements are not addressed during the information analysis phase of software engineering is a valid option as if security requirements are included from the information gathering and analysis phase; then subsequent stages will be addressing those security artifacts.

16. **A.** Fuzzing is a technique in which a large amount of random data is sent to the application, usually larger than expected by the application, to the input channels of an application to provoke a crashing of the application for detection of application crashes (e.g., caused by buffer overflows, etc.) that might be security-critical. SQL injection and cross-site scripting is peculiar to websites.

17. **C.** From a software maintenance perspective, the security testing of patches is particularly important: Patches need to be tested thoroughly (i.e., against all possible attacks and all system configurations the patch can be applied) to ensure that a customer fixes bugs and their system is not accidentally exposed to new vulnerabilities. Patches should be downloaded from a trusted source.

18. **B.** If the frequency of employees switches jobs regularly, it will be beneficial for the SEMAIS to develop a configuration management system for version management and source code archival. A Project manager cannot handle self-handle the project. Moreover, perks and pay package is not the guarantee of employees' retention.

19. **B.** All the mentioned options are specific to change management except that the network administrator can make changes without management approval as every change should be approved by management.

20. **A.** Buffer overflow vulnerabilities are best addressed by implementing bounds checking. The software can neither be run in a sandbox environment, and a standalone program in practical scenario nor memory releasing is effective for buffer flow-related attacks.

21. **B.** If the software is utilizing maximum memory resources on the system where it is deployed, and the system is used to halt frequently, the programmer has not used a garbage collector to release memory after its use.

22. **D.** Processes need to be isolated, which can be done through segmented memory addressing, encapsulation of objects, time multiplexing of shared resources, naming distinctions, and virtual mapping.

23. **C.** Employing a third-party firm to perform penetration testing requires a signed non-disclosure agreement (NDA). Output of the penetration testing is a detailed report enlisting vulnerabilities across IT infrastructure. Third-party penetration testing firms do not hire hackers for testing; instead, it is considered bad practice.

24. **A.** Penetration testing is a sequential process; the process in which all ports and services are running on a system is enlisted/found is known as enumeration. During enumeration, information is systematically collected, and individual systems are identified. The pen testers examine the systems in their entirety; this allows them to evaluate security weaknesses.

25. **B.** Vulnerabilities should not be exploited on a running system until backup of critical as exploitation on a running system can have a catastrophic effect. Moreover, posting vulnerabilities on an internet forum is not advisable because it will make the task easy for everyone.

26. **D.** Software developers used to have a maintenance hook for maintaining software, future patching, and enhancement. Maintenance hook, if discovered by the hackers, can be misused for installing rootkits and malware.

27. **C.** Keying materials are used in cryptographic constructs, and the entire security of the cryptographic construct depends upon the keying material. If keying material is not handled correctly (keying material residing in the plain on hard disk, memory, etc.), it can jeopardize software security.

28. **D.** The most effective way to determine how controls function within the software is to review software control features against all possible options with all probable input parameters.

29. **B.** Black box testing and white box testing are both approaches for software testing. Black box testing deals with the input and output of software; white box testing deals with source code details. No technique can be preferred over another according to the testing scenario.

30. **D.** All the mentioned options are specific to the network administrator's logging responsibilities except that each logging host's clock is not synched to a common time source. Each logging host's watch should be synched to a common time source.

31. **A.** Logs should be consolidated to repositories such as Security Information and Event Management (SIEM) systems. Firewall is used at the gateway for traffic access/entry into a network. IDS is used for intrusion detection. A router is a routing device.

32. **C.** Web proxies are intermediate hosts through which websites are accessed, not the non-intermediate ones. All the other options are characteristics of web proxies.

33. **B.** All the mentioned options can be a candidate for system events to be attended by a network administrator, but the most critical one is failed login attempts. A failed login attempt can indicate a possible intrusion by a hacker.

34. **D.** Usage information such as the number of transactions occurring in a certain period (e.g., minute, hour) and the size of transactions (e.g., email message size, file transfer size) can be helpful for certain types of security monitoring, but database startup and shutdown is not the usage criteria.

35. **A.** SEMAIS should encrypt the log and calculate its hash for the sake of log confidentiality and integrity, respectively. As the log is being calculated remotely to a central location across the US, the log's privacy and integrity should be addressed. Attackers are interested in logs and are used to manipulate them for hiding attack signatures.

36. **C.** Memory managers use various memory protection mechanisms, as the base (beginning) and limit (ending) addressing, address space layout randomization. Data execution prevention. Data execution authorization is not advisable as one process can use another process address space, leading to various attacks.

37. **D.** A mix of balance where low-level instructions to be executed in user mode and high-level instructions in a privileged way is the best option suited for this question. As a software tester and quality assurance, you plan for access restriction and minimize software user's controls. Neither all high-level instructions nor all instructions to be executed in user mode will give more access to users.

38. **A.** Real User Monitoring (RUM) is an approach to web monitoring that aims to capture and analyze every transaction of every user of a website or application. Also known as real user measurement, real-user metrics, or end-user experience monitoring (EUM), it is a form of passive monitoring, relying on web-monitoring services that continuously observe a system in action, tracking availability, functionality, and responsiveness.

39. **A.** Synthetic performance monitoring, sometimes called proactive monitoring, involves having external agents run scripted transactions against a web application. Unlike RUM, synthetics do not track real user sessions. First, the script executes a known set of steps at regular intervals from a known location, and its performance is predictable. That means it is more useful for alerting than often noisy RUM data. Second, it occurs predictably and externally, making it better to assess site availability and network problems.

40. **C.:** Database monitoring uses synthetic transactions to monitor the availability of a database. Synthetic performance monitoring, sometimes called proactive monitoring, involves having external agents run scripted transactions against a web application. Real User Monitoring (RUM) is an approach to web monitoring that aims to capture and analyze every user's transaction of a website or application. SQL injection is a code injection technique used to attack data-driven applications, in which nefarious SQL statements are inserted into an entry field for execution.

41. **D.** SEMAIS management is responsible for enforcing remedial measures mentioned in the audit report. Employees data custodian and network administrator has to take measures as per their roles, but controls implementation and making it part of SEMAIS security policy is the responsibility of SEMAIS management.

42. **B.** Penetration testing is a multi-stage process and sequential process. Planning is working with a targeted customer to develop a testing plan with defined objectives, scope, and rules of engagement. Information gathering is a phase in which information about targeted infrastructure (hosts, servers, applications, etc.) is collected. Vulnerabilities are discovered across the targeted infrastructure and services running. Discovered vulnerabilities are reported to the client.

43. **B.** Threat modeling is not used to diminish all risk as all risk cannot be diminished at all. All other options are specific to threat modeling as it is used to identify threats, their impact, and potential countermeasures to be adopted.

44. **C.** The state machine model dictates that a software/system should start up securely, carry out secure state transitions, and even fail securely. Therefore, if the software/system encounters something it deems unsafe, it should change to a more secure state for self-preservation and protection.

45. **B.** Buffer overflow, or buffer overrun, is an anomaly where a program, while writing data to a buffer, overruns the buffer's boundary and overwrites adjacent memory locations. This is a particular case of the violation of memory safety. Fuzz testing or fuzzing is a software testing technique, often automated or semi-automated, that involves providing invalid, unexpected, or random data to the inputs of a computer program. SQL Injection refers to an injection attack wherein an attacker can execute malicious SQL statements (also commonly referred to as a malicious payload) that control a web application's database server. Cross-site scripting (XSS) is a type of computer security vulnerability typically found in web applications. XSS enables attackers to inject client-side scripts into web pages viewed by other users. Attackers may use a cross-site scripting vulnerability to bypass access controls such as the same-origin policy.

46. **D.** The best and most economical way of software testing is during development and at each stage of development for accurate results. Software design can be error-prone. Software testing cannot be tested after deployment as it is easy to remediate errors in development, not after deployment.

47. **B.** If SEMAIS threat protection controls remain updated, nothing should be advised. Investments and consultation as well when controls are updated. SEMAIS should train HR on cybersecurity awareness.

48. **C.** A new version of the software should be treated as new software. It should be tested in totality, the amended part/module, and the previous part/module, as changes may impact the software's overall functionality.

49. **A.** Negative testing does not determine that your application works as expected. It is specific to positive testing. All other options are specific to negative testing. For Example, an application contains a textbox, and as per the user's requirements, the textbox should accept only certain strings. Positive testing is the type of testing performed on the system by providing valid data as input. It checks whether an applicant behaves as expected with positive information.

50. **D.** In the U.S., federal agencies are subject to the Federal Information Security Management Act (FISMA). FISMA requires agencies to audit themselves and have an independent auditor review their information security implementation at least annually. FISMA does not apply to all organization worldwide

51. **B.** Many organizations rely upon Statement on Auditing Standards (SAS) 70 to gain overall comfort over outsourced activities. FIPS 140-2 is specific to cryptographic module testing. FISMA requires agencies to audit themselves and have an independent auditor review their information security implementation annually. NIST SP 800-30 deals with risk management.

52. **C.** The correct sequence is Plan, Do Check, Act. Planning is to Establish ISMS policy, objectives, processes, and procedures relevant to managing risk and improving information security to deliver results by an organization's overall policies and objectives. Do is to implement and operate the ISMS policy, controls, processes, and

procedures. Check access and, where applicable, measure process performance against ISMS policy, objectives, and practical experience and report the results to management for review. The act is to take corrective and preventive actions based on the internal ISMS audit and management review results or other relevant information to achieve continuous improvement of the ISMS.

53. C. When selecting a security testing method or tool, the security practitioner must consider many different things, including attack surface and supported technologies. Attack surface will identify other security testing methods to find different vulnerability types. Security testing tools usually only help a limited number of technologies (e.g., programming languages). If a tool supports multiple technologies, it does not necessarily endorse all of them equally well.

18. Domain 7: Security Operations - Questions

1. **Which one of the following is the most important for digital evidence?**

   A. Digital evidence is volatile in nature and requires timely action.

   B. Digital evidence is non-volatile in nature and has no time limitations.

   C. Digital evidence is challenging to prove in a court of law.

   D. Digital evidence to be treated like material evidence security operations.

2. **Which one of the following is not relevant to digital evidence collection?**

   A. Identify the scene for digital evidence collection.

   B. Protect the environment from where evidence is collected.

   C. Allow a degree of contamination for large evidence space.

   D. Collect evidence in a timely and efficient manner.

3. **The attackers are attacking the SEMAIS web server, and hosted websites are not accessible. The traffic originated from specific IPs. What is the root- cause and remediation step to partake?**

   A. Configure web server for better accessibility.

   B. Identify injection points for the hosted web.

   C. Host web site with some other Internet service provider.

   D. The suspicious IPs are launching distributed denial of service attacks. Block those IPs for better accessibility.

4. **SEMAIS has updated and configured its IT infrastructure to counter threats by employing a defense-in-depth strategy. Still, there are reports related to information security-related incidents. What event or activity could be causing the issue if baseline settings and configuration items are in place?**

   A. Information security controls are not configured correctly.

   B. Employees of SEMAIS require training.

   C. Defense-in-depth strategy is not in place.

   D. Top management of SEMAIS should take action.

5. **What is the most important consideration for digital/electronic evidence to serve as legitimate evidence in the court of law?**

   A. The chain of custody of the digital/electronic evidence is verifiable.

   B. Authenticity and integrity of digital/electronic evidence is verifiable.

   C. Chain of custody and authenticity/integrity of the digital/electronic evidence is verifiable.

   D. Digital/electronic evidence is not acceptable in a court of law.

6. **Which one of the following is not specific to digital forensic of digital/electronic evidence?**

    A. Digital/electronic evidence needs to be authentic, accurate, complete, convincing, and admissible.

    B. Digital/electronic evidence needs to be authentic, accurate, complete, convincing, and non-admissible.

    C. Digital/electronic evidence needs to be authentic, accurate, complete, non-convincing, and admissible.

    D. Digital/electronic evidence needs to be non-authentic, accurate, complete, convincing, and admissible.

7. **SEMAIS has a digital forensic platform for identifying incidents and collecting evidence. SEMAIS has received a hard disk from a client with infected malware. What will be the correct action for analyzing the hard disk drive?**

    A. Scan hard disk drive with antivirus.

    B. Make an image/copy of the hard disk drive before executing forensic analysis.

    C. Try to identify suspicious files on the hard disk drive.

    D. Identify malware signatures on the hard disk drive.

8. **SEMAIS network has imprints of information security-related incidents. Which answer represents the most convenient method to analyze intrusion and incidents?**

    A. Configure network controls properly.

    B. Check rules of perimeter firewall.

    C. Block open ports on the server.

    D. Analyze and examine data from network logs and network activity.

9. **SEMAIS hosted web server is infected with a trojan. After performing application updates via an unauthorized source. Which answer would provide identification and analysis of the trojan?**

    A. Download updates from the authentic source.

    B. What and where files were installed or altered on the infected systems.

    C. What communications channels were opened (ingress and egress).

    D. Identification of any upstream destination addresses.

10. **SEMAIS gateway router has been compromised and routes traffic to un-identified locations. There is a strong suspicion that attackers compromised the router firmware. What is the best step to identify whether the router firmware was compromised?**

    A. A router is routing traffic to unidentified locations.

    B. Match the hash of the router firmware with its vendor's supplied hash.

    C. Change configuration of the router.

    D. Replace the router with the new one.

11. **Which answer serves as the best method to preserve a standalone hard disk drive containing evidence?**

    A. Place the hard disk drive in the magnetic field to preserve the evidence.

    B. Induce that the hard disk drive is the static electric field.

    C. Plug the hard disk drive with a non-compatible system.

    D. Protect the hard disk drive from the magnetic and static electric field.

12. **The main hurdle in bringing cyber attackers to justice is their location, laws, and perspective on handling cyber criminals. Which answer calls for resolving jurisdiction-related issues?**

    A. Cyber criminals should be investigated and trialed in the hosted country.

    B. Cyber criminals should be investigated and trialed in the hosted country where they committed crimes.

    C. An international forum/agreement should be established for cyber criminals, irrespective of their physical location.

    D. Cyber criminals cannot be investigated and trialed.

13. **SEMAIS management has a strong suspicion that an employee leaked vital information to an unknown source. Which control would help to monitor collected evidence against the employee?**

    A. A host-Based Intrusion detection system

    B. A network-Based Intrusion detection system

    C. Network-Based Intrusion Prevention system

    D. Perimeter firewall

14. **SEMAIS has a hosted server that provides service to several clients. An intrusion detection system (IDS) deployed at SEMAIS DMZ generates a false positive for the client. What can remedial measures be implemented to avoid false positives?**

    A. Replace IDS with Intrusion Prevention System (IPS).

    B. Ignore false positives.

    C. Replace IDS with firewall.

    D. Properly configure and tune the IDS so that trusted traffic is not treated as threat vectors.

15. **Which answer is not specific to Security Information and Event Management (SIEM)?**

    A. Store raw information from various systems logs.

    B. Aggregation of information in multiple repositories.

    C. Normalize the information to make comparisons more meaningful.

    D. Analytical tools that can process, map, and extract target information.

16. SEMAIS has suspicion that its publicly hosted servers are being used as zombies. Which answer provides the best solution to stop the incident?

   A. Egress filtering at perimeter devices of SEMAIS.

   B. Ingress filtering at publicly hosted servers SEMAIS.

   C. Scan the publicly hosted servers with updated antivirus.

   D. Limit access to publicly hosted servers.

17. SEMAIS is planning to implement a data loss prevention (DLP) platform. The platform will prevent classified data leakage. Which answer provides the top concern that SEMAIS may consider?

   A. Implement mandatory access control to access classified data.

   B. Implement role-based access control to access classified data.

   C. Configure perimeter devices to stop leakage of data.

   D. Implement DLP to protect confidential data in all its forms and manifestations.

18. The process of hiding data within graphics, pictures, or images is referenced as which security concern?

   A. Cryptography

   B. Steganography

   C. Cryptanalysis

   D. Watermarking

19. Which one of the following is not specific to the configuration management (CM) process?

   A. Configuration management establishes and maintains the integrity of the product, system, or item managed throughout its lifecycle within the organization.

   B. Configuration management refers to a discipline for evaluating, coordinating, approving or disapproving, and implementing changes in artifacts used to construct and maintain software systems.

   C. Configuration management is intended to eliminate the confusion and error brought about by different versions of artifacts.

   D. Configuration management has nothing to do with the naming convention of artifacts.

20. To manage the IT operations of SEMAIS, which one of the following is most appropriate?

   A. Maintaining operational resilience across all tentacles.

   B. Controlling and auditing privileged accounts periodically.

   C. Protecting valuable assets by taking all possible measures.

   D. To ensure service consistency and effectiveness.

21. SEMAIS has provided full rights to system resources for all network administrators. The Chief Networking Officer (CNO) has decided to change the permissions due to illegitimate access and inside threats. Which answer does not demonstrate an action the CNO will take?

    A. The network administrator of SEMAIS should be given maximum privilege across systems and IT infrastructure.

    B. Network administrator duties should be separated.

    C. Activities of the network administrator should be monitored.

    D. System/network administrators should be subject to job rotation.

22. What procedure is appropriate for controlling identity management across a large enterprise where frequent resignation and roles switch occurs?

    A. Implement job rotation in the enterprise.

    B. Implement separation of duties in the enterprise.

    C. Implement the least privilege in the enterprise.

    D. Validate user accounts frequently.

23. SEMAIS deals with a third-party organization for IT provision. By formalizing a service level agreement with the company, what should be the least concern for management?

    A. Service availability the entire year and 24/7.

    B. Quality of service and defect rate of deliverables.

    C. The third-party share value in the trade market.

    D. IT security of services to be provided.

24. SEMAIS management travels globally for business operations. SEMAIS management has been a victim of laptop theft; the laptop contained confidential data. As a security consultant, what will you suggest?

    A. Encrypt the laptop-mounted hard disk drive to protect confidential data.

    B. Access confidential data from a remote site by using the internet.

    C. Stop using the laptop for business meetings, use personal data assistants (PDAs), tabs, and other mobile devices.

    D. SEMAIS management should take care of laptops during meetings.

25. Cloud storage is gaining popularity because of its convenience and affordability. Which one of the following should be your primary concern related to cloud storage?

    A. Cloud data is stored in various locations where isolation of physical access to information may fail.

    B. It increases the number of networks over which the data travels.

    C. Encryption keys kept by the service user and the service provider has limit access to the data

D. When the cloud is sharing storage and networks with many customers, other customers can access their data.

26. **SEMAIS has introduced screening and background checks for its employees. Which background will the investigation category be least problematic for SEMAIS?**

    A. Employees having proven criminal records.

    B. Employees involved in financial embezzlement.

    C. Employees involved in lawsuits.

    D. Employees used to have traffic violation tickets.

27. **SEMAIS used to have user accounts for accessing the services across SEMAIS IT infrastructure. Which one of the following is not to be considered when auditing and reviewing accounts?**

    A. Users' inactive accounts should be audited and reviewed.

    B. Users' accounts should not be audited and reviewed when they resign.

    C. Whenever users get into the new role.

    D. Whenever users' have been posted to the company's other premises.

28. **SEMAIS collects confidential data from its clients and uses the information to build new business requirements. Due to recent data breaches, SEMAIS management has decided to protect personal data. Which one of the following will be most important in protecting confidential data?**

    A. Company's and clients' confidential data to be protected in storage, transit, and processing as per SEMAIS policy.

    B. Data owners must work with the information security program and officer to ensure the protection of data.

    C. Employees of SEMAIS should take care of handling data.

    D. SEMAIS management should classify data as per its importance.

29. **SEMAIS headquarters occasionally host visits for clients and vendors. The vendors and clients are allowed to have meetings on operational issues. Which one of the following should not occur during the sessions?**

    A. Clients' and vendors' records should be maintained.

    B. Clients' and vendors' physical access should be restricted to their place of work.

    C. Clients and vendors should be given access to the company's resources.

    D. Clients and vendors should be given visitor cards for display.

30. **SEMAIS owns a datacenter that hosts critical IT services. Which one of the following is considered a high-risk when securing the datacenter?**

    A. Datacenter should be access restricted with biometric-based access control.

    B. Only limited users should be allowed to access datacenter.

    C. Systems should not be visible from the outside of the datacenter.

D.   Everyone should be given access to the datacenter.

31. **To protect SEMAIS software from virus attacks, which one of the following will be most economical?**

   A.   Install antivirus software from a world-renowned vendor of antivirus.

   B.   Scan the network traffic for malware attacks.

   C.   Users should have read and execute permissions.

   D.   Employ in-depth defense strategy for mitigating virus attacks.

32. **SEMAIS portable and mobile devices are prone to data leakage. As a security officer, which of the following would you not implement to counter the data leakage?**

   A.   Require portable and mobile devices to turn off encryption methods.

   B.   Implement mandatory encryption with strong authentication.

   C.   Monitoring and logging of information transferred.

   D.   Implement remote wipe capability and geo-locate capability.

33. **Degaussers are used to remove hard drive data. To remove the hard drive data, which of the following degausser properties is not recommended?**

   A.   Degausser with maximum coercivity to be used.

   B.   Degausser with minimum coercivity to be used.

   C.   Degausser with approved coercivity to be used.

   D.   Degausser should be avoided as much as possible.

34. **One of SEMAIS critical servers was attacked and discovered that the server is self-rebooting and unresponsive. As an information security responder, what action would you recommend restoring operations? Your main concern is downtime and loss of evidence?**

   A.   Create an image of the server first to preserve evidence and then reboot it.

   B.   Prepare another machine with a similar configuration.

   C.   Hot reboot the system.

   D.   Cold reboot the system.

35. **Employees of SEMAIS detected malicious software behavior before determining a data compromise had occurred. Which of the following probably prohibited employees from sharing vital information with the security incident department?**

   A.   Employees are not well trained for detecting malicious behavior.

   B.   Employees fear management's suspicion about themselves.

   C.   It is not the employee's responsibility to detect attack signatures.

   D.   Employees should be imparted advanced level training in the cybersecurity field.

36. **Which of the following IDS system can detect persistent advance threats (APT)?**

    A. Signature- or Pattern-Matching IDS

    B. Protocol Anomaly-Based IDS

    C. Statistical-Anomaly-Based IDS

    D. No IDS can detect APTs

37. **Which one of the following is not specific to log management?**

    A. Logs from all the controls should be collected to a central location.

    B. Logs should be reviewed periodically.

    C. Logs authenticity and integrity should be ensured.

    D. Logs should not be archived.

38. **To protect SEMAIS IT infrastructure from cyber threats, which action should SEMAIS implement?**

    A. SEMAIS should contact other business partners.

    B. SEMAIS should have an agreement with US-CERT.

    C. SEMAIS should augment its already deployed cyber controls.

    D. SEMAIS should buy cyber insurance.

39. **What is the difference between vulnerability assessment and penetration testing?**

    A. Vulnerability assessment is a precursor to penetration testing.

    B. Vulnerability assessment and penetration testing are the same.

    C. Penetration testing is a pre-cursor to vulnerability assessment.

    D. Vulnerability assessment and penetration testing are not the same.

40. **SEMAIS management must decide whether an audit should be conducted by its internal team or a third-party vendor. Which of the following is a strong argument for selecting third-party auditing?**

    A. In-house auditing will save finances.

    B. A third-party audit will identify more loopholes.

    C. A third-party audit can leak SEMAIS secrets.

    D. A third-party audit will make SEMAIS threat profile public.

41. **Which access control concept cannot provide anomalous data?**

    A. Attempts to access restricted files.

    B. Multiple failed logon attempts.

C. Users are logging in at office timings.

D. Unexplained changes to system clocks.

42. **SEMAIS web server was attacked through half-open TCP connections. Which of the following will be used to detect this type of attack?**

   A. Protocol anomaly IDS

   B. Application-level firewall

   C. Statistics anomaly IDS

   D. Signature-based IDS

43. **An essential aspect of Security Operations is to make notifications about incidents. Which of the following is not correct for notifications?**

   A. Concerning Staff should be notified in time.

   B. All employees of the company should be notified.

   C. The process of notifying should be documented.

   D. The mechanism for notifying should be efficient.

44. **Which one of the following is not specific to change management?**

   A. Changes are required to be logged.

   B. Change made to be tested and verified.

   C. Every change should have its ownership.

   D. Changes do not require management approval.

45. **Which of the following is least discussed with end-users regarding email retention policies?**

   A. Privacy policy for email

   B. Auditor review of email retention

   C. Length of retaining

   D. Backup method

46. **You have been hired as an ethical penetration tester; what is your first step in conducting penetration testing?**

   A. Approval of change management.

   B. Development of detailed test plan.

   C. Formulation of management control objective.

   D. Team formulation.

47. SEMAIS is planning to test its recovery plan for the first time. One of the following is a recommendation when management is concerned about the physical relocation of its staff, IT infrastructure, and training employees about business continuity planning?

    A. Structured Walk-Through Test

    B. Functional Drill/Parallel Test

    C. Full-Interruption/Full-Scale Test

    D. Simulation Test

48. Which one of the following is most important before deploying software updates?

    A. Full disclosure information about the threat that the patch addresses is available.

    B. The patching process is documented.

    C. The production systems are backed up.

    D. An independent third party attests to the validity of the patch.

49. SEMAIS is planning to outsource its IT systems. Which one of the following is the most important for SEMAIS since its outsourcing work?

    A. All regulatory and compliance requirements must be passed on to the provider.

    B. The outsourcing organization is free from compliance obligations.

    C. The outsourced IT systems are free from compliance obligations.

    D. The provider is free from compliance obligations.

50. The strategy of forming defensive layers around an asset is known as which of the following?

    A. Secured Perimeter

    B. Defense-in-Depth

    C. Reinforced Barrier Deterrent

    D. Reasonable Asset Protection

51. Which one of the following defines the duration of time and a service level within which a business process must be restored after a disaster to avoid unacceptable consequences associated with a break in continuity?

    A. Recovery Point Objective (RPO)

    B. Mean time between failures (MTBF)

    C. Mean time to repair (MTTR)

    D. Recovery Time Objective (RTO)

19. Domain 7: Security Operations - Answers and Explanations

1. **A.** Digital evidence is volatile in nature and requires timely action. Digital evidence is acceptable in the court of law if collected, identified, and preserved correctly. Digital evidence is different from material evidence, and care should be adopted in their collection.

2. **C.** All are relevant to digital evidence collection except that "allow a degree of contamination for large evidence space" as contamination can destroy the actual evidence or make it irrelevant.

3. **D.** The traffic seems to be originated from specific IP s is indicating the suspicious IPs are launching imprints for distributed denial of service attack. Block those IPs for better accessibility. All other options are not relevant.

4. **B.** SEMAIS has updated and configured its IT infrastructure to counter prevalent threats by employing a defense-in-depth strategy. There are still reports about information security-related incidents that employ that SEMAIS controls (baseline configurations). Still, its employees are not appropriately trained. SEMAIS should conduct training for its employees. All other options are not relevant; SEMAIS management can take disciplinary action once employees are trained.

5. **C.** Digital/electronic evidence is acceptable in the court of law if the chain of custody and authenticity/integrity of the digital/electronic evidence are verifiable. The chain of custody refers to the who, what, when, where, and how the evidence was handled – from its identification through its entire lifecycle, which ends with destruction or permanent archiving. Any break in this chain can cast doubt on the integrity of the evidence and the professionalism of those directly involved in either the investigation or collecting and handling the evidence. Ensuring the authenticity and integrity of evidence is critical. Suppose the courts feel the evidence or its copies are not accurate or lack integrity. In that case, it is doubtful that the evidence or any information derived from the evidence will be admissible.

6. **A.** The exact requirements for the admissibility of evidence vary across legal systems and between different cases (e.g., criminal versus tort). At a more generic level, evidence should have some probative value, be relevant to the case at hand, and meet the following criteria (often called the five rules of evidence): be authentic, be accurate, be complete, be convincing, and be admissible.

7. **B.** The correct action for forensic analysis of the hard disk drive is to first make an image/copy of the hard disk drive before any evidence collection. All other options are subsequent stages of the malware analysis on the hard disk drive.

8. **D.** Analyzing network logs for intrusions is the most successful method. The logs contain data timestamps and information on the intrusive attack.

9. **A.** Download updates from the authentic source are a countermeasure to stop trojan from installation, not the trojan analysis. All other options are related to the identification and analysis of the trojan.

10. **B.** The foremost step to identify that router's firmware is compromised is to match the hash of the router firmware with its vendor's supplied hash. If hashes are different, it is an indication that router firmware has been infected.

11. **D.** To preserve a standalone hard disk drive from loss of evidence, avoid hard disk drive from a magnetic and static electric field. As magnetic fields and even static electricity can render specific electronic equipment, such as data storage devices or disks unusable and unreadable.

12. **C.** Since national boundaries effectively disappear when considering many cybercrimes, jurisdiction is another complicated matter. Countries differ in civil and criminal offense standards, substantive and procedural law, data collection and preservation practices, and other evidentiary and juridical factors. It calls for an international forum/agreement for the investigation and trial of cybercriminals, irrespective of their physical location and country's laws.

13. **A.** An IDS can also be used on individual host systems to monitor and report on file, disk, user activities, and process activity on that host. When used in this way, it is referred to as a host-based IDS or HIDS.

14. **D.** Properly configure and tune the IDS so that trusted applications' traffic is not treated as a threat vector. A critical operational requirement for establishing IDS capabilities is the need to adjust the IDS to the unique traffic patterns generated by the organization. For example, without proper tuning, the activity associated with a company's custom-developed application may appear to an IDS as unwanted or suspicious activity, forcing the generation of multiple alerts.

15. **B.** All other options are characteristics of SIEM except that SIEM aggregates the information in multiple repositories. A SIEM is used to aggregate the information and log from various sources to a single repository.

16. **A.** As SEMAIS publicly hosted servers are being used as zombies to launch an attack on other organizations. It is recommended to implement egress filtering at perimeter devices of SEMAIS to unknown destinations. Egress filtering is the practice of monitoring and potentially restricting the flow of information outbound from one network to another. Typically, the information flow from a private computer network to the Internet is being monitored and controlled. TCP/IP packets sent out of the internal network are examined via a router, firewall, or similar edge device. Packets that do not meet security policies are not allowed to leave the network. Egress filtering helps ensure that unauthorized or malicious traffic never leaves the internal network.

17. **D.** DLP objectives can be met by considering all forms and manifestations are of data, i.e., data at rest, data in motion, and data in use. Each of these three states of data is addressed by a specific set of technologies provided by DLP solutions.

18. **B.** Steganography is the science of hiding information. Whereas cryptography aims to make data unreadable by a third party, the purpose of steganography is to hide the data from a third party. Cryptanalysis is the science of breaking codes and cryptographic algorithms.

19. **D.** All other options are characteristics of configuration management except that CM has nothing to do with the naming convention of artifacts. CM also ensures the naming convention of artifacts.

20. **B.** All the mentioned options are fundamental for the security operations of SEMAIS. The most considerable one is controlling and auditing privileged accounts of SEMAIS periodically. Security operations must maintain strong control over the number and types of accounts used on systems. This requires careful supervision over the management of accounts given privileges on IT systems, such as service accounts and accounts used to execute scripts.

21. **A.** System/network administrators enjoy the highest level of privilege in any organization; therefore, any organization should pay attention to system/network administrators' accounts and activities. The network administrator of SEMAIS should be given the least privilege on the need-to basis across all systems and IT infrastructure. If possible, the system administrator's actions should be logged and sent to a separate system that the system administrator does not control. The logs should be reviewed with change or configuration management requests to determine if only authorized actions occur. An administrator should not have the ability to engage in malicious activities without collision and separation of duties to be enforced. System administrators should be subject to job rotation. Job rotation ensures another individual must perform the original system administrator's duties and review their work.

22. **D.** Job rotation, separation of duties, and least privilege are the principles for smooth functioning and secure operation of an enterprise. This question is related to user identity management, so the user account must be validated from time to time. Reviews of account activity are necessary to determine the existence of inactive accounts. Those accounts found to be inactive due to the departure of an individual from the organization should be removed from the system. Accounts that are inactive due to extended leave or temporary duties should be disabled.

23. **C.** All the factors are considered for making service agreements with an organization, but the least important to be considered is the knowledge of the company, big name, and share value in the trade market.

24. **A.** A laptop may contain a lot of sensitive data. You need to encrypt the data with encryption software should the computer be lost or stolen. Laptops do not have a built-in encryption system that is activated by simply using the passcode. By only having the passcode activated on a computer, a skilled person can often crack it in less than five minutes and read everything stored on the hard drive. The only way to ensure your data is secure is to encrypt the hard drive on your laptop.

25. **C.** There is several concerns that the security practitioner needs to consider regarding cloud-based storage in the enterprise. The most important to consider is that encryption keys remain with users, not with the service provider. All other options should also be taken into account.

26. **D.** Background checks and investigations are a valuable tool for determining an individual's trustworthiness and the likelihood of compliance with organization policy. In all mentioned categories of employees, the employees having traffic violation tickets will be the least problematic for the SEMAIS.

27. **B.** Reviewing of account activity is necessary to determine the existence of inactive accounts. Those accounts found to be inactive due to the departure of an individual from the organization should be removed from the system. Accounts that are inactive due to extended leave or temporary duties should be disabled. Ideally, individuals or their supervisors would promptly report temporary or permanent departures of system users to the appropriate system or security administrator.

28. **A.** All the mentioned options are equally important for protecting client's and company's confidential data. The most important is to protect data in all its forms and manifestations, i.e., storage, transit, and processing. Moreover, when the company's policy dictates data security, all the other options will be afforested.

29. **C.** Clients and vendors should have no access to the company's resources unless required and sanctioned by the SEMAIS management. Moreover, the clients' and vendors' access should be restricted. All other options are necessary to ensure operational security.

30. **D.** A datacenter should have access restrictions. All other options are imparting towards datacenter secure operations except that the employees of SEMAIS are trustworthy, and everyone should be given access to datacenter for speedy operations. Employees' trustworthiness does not entitle them to more privileges.

31. **C.** The question is a bit tricky; all mentioned options can be used for the protection of malware in one way or the other, but the most economical, most accessible, and convenient way is that users should have read and executed permissions for software as some viruses infect executable content through modification of the binary. Suppose the user does not have to write, modify, or delete permissions to system binaries. In that case, the virus will be unable to affect these files when executing in the context of an ordinary user.

32. **A.** As an information security officer of SEMAIS, you should recommend all mentioned options except portable and mobile devices' authentication before connecting to SEMAIS IT infrastructure with no encryption enabled. Without encryption, compromise of data cannot be guaranteed.

33. **B.** Specialized hardware devices known as degaussers can be used to erase data saved to magnetic media. The amount of energy needed to reduce the magnetic field on the media to zero is known as coercivity. It is important to make sure that the coercivity of the degausser is of sufficient strength to meet object reuse requirements when erasing data. If a degausser is used with low coercivity, then a remanence of the data will exist. Therefore, a degausser with minimum coercivity should not be used.

34. **D.** In this case, the priority is clear that get the critical server should be operational. Simultaneously, the information security responder wants to preserve as much information as possible for investigative purposes. The system has been attempting to perform an emergency system restart (by rebooting itself), but it has been unable to return to normal service. While a warm reboot (or graceful reboot) is not likely going to work, perhaps a cold reboot, which shuts the system down completely, may be most suitable.

35. **B.** Employees can become fearful about making reports concerning suspicious behavior. This derives from strict and regulated interrogation that poses employees as a violator.

36. C. Statistical-Anomaly-Based IDS are recommended for detecting Advanced Persistent Threats (APTs). Signature- or Pattern-Matching IDS examines the available information (logs or network traffic) to determine if it matches a known attack. Protocol Anomaly-Based IDS examines network traffic to determine if what it sees conforms to the defined standard for that protocol, as defined in a Request for Comment (RFC). Statistical-Anomaly-Based IDS establishes a baseline of normal traffic patterns over time and detects any deviations from that baseline. Some also use heuristics to evaluate the intended behavior of network traffic to determine if it is intended to be malicious or not. Most modern systems combine two or more of these techniques to provide a more accurate analysis before it decides whether it sees an attack.

37. D. All the mentioned options are specific to log management except that the log should not be archived. Logs should be archived as per the company's policy for threat identification or futuristic threats.

38. B. SEMAIS should have an agreement with US-CERT for attack protection and identification. National level CERT helps enterprises in all cyber aspects. Buying cyber insurance and augmenting already deployed controls is not the solution.

39. A. Vulnerability assessment is a precursor to penetration testing. Vulnerability assessment identifies weaknesses in an enterprise's security posture, whereas penetration testing tries to exploit identified vulnerabilities.

40. B. Third-party audits will identify more loopholes than in-house auditing as an in-house team is tuned and accustomed to security controls for which they have been working. An independent third party typically performs a security audit to the management of the system. The audit determines the degree to which the required controls are implemented. The system maintenance or security personnel conducts a security review to discover vulnerabilities within the system. Exposure occurs when policies are not followed, misconfigurations are present, or flaws exist in the hardware or software of the system. System reviews are sometimes referred to as vulnerability assessments.

41. C. Anomalies can be variety in numbers. Users logging in at office timings are not to be considered as an anomaly.

42. A. Protocol anomaly-based IDS will be used to detect attacks related to protocol anomaly. Protocol anomaly detection works by understanding the network protocols, which generally requires having a protocol engine for each network protocol and checking or validating known abuses' inputs. Much of this is part of the essential operation of the firewall, creating sessions, matching packets to flows and sessions, and closing sessions.

43. B. Only relevant staff should be notified about any information security incident. Any notification across the enterprise will cause panic and will make recovery procedures more difficult.

44. D. The company has a change management process in which all staff personnel is entitled to change. Management can review, authorize, supervise, unauthorize and revoke changes as per company policies. Changes are logged and reviewed so that staff members are accountable for their respective changes and no one can make unauthorized changes.

45. D. The backup method is not an important factor to discuss with end-users regarding email retention.

46. C. Penetration testing depends upon the organization, its security objective, and management's goal.

47. A. A tabletop exercise/structured walk-through test is considered a preliminary step in the overall testing process and may be used as an effective training tool; however, it is not a preferred testing method. Its primary objective is to ensure that critical personnel from all areas are familiar with the BCP and that the plan accurately reflects the organization's ability to recover from a disaster. A walk-through drill/simulation test is somewhat more involved than a tabletop exercise/structured walk-through test. The participants choose a specific event scenario and apply the BCP to it. Functional drill/parallel testing is the first type of test that involves the actual mobilization of personnel to other sites to establish communications and perform basic recovery processing as outlined in the BCP.

48. C. Prior to deploying updates to production servers, make certain that a full system backup is conducted. In the regrettable event of a system crash, the server and data can be recovered without significant data loss due to the update. Additionally, if the update involved propriety code, it will be necessary to copy the server or application image to the media librarian. The presence or absence of complete disclosure information is good to have, but not a requirement as the patching process will have to be a risk-based decision as it applies to the organization. Documentation of the patching process is the last step in patch management processes. Independent third-party assessments are not usually related to attesting patch validity. Full-interruption/full-scale test is the most comprehensive type of test. In a full-scale test, a real-life emergency is simulated as closely as possible. Therefore, comprehensive planning should be a prerequisite to this type of test to ensure that business operations are not negatively affected.

49. **A.** An organization's obligations for due care extend to its business partners; therefore, all regulatory and compliance requirements must be passed to the provider.

50. **B.** In the concept of defense-in-depth, barriers are arraigned in layers. The level of security grows progressively higher as one comes closer to the center or the highest protective area. Defending an asset with multiple postures can reduce the likelihood of a successful attack; if one layer of defense fails, another layer of defense will hopefully prevent the attack, and so on.

51. **D.** Recovery Time Objective (RTO) is the earliest period and a service level within which a business process must be restored after a disaster to avoid unacceptable consequences. Recovery Point Objective (RPO) is the acceptable amount of data loss measured in time. Meantime between failures (MTBF) is the predicted amount of time between inherent failures of a system during operation. Meantime to repair (MTTR) measures maintainability by representing the average time required to repair a failed component or device.

20. Domain 8: Software Development Security - Questions

1. Software products are getting popular over hardware products in the realm of information security and network security. Which of the following factor makes software products more promising as compared to hardware products?

    A. Software is customizable.

    B. Software is cost-effective.

    C. Software is easy to develop.

    D. Software performance is better.

2. Software is more prone to vulnerabilities and exploits. Which one of the following is most pertinent to software vulnerabilities and exploits?

    A. Poor programming practices.

    B. Vendor competition for early releases and marketing.

    C. Security requirements are not addressed during design phases.

    D. Lack of information security professionals in the ranks of software developers.

3. Systems Development Life Cycle (SDLC) is employed for the development of software products. Which one of the following is not an SDLC process/phase?

    A. System design specifications

    B. Development and implementation

    C. Testing and evaluation control

    D. Revisions and system replacement

4. SEMAIS is planning to launch a website backed with a database to store clients' data. As a security professional, what will you recommend to the SEMAIS web developer?

    A. No SQL injection point for an attacker to be supplied.

    B. Graphics should be well designed.

    C. DDoS protection mechanism to be adopted.

    D. A website should be easily accessible.

5. As a security professional of SEMAIS, which answer would be of less concern for data security?

    A. Does the information have special value or sensitivity; therefore, it requires special protection?

    B. Will application operation risk exposure of sensitive information?

    C. Even if the original data is of low sensitivity, does the resultant information have a higher value?

    D. The development team is maintaining version control of software under development.

6. If a client has security concerns during the SDLC, a company can address the concerns at which SDLC stage?

   A. Testing phase

   B. Design phase

   C. Requirement gathering and analysis phase

   D. Implementation phase

7. Which of the following SDLC stage poses the most important security-enabled software, considering that software meets its functional requirements and security requirements?

   A. Design phase

   B. Testing phase

   C. Implementation phase

   D. Requirement gathering and analysis phase

8. Which of the following is not the intention of SDLC models?

   A. Reduce software development failures.

   B. Improve the cost of the software.

   C. Meet schedules.

   D. Produce a higher quality product.

9. SEMAIS deployed a third-party software program on its IT infrastructure. The software was passed all functional tests. SEMAIS was planning to upgrade its IT infrastructure and requested the third-party vendor to make changes. Which answer is not valid for the software change?

   A. Risk analysis and recertification of the changed software will not occur.

   B. Any software changes will not disable or circumvent the security features.

   C. Changed software will not exfiltrate sensitive data.

   D. The software will operate perfectly.

10. SEMAIS financial department is requesting a software upgrade because the current software is outdated and causes latent issues. When performing the upgrade, which answer would not support a secure software update?

   A. Seek approval of management for new software.

   B. Download the software from the internet and start using it.

   C. The functionality of the software to be verified.

   D. Cost-benefit analysis and relevance of software in IT infrastructure to be verified.

11. SEMAIS software program "Unique Access" has been validated to have exploitable vulnerabilities as per the security audit. Which answer is the best recommendation for addressing the vulnerabilities?

    A. Ask the vendor for desired patches.

    B. Implement countermeasure by deploying other controls.

    C. Download patches from an unidentified source.

    D. Discard vulnerable software.

12. SEMAIS has been tasked to develop a software program for a client. To meet the client's requirements, SEMAIS outsourced 50% of the project. Who will be responsible for integrating the software?

    A. CEO of SEMAIS

    B. Quality assurance manager

    C. Project manager of the software program

    D. Outsourced development team

13. Which of the following is not specific to DevOps?

    A. Develop and test against production-like systems.

    B. Deploy with repeatable, reliable processes.

    C. Monitor and validate operational quality.

    D. No feedback from stakeholders.

14. Which answer provides the best advantage to using the waterfall model?

    A. Demands heavy overhead in planning and administration.

    B. Patient in the realization of software.

    C. Provides deliberate consideration and planning.

    D. Non-iterative model in nature.

15. ISO 27000 emphasizes the implementation of an Information System Management System (ISMS) across an enterprise. Which model follows the ISO 27000 standard for ISMS?

    A. Waterfall model

    B. Spiral Model

    C. Iterative model

    D. Non-iterative model

16. **Which answer is not specific to the cleanroom model and software development?**

    A. More time in the testing of software consumed.

    B. It is used to produce defect-free software.

    C. Employed for high-quality software.

    D. Cleanroom software development focuses on defect prevention rather than defect removal.

17. **When providing a description and probable software functionality, which the SEMAIS development team can deploy the model?**

    A. Waterfall model

    B. Cleanroom model

    C. Capability maturity model

    D. Prototyping model

18. **SEMAIS competes with its competitors to market a quick software product. To safeguard SEMAIS interests, which one of the following models would you recommend for software development?**

    A. Jump start the software.

    B. Capability Maturity model

    C. Rapid Development model

    D. Waterfall model

19. **The set of applications used to manage large, structured sets of persistent data is known as which answer?**

    A. Database management system

    B. ActiveX

    C. Applet

    D. Enterprise application

20. **A database that is used to store confidential data should provide all the following except.**

    A. Confidentiality of data

    B. Integrity of data

    C. Access control mechanism for users.

    D. Database query language

21. A security auditor is auditing a database management system (DBMS). From a security perspective, which one of the following is a major concern for SEMAIS?

    A. Database management system

    B. Database Schema

    C. Database query language

    D. Data residing in the database

22. Which of the following is not specific to the relational DBMS model?

    A. Data structures are called either tables or relations.

    B. Data is stored as objects.

    C. Integrity rules on allowable values and combinations of values in tables.

    D. Data manipulation agents that provide the relational mathematical basis and an assignment operator.

23. A database administrator types in a query to reference a specific key. The key also references keys in other tables. What type of key is being described?

    A. Primary key

    B. Candidate key

    C. Candidate key

    D. Foreign key

24. To maintain the integrity of relational DBMS, which one of the following is necessary?

    A. Entity integrity and referential integrity

    B. Entity integrity

    C. Referential integrity

    D. Data integrity

25. Structured Query Language (SQL) is used to interact with DBMS. Which one of the following is not specific to SQL?

    A. SQL was developed by IBM and is an International Organization for Standardization (ISO) and American National Standards Institute (ANSI) standard.

    B. SQL is specific to each DBMS.

    C. SQL is used as a data manipulation language.

    D. SQL provides the users with a high-level view of the data.

26. A DBA is attempting to integrate new access controls for a DBMS. The control provides grant functionality to a remote database. Which one of the following accurately describes the control?

    A. Table

    B. Schemas

    C. View

    D. Tuple

27. An employee has modified the SEMAIS database. As a database administrator of SEMAIS, which command will enable you to view the database's last state?

    A. COMMIT

    B. ROLLBACK

    C. SAVEPOINT

    D. SET TRANSACTION

28. As an information security expert, what can you recommend to the SEMAIS database designing team to protect users' passwords and hosted services?

    A. Store passwords in encrypted form.

    B. Store passwords in plain form.

    C. Store passwords in some other database.

    D. Do not store users/clients' passwords in the database.

29. SEMAIS has started an online shopping portal. A discussion has been prompted to secure the database from attackers. Which Tier model protects web and backend databases from attackers?

    A. Three-tier approach

    B. Two-tier approach

    C. Single-tier approach

    D. No-Layered approach

30. Which one of the following is not a benefit of data mining?

    A. Data mining is used to reveal hidden relationships, patterns, and trends in the data.

    B. Data mining is a decision-making technique.

    C. A large repository of data is required to perform data mining.

    D. Detailed data about individuals obtained by data mining that violate privacy.

31. Which of the following is not an attack on DBMS?

    A. Aggregation

B. Cross-site request forgery

C. Concurrency

D. SQL injection attack

32. **Neural networks are specific artificial intelligence (AI) methods used widely in computing. Which one of the following is not specific to neural networks?**

   A. Neural networks are specific AI methods used to develop classification, regression, association, and segmentation models based on the way neurons work in the human brain.

   B. The neural net method organizes data into nodes arranged in layers, and links between the nodes have specific weighting classifications.

   C. The neural network helps detect the associations among the input patterns or relationships.

   D. Value and relevance of the decisions made by the neural network decrease with time and passage of experience.

33. **Most of the attacks today are being launched on websites. Which one of the following makes websites most vulnerable as compared to other software applications?**

   A. Websites are publicly available and widely accessible resources.

   B. Websites are also the primary interface for e-commerce.

   C. Web-based systems are tied to the production or internal systems of an organization.

   D. Most intrusion detection controls are relaxed to increase web performance.

34. **SEMAIS is planning to launch an e-commerce website. It has been reported that previous websites had authentication issues, and vendor credentials were never removed. What control procedure should the company consider before launching the website.**

   A. Do not hard code the authentication credentials.

   B. Use account lockout and extended logging and audit.

   C. Ensure administrative interfaces are removed or secured appropriately.

   D. Protect all authentication traffic with encryption.

35. **Cookies are used to recover the stateless property of Hypertext Transfer Protocol (HTTP). Which of the following is not pertinent to cookies security?**

   A. Do not use cookies.

   B. Cookies should be time validated.

   C. Use random and unique indicators for cookies.

   D. Cookies should retain plain confidential data.

36. **Which answer is falsely stated when only valid, authorized, and authenticated users can access the data?**

   A. The system or software provides some type of granularity for controlling such permissions.

   B. Permissions related to the use of the data cannot be controlled and managed.

C. Encryption or other appropriate logical controls are available for protecting sensitive information.

D. Audit trails are in place to provide assurance of the functional security controls.

37. **Which of the following advocates using open-source software vs. closed software in terms of security?**

A. Open-source software is free of cost.

B. Open-source software is readily available.

C. Open-source software is verified and tested by the community.

D. Open-source software is continuously developed.

38. **An application has been categorized as a Level II threat based on recent programming errors. The report states that: Application "Hack" has been classified as a high-level risk, and the results are based on prior agreements and software development plan. According to the report, which answer is attributed to buffer overflow attack?**

A. Poor programming practices by developers.

B. Deployed software is not configured properly.

C. Buffer flow has nothing to do with software attacks.

D. The development team does not perform requirement gathering and analysis.

39. **SEMAIS is developing software and hardware requirements through a business partnership. A client has expressed concern about the efficiency and performance of the software. To address the client's concern, which language should the SEMAIS development team implement?**

A. Low-level language for both hardware and software.

B. Low-level language for hardware and high-level language for software.

C. High-level language for both hardware and software.

D. High-level language for hardware and low-level language for software.

40. **Software programmers widely use JavaScript language. There are various schemes and programmatic functions that allow developers to interface with JavaScript platforms. Which one of the following statements is not specific to the JavaScript development platform?**

A. JavaScript is specific to web technology.

B. It is interpreted by the user's web browser and allows control over most of the web browser features.

C. It is not Java and has no relation to Java.

D. JavaScript is only used for desktop applications.

41. **SEMAIS has developed an application to process classified data. To avoid data leakage from the application and spillage of classified data, what control measure can SEMAIS implement?**

A. Do not process classified data by the application.

B. Run the software in a sandbox.

C. Avoid using other software on the same system.

D. Implement access control at the user level.

42. **A developer has opened a text file to see the contents of a code. Upon reviewing the information, he notices that a refined method for software coding needs to occur. The method must provide an independent platform that allows developers to write human-readable code, not machine code. Which answer provides the developer with the solution to read the code?**

A. Compiles source code into a sort of pseudo-object code called bytecode.

B. Develop software for each independent platform.

C. Only develop software for the desired platform.

D. Compile source code in object code.

43. **Object-oriented programming is preferred over structured programming. Which one of the following is the most promising feature of object-oriented programming?**

A. Ease of use.

B. Efficient memory utilization.

C. Object reusability.

D. Class abstraction and inheritance.

44. **SEMAIS is developing software for one of its clients. It is discovered that the software hangs and consumes maximum resources during testing. What error could be causing the issue?**

A. Increase hardware resources, i.e., random access memory (RAM) & hard disk in the system.

B. Memory does not release.

C. Change testing strategy for software.

D. The software has no issue; use it in its current condition.

45. **SEMAIS development team is developing a cryptographic software program. The team is planning to use a publicly available software library. What should be the primary consideration for using the library?**

A. The software library should be efficient.

B. Software libraries should support all possible cryptographic algorithms.

C. The software library should provide a programming interface.

D. Verify that cryptographic algorithms are implemented correctly.

46. **What causes a website redirection attack?**

A. Hosted web server is misconfigured.

B. Firewall rules are not applied properly.

C. The browser is not processing the site.

D. The attacker is manipulating a uniform resource identifier (URL) in Unicode format.

47. Which aspects of malware and viruses are considered the most dangerous?

A. Malware infecting files and programs.

B. The antivirus does not detect malware.

C. Malware communicating with its command and control center.

D. Malware renaming specific files.

48. Which one of the following is true about trojans?

A. Trojans are viruses.

B. Trojans are malicious applications.

C. Trojans can propagate by themselves.

D. Trojans are undetectable.

49. When attempting to acquire sensitive data from bank accounts through email or website, fraud is defined as which attack?

A. Phishing

B. Whaling

C. Social engineering attack

D. Brute force attack

50. Distributed Denial of Service (DDoS) Zombies are known as which one of the following?

A. Zombies protect against DDoS attacks.

B. Zombies facilitate in launching the DDoS.

C. Zombies are attackers launching DDoS.

D. Zombies have no relevance to DDoS.

51. To protect SEMAIS IT infrastructure from malware, which one of the following would not be recommended?

A. Disable Windows Script Host, ActiveX, VBScript, and JavaScript. Do not send HTML-formatted emails.

B. Do not accept and double-click email attachments that seem to be malicious and from an unauthentic source.

C. Use more than one scanner and scan everything.

D. SEMAIS employees should have a stronger password for better protection.

21. Domain 8: Software Development Security - Answers and Explanations

1. **B.** Although software performance is slower than similar hardware products, the software is customizable, easy to develop, and cost-effects. The most important factor is that software products are cost-effective.

2. **C.** All the mentioned options, i.e., poor programming practices, early release competition, security requirements are not addressed during design phases, and lack of information security professionals in the ranks of software developers, are pertinent to software-related bugs and vulnerabilities. Still, the most important is to address security requirements from the design phase.

3. **D.** A project management tool that can be used to plan, execute, and control a software development project is the systems development life cycle (SDLC). The SDLC is a process that includes systems analysts, software engineers, programmers, and end-users in the project design and development. Revisions and system replacement are not part of SDLC; instead, it is part of the system life cycle.

4. **A.** When a website is backed with a database to store clients' data, a security professional should recommend providing no SQL injection point to enable the website to be developed. DDoS is a network attack and nothing to do with development. All other options are not security-relevant.

5. **D.** All the mentioned options should concern the security practitioner except that the development team maintains version control of software under development as version control is the primary responsibility of the development team, not the security practitioner.

6. **C.** Since the client has security concerns, information security staff should be incorporated in the development process from the requirement gathering and analysis phase to understand the client's requirements better and communicate them to the development team.

7. **A:** The design phase of software development seems to be most important for security-enabled software, considering that software meets its functional requirements and security requirements. The design phase includes all activities related to designing the system and software. In this phase, the system architecture, system outputs, and system interfaces are designed. Data input, data flow, and output requirements are established, and security features are generally based on the overall security architecture for the company.

8. **B.** Improve the cost of software is not the intention of software. Rather SDLC intends to complete the software within an estimated budget. SDLC is intended to reduce software development failures, improve cost estimates, meet schedules, and produce a higher quality product.

9. **D.** Previous behavior and functioning of software do not guarantee that a new changed version will work. Therefore, periodic risk analysis and recertification of sensitive applications are required when significant changes occur.

10. **B.** Download the software from the internet and start using it is not recommended because SEMAIS management has not yet approved the software installation at its IT infrastructure.

11. **A.** The most recommended for addressing software vulnerabilities is to ask the vendor for patches. Patches should not be downloaded from an unidentified source. Moreover, discarding software is not the solution because it will cause SEMAIS monetary effects.

12. **C.** Project management is responsible for software integration. Integrated Product and Process Development (IPPD) is a management technique that simultaneously integrates all essential acquisition activities with multi-disciplinary teams, optimizing the design, manufacturing, and supportability processes. IPPD facilitates meeting cost and performance objectives from product concept through production, including field support.

13. **D.** DevOps encompasses the already popular programming concepts of agile development, continuous integration, and continuous delivery and extends into the social aspect of IT by placing a premium on the importance of tearing down walls that divide development, operations, support, and management teams.

14. **C.** From the perspective of business in general, the disadvantage of the waterfall model is that it demands a heavy overhead in planning and administration. It requires patience in the early stages of a project. These same factors are considered an advantage in the security community because they force careful consideration and planning. It can inhibit a development team from pursuing concurrent phases or activities. This limit slows initial development, but it ensures that adhoc additions are minimized.

15. **B.** ISMS implementation is based on four sub-stages, i.e., Plan-Do-Check-Act (PDCA) model. The PDCA model is spiral in nature, which predicates continuous risk assessment.

16. **A.** The goal is to write the code correctly rather than find the problems once they are there. Essentially, cleanroom software development focuses on defect prevention rather than defect removal. In order to achieve this, one should spend more time in the early phases, relying on the assumption that the time spent in other phases, such as testing, is reduced.

17. **D.** SEMAIS will employ Prototyping model to describe the probable functionality and desirable features of the software. Prototyping is allowing users to evaluate a developed proposal and try the proposed solution before implementation. It also helps to understand user requirements and may not have been considered by the developer during product design.

18. **C.** A form of rapid prototyping requires strict time limits on each phase and relies on tools that enable rapid development.

19. **A.** A database management system (DBMS) is a suite of application programs that typically manage large, structured sets of persistent data. It stores, maintain, and provides access to data using ad-hoc query capabilities. The DBMS provides the structure for the data and some language for accessing and manipulating the data. The primary objective is to store data and allow users to view the data. ActiveX is a software framework created by Microsoft that adapts its earlier Component Object Model (COM) and Object Linking and Embedding (OLE) technologies for content downloaded from a network, particularly from the World Wide Web. An applet is any small application that performs one specific task that runs within the scope of a dedicated widget engine or a more extensive program, often as a plug-in. An enterprise application can be of any type.

20. **D.** This question is a bit tricky. A DBMS provides query language by default; therefore, it is not pertinent from a security perspective. From a security perspective, confidentiality, integrity, and access controls are more important.

21. **B.** From a security auditing perspective, the database schema is more vital than other options. It will reveal the whole structure of the database, and the entire database can be compromised. The database schema defines what the data is and how it is stored, how it relates to other data, and who can access, add, and modify the data.

22. **B.** The relational model is based on set theory, predicates logic, and provides a high level of abstraction. All the mentioned options are specific to relational DBMS except that data is stored as objects.

23. **D.** The primary key is an attribute or set of attributes that uniquely identifies a specific instance of an entity. Each table in a database must have a primary key that is unique to that table. It is a subset of the candidate key. Any key that could be a primary key is called a candidate key. The candidate key is an attribute that is a unique identifier within a given table. One of the candidate keys is the primary key, and the others are called alternate keys. Primary keys provide the sole tuple-level addressing mechanism within the relational model. The foreign key in a relational model is different from the primary key. The foreign key value represents a reference to an entry in some other table. If an attribute (value) in one table matches those of the primary key of some other relation, it is considered the foreign key.

24. **A.** The two integrity rules of the relational model are entity integrity and referential integrity. The two rules apply to every relational model and focus on the primary and foreign keys. These rules derive from the Clark and Wilson integrity model. The tuple must have a unique and non-null value in the primary key in the entity integrity model. This guarantees that the immediate key-value uniquely identifies the tuple. The referential integrity model states that for any foreign key value, the referenced relation must have a tuple with the same value for its primary key.

25. **B.** An advantage of having a standard language is that organizations can switch between different database engine vendor systems without rewriting all their application software or retrain staff. All other are specific to SQL.

26. **C.** Views define what information a user can view in the tables – the view can be customized so that an entire table may be visible, or a user may be limited to only seeing just a row or a column. Views are created dynamically by the system for each user and provide access control granularity. The columns and rows of the data are contained in tables. Schemas describe the database structure, including any access controls limiting how users view the information contained in the tables. Tuples are rows/records in a table.

27. **B.** COMMIT saves work that has been done. SAVEPOINT identifies a location in a transaction to which you can later roll back, if necessary. ROLLBACK restores the database to its state at last. SET TRANSACTION changes transaction options such as what rollback segment to use.

28. **A.** As primarily security lies in the password, the username can be stored in a simple form, but the password must be kept in encrypted form to save them from compromise.

29. **A.** The tiered approach can add to security because the users do not connect directly to the data. One method for Internet access is to create a tiered application approach that manages data in layers. However, there can be many layers; however, the most typical architecture uses a three-tier approach: presentation layer, business logic layer, and data layer. This is sometimes referred to as the Internet computing model because the browser is used to connect to an application server that connects to a database.

30. **D.** Data mining is another process (or tool) for discovering information in data warehouses by running queries against the data. A large repository of data is required to perform data mining. Data mining is used to reveal hidden relationships, patterns, and trends in the data warehouse. Data mining is a decision-making technique based on a series of analytical techniques taken from mathematics, statistics, cybernetics, and genetics. The methods are used independently and in cooperation with one another to uncover information from data warehouses. A disadvantage of data mining is that it might reveal information contrary to the privacy policy.

31. **B.** Cross-site request forgery is an attack on web site, and it has nothing to do with the database. The ability to combine non-sensitive data from separate sources to create sensitive information is known as aggregation. A concurrency attack is when actions or processes run simultaneously; they are said to be concurrent. Problems with concurrency include running processes that use old data, updates that are inconsistent, or having a deadlock occur. SQL injection attack is used to compromise databases by SQL queries; it is mainly a web-related attack on the database.

32. **D.** All the mentioned options are specific to neural networks except that value and relevance of the decisions made by the neural network decrease with time and passage of experience. Neural network decision gets mature with the passing of time and expertise.

33. **A.** All the mentioned options contribute to web-related attacks, but most threatening websites are publicly available resources and an easy target for attackers.

34. **C.** All the mentioned options are necessary for website security, but the most important is to ensure that administrative interfaces are removed or secured appropriately. A compromise of administrative interfaces will compromise the entire site and other security features as well.

35. **D.** All the mentioned options are necessary for cookie security except that cookies should retain plain confidential data. Cookies should always be encrypted, and if cookies are decrypted for extracting data, the decoded data should be flushed from the local hard disk on task completion.

36. **B.** All the mentioned options are security requirements for applications and databases except that the data's permissions cannot be controlled and managed.

37. **C.** Open-source software is verified and tested by the community. Their code is rigorously tested by the community, making open-source software more promising in terms of security. All other options are specific to open-source software.

38. D. Most software is vulnerable to buffer overflow attacks, and this vulnerability is induced in software by poor programming practices of developers.

39. B. Low-level language for hardware and high-level language for software is the most recommended option as the client is conscious about performance. The high-level language will facilitate software development, and the low-level language supports hardware efficiency.

40. D. JavaScript is not specific to desktop applications; instead, it is specific to web technology. JavaScript is a language mostly used in webpages. However, it is not Java and has no relation to Java. It is interpreted by the user's web browser and allows control over most of the web browser features.

41. B. As the software is susceptible to classified data leakage, it is recommended to run the software in a sandbox so that other processes running on the same system cannot read data from the software's memory.

42. A. Pseudocode is an informal high-level description of the operating principle of a computer program or other algorithm. It uses the structural conventions of a programming language but is intended for human reading rather than machine reading.

43. C. All the mentioned options are properties and benefits of object-oriented programming. The most promising feature of object-oriented programming is object reusability.

44. B. Security weaknesses and vulnerabilities at the source-code level (e.g., buffer overflow, escalation of privilege, input/output validation). As software is used to hang and consume maximum resources of the system during testing; it is advisable to ask programmers to release memory from the source code of the software for efficient utilization of system resources.

45. D. The primary consideration for using the library should be to verify that all cryptographic algorithms are implemented correctly and do not exfiltrate the security parameters.

46. D. A redirect attack happens when an attacker redirects a web browser to an alternate site. A firewall can intercept this traffic through the detection of a Uniform Resource Locator (URL). However, when the URL was expressed in a Unicode format, the firewall would likely fail to recognize the content rather than ASCII. In contrast, the web browser would convert the information without difficulty.

47. C. All the techniques of malware and viruses can be dangerous, and they can have a tremendous impact on the system and exploitation capability. The most dangerous exploitation is malware communicating with its command and control center. In this way, malware will provide a permanent gateway for an attacker.

48. B. Trojans (Trojan horse) programs are the largest class of malware, aside from viruses. A Trojan is a program that pretends to do one thing while performing another unwanted action.

49. A. Phishing attempts to get the user to provide information that will be useful for identity theft-type frauds. Although phishing messages frequently use websites and confuse the origin and ownership of those sites, minimal programming, malicious or otherwise, may be involved. Phishing is unadulterated social engineering or deception. Whaling is a type of phishing aimed to target the top management of the company. A brute force attack is aimed at trying all probable values.

50. B. Zombies have relevance to DDoS and are used to facilitate the DDoS attack. Zombies are compromised systems used by the attacker for launching an attack.

51. D. All the mentioned options are necessary for protecting against malware, but a strong password has no relevance to malware protection.

22. Comprehensive Examination - Questions

1. A new laptop has been configured to have anti-virus software, network access control policies, and full disk encryption. The overall objective is to protect the computer from attacks and control access when in a remote environment or VPN configuration. What security measure has been selected to protect the laptop? Choose the best answer.

   A. Unnecessary services and applications have been blocked to contain perimeter attacks.

   B. A network control solution has been configured for the VPN.

   C. Network access translation devices have been installed for the organization.

   D. The organization has installed endpoint security products to protect the laptop.

2. A senior security architect is developing change procedures to address system protection for various access control principles. Under the plan, audit monitoring and logging that address user restrictions to software files must be addressed. The security architect has decided to implement network-based security technologies to capture logging activity. Which of the following technologies supports the change procedures?

   A. Isolate protection rings within OS platforms for logged data.

   B. Virtualize different environments.

   C. Design an intrusion system to capture threat and log data.

   D. Implement a trusted platform module to control traffic behavior.

3. A Privacy officer has just instituted a new policy that data must be deleted after use. An employee within the Human Resource department violates the policy a week after the CEO approved the policy. The corporate guidelines did not address the appropriate action for violating the policy. What would be an excellent follow-up step for the company to consider?

   A. Remove and transparency from the current policies.

   B. Mandate the enforcement of the OECD policy and procedures.

   C. Have the organization complete enterprise-wide training on privacy and counsel the employee.

   D. Research new data protection strategies for the organization.

4. A wireless network has been designed with various services to support authentication using the Wired Equivalent Privacy (WEP) protocol. The authentication technology will have the following parameters: 1) the computer sends a request for authentication to the access point, 2) the access point responds by generating a sequence of characters called a challenging text for the computer, and 3) the computer encrypts the challenge text with its WEP key and transmits the "message" back to the access point. Which of the following technologies addresses the authentication technology used for WEP?

   A. Closed System Authentication that has shared keys.

   B. Open System Authentication that requires all devices to generate a shared response.

   C. Shared Key technology that provides an encrypted channel.

   D. Open Key Authentication that does not allow encrypted data.

5. A Security Engineer has developed a control to support data in transit over a secured communication path. The protocols selected require confidentiality for all data routed between gateways and host devices. What technology has the Security Engineered used?

   A. End-user tunneling over encrypted communication paths.

   B. Link Encryption

   C. End-to-End encryption

   D. Cryptography and packet transfer

6. Alice and Bob wish to exchange data using PKI technology. What would be the proper exchange of data if Alice encrypted information to Bob with his private key?

   A. Bob performs symmetric encryption twice.

   B. This is abnormal for key exchange and may introduce the possibility of key compromise.

   C. Alice encrypts with the public key, and Bob decrypts with Alice's private key.

   D. Encrypt with both private keys.

7. As a Privacy Officer, you want to integrate security controls that support the collection of personal data. After reviewing several references, you decide to use the OECD Privacy Principle. Which principle below supports your decision?

   A. Data Quality Principle

   B. Purpose Specification Principle Use

   C. Limitation Principle

   D. Collection Limitation Principle

8. Baseline deployments are designed to support what specific resources?

   A. Audit and accountability standards.

   B. Configuration reports that discuss change specifications.

   C. Needs protection and resources for compliance.

   D. Those are designed within the safeguard requirements that align with the system.

9. When collecting private data, why must organizations inform the user of such action?

   A. As an act of policy in following the Use Limitation principle.

   B. To develop a general policy of openness.

   C. As a method to maintain data quality.

   D. To gain consent for approval and use of distribution.

10. When data has been classified with privacy controls, which role is responsible for enduring the controls are updated?

    A. Privacy Officer

    B. Data Owner

    C. Information System Security Officer (ISSO)

    D. Data Custodian

11. When data is described based on its impact on business operations, it can best describe what term?

    A. Reputation Risk: Loss of data will cause significant damage.

    B. Data confidentiality is required by law, policy, or contractual obligation.

    C. Classifying data according to protection needs.

    D. Classifying data according to availability needs.

12. When developing countermeasures to deploy against data mining, what should an organization consider?

    A. The protection needs and how to link encryption mirrors end-to-end traffic.

    B. Transparent routing of data.

    C. Whether inference attacks will occur.

    D. Whether a link session will terminate.

13. When reviewing the data profile for information saved to a company shared location, the user notice that every document has the following label "This critical information is mandated by law (HIPAA, GLBA) or required by private contract." What would be the best description for this marking?

    A. A compliance risk profile that describes the availability of data.

    B. A compliance risk describes the protection need for the information.

    C. The need for protection as it relates to availability.

    D. Loss of the confidentiality or integrity of the information could cause harm to individuals.

14. Which of the following does not support a baseline security standard?

    A. Which enterprise component can be protected?

    B. Change control for the asset SLA

    C. What security level should be applied.

    D. Should the same baseline be deployed enterprise-wide?

15. During normal operations, a security practitioner has discovered IP addresses that are not filtered. To control the risks, what would be a possible solution?

    A. Change the IP scheme for the organization firewall.

    B. Block IPSEC from Layer 3.

    C. Update access requirements within the access boundaries and gateway devices.

    D. Update all Layer 3 devices to send alerts to the IDS for restricting unauthorized traffic.

16. As a CIO, you must develop a decision on risk and budget constraints for your organization. You receive a report that states the SLE is at $10,000. To understand the detailed procedures at why the SLE is at $10,000, what information should the IT department present?

    A. The qualitative value of the asset and what cost consideration is required to maintain critical data.

    B. Qualitative value of the risk management program and cost-benefit for the SLE.

    C. The exposure factor and asset cost consideration.

    D. The impact of the ALE and its quantitative value after a risk assessment.

17. A company policy states that the business owners must take responsibility for risk and implement changes as required. During a security assessment, a business owner was notified that a critical risk was found within its data handling procedures. What would be the first step in investigating the issue?

    A. Investigate all shared responsibilities and assign the responsibility to appropriate business units.

    B. Notify the CIO and take appropriate action by meeting with the data custodian. Discipline the data custodian and update policies to reflect responsibilities.

    C. Considering this was an operative risk.

    D. The CIO should take full responsibility despite what the policy states, and the business owner should assist with any matters.

18. A Security Engineer from an external partner has been hired to configure new firewall settings. When the individual arrives at an organization, what would be a logical security approach to conducting business relationships?

    A. Perform account reviews for the Engineer to perform their task.

    B. Omit non-disclosure agreements from the relationship.

    C. Conduct an investigation and provide oversight to external business relationships.

    D. Require three forms of identification from the Security Engineer.

19. After a risk assessment has been completed, an organization decides to uninstall the chat service from its network. Based on the decision, what risk decision was considered by the organization?

    A. Passed the risk onto another entity for management.

    B. Eliminated the risk through software uninstall.

    C. Based on chat service as a low priority, the risk was accepted.

D. Avoided risk implications through removing chat service.

20. **An assessor has completed a security assessment for a significant application and decides to draft a report on its outcome. During the assessment, he discovered several active malware programs. As part of his report, which is the best solution to present the information?**

A. Examine human threats for inducing vulnerabilities.

B. Perform a new security assessment after the vulnerability scans are executed.

C. Examine a new framework to address the risk.

D. Address the malware issue and all exploitation patterns while considering vulnerable access points.

21. **As a Security Engineer, you have been tasked to use new technologies to help reduce risks associated with network traffic. Which of the following would you select as a tool of choice to minimize the risks?**

A. A detection system that screens gateway traffic based on IP ranges and feeds from various sources.

B. An intrusion detection system that provides system alerts and an IPS that restricts unauthorized gateway access.

C. An intrusive system with open firewall traffic.

D. Implement a VPN, VLAN, and Open Access to Port 23 for traffic analysis.

22. **During a threat assessment, a Security Engineer has discovered an attack method where a hacker can send a fake website to gain information about the corporate security posture. What level of attack should be included with the Threat Model?**

A. Website attack where propriety information is shared.

B. Social engineering attack that provides data about the company to employees.

C. A phishing attack that may use social patterns to determine security access points.

D. Threat attack that uses new vulnerabilities.

23. **To determine the risk valuation for a particular asset, an organization must determine what significant concept?**

A. The market analysis for the security product being evaluated.

B. Whether the asset is considered tangible or intangible to an organization.

C. Whether the impact causes corporately loss.

D. The true value for copyrights and trademarks and their risk association.

24. **The implementation of an anti-virus solution will support what control method?**

A. Technical and

B. Administrative Detective

C. Compensation

D. Technical as it relates to Preventive and Corrective controls.

25. The overall goal of personnel security policies is to establish compliance for employees to meet corporate security goals. Which of the following supports the statement?

   A.   Investigative security should emphasize employee audits for compliance.

   B.   Policies should require an organization to conduct preliminary checks on potential employees.

   C.   Ensure all individuals are qualified for new tasks.

   D.   Perform random job rotation duties to cross-train employees.

26. The process of selection countermeasures should consider what security methodology?

   A.   Control selection that reduces risks without audits.

   B.   Has the potential to reduce risk costs associated with changing budgets.

   C.   Align to security and risk vision for the governance team.

   D.   Derived from a trusted source and protects the availability of assets.

27. To accurately develop a threat model, an organization must consider what factors?

   A.   The overall software landscape and any potential risks.

   B.   The security architect and the SDLC compliance activities.

   C.   The current state of vulnerabilities impacts information systems, applications, risks, and countermeasures selection.

   D.   Attack scenarios and the current state of the security posture.

28. To implement privacy for physical controls, an organization must consider what potential issue?

   A.   Whether the policies align with the organization's goals and privacy objectives.

   B.   Does the policy enforce investigative rights for issues outside regular working hours?

   C.   Whether the company facility requires particular policies.

   D.   How often criminals break privacy policies and regulations.

29. To reduce threat exploitation, an enterprise may resort to what security control method?

   A.   Change the system configuration periodically.

   B.   Mandate security and risk management as a single source of protection needs.

   C.   Implement controls by assessing new standards.

   D.   Implement regulatory control standards that continuously access employee activities and establish a framework of trust with vendors.

30. **When controls are implemented, the overall selection for the controls should consider what component within the security architect? Choose the best answer.**

    A. The security framework and what steps support the implementation details.

    B.   Auditing standards and accountability for the control implementation.

    C. What risks will be avoided by removing applications?

    D. Change management and version control for software updates and policy configurations for the enterprise architect.

31. **When new security personnel enter the data center, he notices a warning sign that displays information sharing outside the organization boundary. What control procedure has been implemented?**

    A. Deterrent control

    B. Preventative Control

    C. Administrative awareness control

    D. Directive Control

32. **When an employee has been terminated, the Security team should proceed to what action once they are notified?**

    A. Disable all accounts and review system access for additional changes.

    B. Delete all accounts and audit the system for possible data breaches.

    C. Check the company policy to ensure the termination process was legal before changing account settings.

    D. Collect token devices and smart cards.

33. **When an organization decides to acquire shared services from a third-party source, what risks should be addressed before the acquisition becomes approved?**

    A. The current state of its baseline and auditing results for potential risks.

    B. What level of training has been completed by employees that manage their systems.

    C. Auditing standards used for the system.

    D. What level of accountability has been imposed on the users who use the system and its services.

34. **When comparing security control implementation to a continuous improvement methodology, the fundamental definition can be defined as which answer?**

    A. Planning for change controls requires sound decisions.

    B. Security checks should be implemented to avoid and differences.

    C. If the change was successful, a control assessor could make additional recommendations.

    D. All change controls should be implemented in incremental steps through the "Do" step of continuous improvement.

35. **Which one of the following statements describes the difference between a vulnerability assessment and a penetration test?**

    A. Vulnerability assessments are cost-related, and penetration tests are not.

    B. Risks for vulnerabilities are best suited for transfer, while penetration tests remove vulnerabilities.

    C. Vulnerability assessments are aimed at finding vulnerabilities, often without regard to exploitation. Penetration testing usually goes more profound, with its goal of exploiting the vulnerability.

    D. A penetration test requires acceptance, and a vulnerability test requires application access.

36. **Which statement best supports the overall objective for a security control assessment?**

    A. Organizations have flexibility in determining which and how many controls are assessed.

    B. Management, operational, and technical controls are omitted for an assessment.

    C. Performing an assessment may not require the tailoring of controls.

    D. Selecting security controls should be the responsibility of the assessor.

37. **Which of the following represents an ALE (Annualized Loss Expectancy) calculation?**

    A. Singe loses expectancy x annualized rate of occurrence.

    B. Gross loss expectancy x loss frequency.

    C. Actual replacement cost - proceeds of salvage.

    D. Asset value x loss expectancy.

38. **You have been hired as a Security Consultant to assess risks for an IDS providing false-positive results. Your initial assessment reveals configurations that are not documented and elevated privileges for all users. Your feedback to the corporate managers must address work accomplished to bring the IDS within compliance and actions taken to resolve the privilege escalation issue. Which answer best describes a solution proposed to the corporate managers?**

    A. Design and implement an access control matrix that supports security personnel role assignments.

    B. Perform risk analysis on potential threats and propose access control standards.

    C. Tune the false-positive settings for the IDS.

    D. Request the organization to integrate a configuration control program.

39. **A Security consultant has decided to examine the clearances and classification scheme used for an organization's privilege access program. He notices that several user's classification access and clearances are expiring within 90 days after reviewing the data. To address this issue, what methodology should the Security Engineer discuss?**

    A. Multi-level security modes of integrity.

    B. Multi-level Security Policy

C. Separation of duties.

D. The concept of interference between two separate groups of processes.

40. **A software program that operates at a Top-Secret level cannot involve information from a lower security level during events, which is developed to ensure that conflicts for critical process control are restricted between security boundaries and memory during data exchange and information sharing. Based on the information provided, which best describes this security concept?**

A. The concept of interference between two separate groups of processes.

B. Biba security model for integrity

C. Separation of duties

D. Clark Wilson Model

41. **An organization has decided to use multiple security standards for its operations. Within each system, numerous classification schemes operate within different security levels. What model is described?**

A. Bell-LaPadula

B. Biba when selecting mandatory access standards.

C. Multi-level security modes of integrity.

D. Covert Channel Analysis

42. **Process termination occurs for a significant software application during a power outage, and non-critical servers remain online and operational through virtual interfaces. After the system comes back online, manual checks identify the system as fully functional, and events trigger the servers to remember an occurring power outage. What security principles apply to this situation?**

A. Fail secure concept for servers.

B. Fault Tolerance.

C. A fault-tolerant system with fail-safe mechanisms.

D. Boundary controls to reduce threats.

43. **During a power outage, ten critical servers shut down and recover without any errors. What security concept supports this process?**

A. Fail secure concept for servers.

B. Boot sequence mirroring.

C. A fault-tolerant system with fail-safe mechanisms.

D. Multi-level security modes of integrity.

44. **One of the most effective access control mechanisms is to restrict users from using information. Which of the following best supports this concept?**

A. Bilba labeling for integrity.

B. Clark Wilson separation of duties.

C. Imposing sensitivity labels.

D. Data Hiding

45. User A has a secret clearance, and User B has a Top-Secret clearance. User B attempts to change data based on User A profile settings. User B receives an error that states: "You do not have rights to change this data." What security model addresses this error?

A. Biba Security Model

B. Trusted Recovery

C. Separation of duties

D. Bell-LaPadula outlines Mandatory Access Control principles.

46. When a computer or network component fails, and the computer or the network continues to function, it is called a fault-tolerant system. For fault tolerance to operate: 1) The system must be capable of detecting that a fault has occurred; 2) The security cannot be breached; 3) When a system crashes, it must restart in a safe and secure mode, not allowing the security to be compromised such as a B3 security rating. This concept best describes what security principle?

A. Information Flow Model

B. Trusted Recovery

C. Fail-Safe operation

D. Fail Secure state

47. SEMAIS has experienced a significant emergency within its datacenter. The initial reports state that the site must execute its disaster recovery plan (DRP) and perform necessary backups for critical applications. The DRP developed proposed offsite storage for all application data as a priority. The last backup completed a backup of user data and shared files. Which method would be most appropriate for SEMAIS to accomplish its backups?

A. Adjust the DRP to execute incremental backup procedures for shared files.

B. Examine critical user data locations to determine the best method for an off-site backup method.

C. Execute an entire backup process as outlined by recovery procedures.

D. Combine the last two differential backups to restore all application data.

48. Your organization has a requirement to audit and monitor logs daily and make reports to the security team. Which role would describe the auditing of the logs?

A. Long-term goals creation

B. Operational goals for auditing backup procedures

C. Strategic Goals

D. Tactical procedures that address a company's vision.

49. A software developer has created a software library with proprietary codes and information for a database program. After two months, the software group requests the code to validate recent vulnerabilities. As part of the requirements, the outcome of the validation results must be re-examined for potential errors. Which of the following statements would best support the group in validating the software?

   A. A bottom-up approach allows interface errors to be detected earlier.

   B. A top-down approach allows errors in critical modules to be detected earlier.

   C. The test plan and results should be retained as part of the system's permanent documentation.

   D. Black box testing is predicted on a close examination of procedural detail.

50. The test policies for the SEMAIS software development team require separate authentication for the development staff and implementation of job rotation. Based on the policy, which would be the best reason for separating the test and development environments?

   A. To restrict access to systems under test.

   B. To control the stability of the test environment.

   C. To segregate user and development staff.

   D. To secure access to systems under development.

51. What is the best description of an enterprise risk management framework?

   A. The early integration of information security requirements into the system development life cycle (SDLC) is the most cost-effective and efficient method for an organization to implement a control strategy.

   B. Provides a disciplined and structured process that integrates information security and risk management activities.

   C. Provides an emphasis on the selection, implementation, assessment, and reference monitoring of security control.

   D. Links risk management processes at the information system level to risk management processes at other system levels.

52. An evaluation criterion has been selected that produces a rating that has F5, E5, and B3. The system has also been given an evaluation that prepares the plan for deployment within the enterprise. Which one of the following describes these evaluations?

   A. The system has been going through a certification phase; under TCSEC, the system is configured for mandatory protection.

   B. A verified protection control measure has been selected, and the system has minimal protection to operate.

   C. The system target of evaluation has exceeded the minimal functionality and assurance rating.

   D. The protection profile has addressed the security target requirements for functionality and assurance.

53. SEMAIS has hired you as a consultant to address client-based vulnerabilities within its architect. After reviewing various audits and reports, you discover that many of the issues are associated with web-based applications for end-user mobile applications. As a control measure, what could you implement to secure the web-based application?

   A. Access control time developed data usage restrictions.

   B. A web-based firewall that identifies applications with vulnerable traffic.

   C. An application that identifies SQL injections.

   D. Layer 3 firewall that blocks unwanted traffic.

54. What control measure is most appropriate in securing an environment for server-based vulnerabilities caused by authentication bypass policies?

   A. Strong authentication and controls to identify key logging programs.

   B. Configuration control standards that restrict shared services.

   C. Remote service protocols that prevent session locks.

   D. Session control parameters for all applications

55. A patient representative has been restricted from gaining access to patients' medical history. The user decides to test the system for access and finds out that his privileges are still valid. The user decides to reduce as much information from sensitive database files so they could gain limited knowledge. What type of security action has the user explored?

   A. Combining non-sensitive information from separate sources.

   B. Data mining of restricted data based on HIPPA violations.

   C. The concept of confidentiality controls.

   D. Inferred sensitive information from a database and aggregation of non-sensitive data.

56. The process of using many nodes that produce a fail-safe operation after child nodes have failed can be called what fundamental type of system?

   A. Client-server architect

   B. Big Data Operation

   C. One that uses parallel database technology.

   D. Distributed form of application storage

57. As a Security Engineer, you have been tasked to develop a security model for a Database Management system. The system has various users with different access levels. The overall objective is to secure the system without affecting the end user's ability to complete tasks. Based on the information provided, what process is being achieved?

   A. Grid computing is being installed to support middle-ware security tasks.

   B. A cloud system architect is being examined to virtualize the security environment at different levels.

C. A restrictive form of database security is used to control data at multiple levels.

D. A client-server architect is being secured for the organization.

58. **As a Security Architect, what design flaw provides the most fundamental risk for a crypto system?**

A. Have functions altered to defeat the very properties they are being used to produce?

B. Registering a certificate without evaluating the risks associated with the user.

C. Tampering of symmetric keys during the exchange of data.

D. Removing an access control data exchange and design that will work within multiple versions of a crypto system.

59. **When accessing an Industrial Control System, a security professional has discovered various authentication failures between the physical nodes and commercial-off-the-shelf (COTS) software used for the system. Part of the assessment is that multiple threats have been identified and graded as a high risk for the environment. Based on the information presented, what threats could the system be facing?**

A. Unauthorized access to resources and use of maintenance access points; and attacks on standard components used in the ICS Network.

B. Malware development for system integrity.

C. SCADA systems will introduce Trojans.

D. Reading and writing new commands with a firewall policy.

60. **During a penetration test, it has been discovered that various web ports are open and accessible to the public. One port has been identified to cause remote code execution threats and open access for crafted validation codes into web applications. After presenting the report to the organization, the company has decided to address web-based vulnerabilities and develop countermeasures based on penetration testing. Which answer describes the outcome of the penetration test?**

A. The company is vulnerable to buffer overflow attacks. Countermeasures should prevent the execution of HTTP scripts in the victim's browser, which can hijack user sessions, deface websites, possibly introduce worms.

B. The company is vulnerable to buffer overflow attacks, and as a countermeasure, they should validate user input via HTTP to prevent unexpected data from being processed.

C. The company is vulnerable to injection flaws, and as a countermeasure, they should validate data HTTP input to prevent unexpected data from being processed.

D. The company is vulnerable to injection flaws, and as a countermeasure, they should use a standard input validation mechanism to validate all HTTP input data for length, type, syntax.

61. **A corporation has decided to deploy mobile devices through its enterprise. Each smartphone will be configured for Bluetooth communication and have unique passwords. Part of the initial requirements is to conduct field testing to identify points of weakness and system failures. After the testing has been completed, the CIO receives a report stating that mobile phones are subjected to bluejacking if deployed with the current technology. As a security expert, what advice would you provide to the CIO to mitigate the potential risk of bluejacking?**

A. Contact the vendor and suggest the risk rating for the Bluetooth-enabled device be lowered since Bluetooth vulnerabilities are at a lower risk profile.

B. Alert and train users to delete and not respond to phrank messages.

C. Change the mobile technology devices and try a device that is less prone to mobile attacks.

D. Develop a countermeasure by placing the device under test into a non-discoverable mode so others cannot identify the mobile Bluetooth device.

62. While a ping sweep was being performed on an active **SCADA** network that controlled 3 meters (9 foot) robotic arms, it was noticed that one arm became active and swung around 180 degrees. The controller for the arm was in standby mode before the ping sweep was initiated. After the initial assessment, it was discovered that proprietary protocols did not communicate echo requests for the computer systems. What countermeasure should an organization consider?

A. Implement protocols that are operable among different software systems.

B. Develop software assurance capabilities that prevent SCADA systems from working upon intrusive events.

C. Implement TCP/IP within its suite of protocols for vulnerability scanning.

D. Develop a block list for ping sweep commands.

63. Cryptographic keys need to change over time to ensure the cryptographic algorithm provides the expected security level. From a management perspective, what should be monitored to ensure keys offer the necessary services.

A. The lifecycle of generation, registration, distribution, usage, storage, deregistration, destruction, and archival.

B. The technology is used to encrypt data across networks.

C. Controls that address protocol standards for different data decoders.

D. The generation of key exchange and registration.

64. Alice and Bob wish to exchange data using a cryptographic method that will allow the fastest data transfer. Each month, they will have to keep track of 10 co-workers who communicate with the same category of keys and report to senior management the number of keys required for the co-workers and type. Which of the following describes the keys used?

A. Public key Infrastructure using 450 keys monthly

B. Symmetric technology and 45 keys monthly

C. Symmetric key standard using five keys monthly

D. Asymmetric keys using 450 keys monthly

65. As a Security Engineer, you have been asked to implement public key infrastructure (PKI) within a network environment. Which of the following describes the PKI technology and implementation standard?

A. Symmetric Cryptography uses PKI to encrypt data through the X.509 protocol suite.

B. Alice and Bob can encrypt with each's private key as a standard.

C. The technology uses X.509 as the protocol standard and requires separate public and private data exchange keys.

D. Authentication is produced via need-to-know principles, and hashing can be integrated as a standard.

66. **As a Security Manager, what would be a fundamental practice for Key Management?**

    A. Using the same key for two different cryptographic processes may strengthen the security provided by one or both processes.

    B. Information protected by cryptographic mechanisms is secure only if the algorithms remain strong and the keys have not been compromised.

    C. The authorized disclosure of a key means that another entity may know the key and use that key to perform computations requiring the key.

    D. A key destruction plan should be developed and followed so that the change over from the old to the new key management system runs as smoothly as possible.

67. **Alice wants to send an email attachment to Bob through email encryption. Once the email has been sent, what fundamental technology ensures that the attachments in the email are authentic?**

    A. Digitally signing the email to provide authentication, integrity, and non-repudiation

    B. Encrypting a message to provide confidentiality.

    C. Hashing a message to provide integrity.

    D. Using a hash value to validate a public key for the signature.

68. **A Security Engineer has been tasked to implement a solution to protect digital media distribution. The solution must ensure that content located on computers can only be accessed with digital rights privileges. Which of the following solutions provide the necessary measures to protect the media?**

    A. A digital watermark verifies the integrity of the data used.

    B. A desktop firewall that restricts inbound data.

    C. Assign a unique ID that verifies the users to have authorized privileges through file integrity checks such as fingerprinting.

    D. Implementation of a key solution that uses USB technology.

69. **A criminal court case has proceeded with a hacker who has been accused of conducting a computer crime. The evidence collected includes encrypted email messages and storage drives that hold essential files. The court has decided to hire an expert to testify in court concerning encrypted email transmission from the hacker. What is the best security services the expert can use as evidence?**

    A. The use of digital signatures where the hacker cannot repudiate the transmission of email messages.

    B. The use of authentication principles to show that each email message was authentic.

    C. The use of data integrity to indicate foul proof of digitized messages.

    D. Non-repudiation that shows the data was sent in plain text over encrypted channels.

70. **Which of the following best describes the secure hash function as it relates to a one-way function?**

    A. Public functions create a hash value, also known as a message digest, by converting variable-length messages into a single fixed-length value.

B. A one-way hash algorithm converts a variable-length message into a condensed representation of the electronic data in the message.

C. It is easy to compute the hash value from the input, but it is extremely difficult to reproduce the hash value.

D. When employed in a digital signature application, the hash value of the message is signed instead of the message itself.

71. **A hacker has attempted to gain access to a major computer system and realized that a secret key must complete the action. What would a fundamental attack method have to occur for the hacker to decipher the secret key?**

   A. A chosen plaintext attack where the hacker could encrypt the information to discover the corresponding cipher text.

   B. A chosen cipher text where the hacker could determine the correct plaintext for the secret key.

   C. A side-channel attack where the hacker could deduce all information based on logical inclusions.

   D. A replay attack where information concerning ciphertext would establish the PKI data exchange format.

72. **During a threat assessment, the physical security officer has discovered that the datacenter maybe located in a high-risk and crime area. Due to the importance of the datacenter, the organization has decided to go ahead with the project. As a physical security control, what should the organization consider?**

   A. The outcome for the vulnerability assessment and operational controls required to have security guards.

   B. Key controls that prevent unauthorized access.

   C. Implementing high curbs and trained security guards that can deter crime.

   D. Implementation of external boundary protection mechanisms to control traffic, entry, and building access.

73. **A security manager has taken his daily rounds of the datacenter and noticed that fiber optic cable was distributed outside the wiring closet. After further reviewing the situation, he finds that the IT team has distributed cabling outside the wiring closet to test new servers. The company policy states that all cables must be routed within cable tubing. What would the finding constitute for the organization?**

   A. A new threat where unauthorized personnel could gain access to the datacenter.

   B. A risk where the organization could lose vital information.

   C. A weakness where the company could be liable for control implementation of standards.

   D. Physical security compromise of resources.

74. **A company's environmental design is under review. The initial assessment has discovered that the building impact assessment was inaccurate and did not involve the entire IT facility. As a security manager, you must re-evaluate the impact assessment and make recommendations for the environmental redesign. The outcome of the assessment revealed that the datacenter was in an older building. If you decide to move the datacenter, what environmental factor would you consider?**

   A. Threats associated with the building design.

   B. Storm and weather assessments for the geographical region.

   C. The central location of the building structure.

D. Risks associated with the move and system downtime.

75. **The physical layout of an organization's datacenter should include cabinets and a storage area to protect media. As part of a physical assessment for a datacenter, what control method should an organization implement to ensure media information is adequately protected?**

   A. Environmental factors that control temperature and humidity for backup tapes.

   B. Physical controls that ensure property damage does not affect the media.

   C. Security access control devices that lock media cabinets after use.

   D. Core location of media within datacenters to withstand natural weather conditions and fires.

76. **Which one of the following answers best describes the policies and procedures to manage the physical and chain of custody for media evidence collected and stored within a datacenter?**

   A. Physical properties should not be altered, and if it does become altered new tags need to be identified.

   B. Everyone who has legitimate access to the evidence must sign the chain-of-custody form.

   C. New tags should never be created unless there is physical damage or the evidence has been transported

   D. Physical location and time of removal for the media will serve as the best evidence that the chain of custody was followed.

77. **A restricted area has been created for the server room at company ABC. The area consists of several servers that hold patients' critical health data. As a new employee, how would you know that the servers are located within a restricted area? Choose the best answer.**

   A. The vendors' information would be identical for each server as well as physical design.

   B. Special colors or markings that deter people from entering the area would be physically located within the server room.

   C. Access control listings would be placed outside the server room to indicate restricted zones.

   D. Preventative and corrective access control markings would be used to warn people on what areas are considered restricted.

78. **A redesign for the physical security with company ABC has resulted in the company upgrading its datacenter security. One area of risk was the open access to the datacenter. To mitigate the open-access issue, what would be the best solution for the organization?**

   A. Implement key cards that require users to authenticate.

   B. Develop a biometric entry system that requires multiple cross-over error rates to help create multiple entry standards.

   C. Require every user to attend a security awareness course that outlines open access and restrictions.

   D. Hire a security guard to check users' access and restrict unauthorized entry.

79. **A risk assessment has resulted in major concerns for an organization's backup and power generation. The backup generator does not supply enough power for the three-day contingency period. The generator has been used before, but under testing methods. To properly obtain the required power during a 72-hour contingency period, what alternative should the organization consider?**

A. Purchase a new generator that is rated with the same specifications.

B. Limit the power for the HVAC and uninterruptible power supply (UPS), so fuel will last longer.

C. Recheck the fuel consumption, power rating, and contract fuel from a distributor.

D. Purchase a backup generator with lower specifications to take over after the primary generator fails.

80. When developing a ventilation system for a datacenter, company ABC has discovered that the building is susceptible to moisture and leaking piping systems that the previous owners did not repair. The company has gathered the piping and fire system diagrams to understand better how to resolve the problem. If the company did not perform its assessment, what would be the most likely problem they would occur?

A. The fire suppression systems would create a dry pipe issue for the sprinkler systems.

B. They could have issues with block ventilation which would ultimately cause condensation to form around electrical equipment.

C. The sprinkler system would activate during normal operation.

D. The vents located behind server racks would cause heat sensors to activate.

81. When deciding on a specific fire suppression system, what fundamental factors should an organization consider before installing fire prevention and isolation equipment?

A. Whether the fire suppression system has an automatic feature to sense fires.

B. The type of fire detectors and their locations within the datacenter.

C. The system and chemical agents used to treat fires.

D. The amount of smoke needs to be isolated due to the ventilation system and air enclosures.

82. Company ABC has decided to change all IP address devices' configuration and security requirements: 123.45.67.34 – 123.48.78.234. The security team has also agreed to implement new address filtering within any device that receives traffic from the IP Address range. What layer and devices are affected by the configuration change?

A. Layer 2 – Routers and Firewall that filter IP Octets starting with 123.XXX.XXX.XXX.

B. Layer 2 – Switches that have Access Control Listings.

C. Layer 3 – Routers and Firewall that filter IP Octets starting with 123.XXX.XXX.XXX.

D. Layer 3 – MAC Address and IP filtering for the specified address range.

83. A network has been established with 50 host machines that require network interface design with a subnet address of 134.56.0.0 and host field of 134.56.0.1 - 134.56.255.254. The team has decided to install secure interface requirements and test each interface using a small software tool. All but one IP Address: 134.56.34.234 was able to pass the security testing. To securely design and test the failing host, what should the team consider concerning the network class?

A. Whether manual diagnostic of the network interface card was completed by the vendor for a Class C Network.

B. Whether IP 134.56.34.234 is a legitimate Class A address based on the IP Address range for the organization.

C. Whether a connection to a socket address designated at 134.56.34.234:127.0.0.1 was successful for a Class B Address.

D. Whether connected to the loopback address at IP 127.0.0.1 indicated failing packets during the integration test for the failing host.

84. **During the design of a Supervisory Control and Data Acquisition (SCADA) system consisting of SCADA hosts, Remote Terminal Units (RTUs), a security architect has discovered that data is transmitted within plaintext the Modbus protocol, and no user authentication parameters are configured. What solution would be an appropriate control measure for the vulnerability when using the Modbus protocol for various systems in a SCADA environment?**

A. Provide an encapsulated security standard using a VPN solution that would isolate Modbus from public or open networks.

B. Implement strong authentication standards within the security control architect.

C. Switch the protocols to use the standard TCP/IP suite of standards.

D. Monitor administrative accounts for unique passwords and use a VPN solution for the SCADA system.

85. **What protocol and technology would help integrate data for SAN storage and communication links, voice, and data securely despite interoperability challenges?**

A. Multi-layer security protocols that combine data paths.

B. Decapsulation of native Fiber Channel frames into Ethernet Frames or Converged technology.

C. Block storage data management protocols.

D. Fiber Channel over IP traffic protocols within a converged network.

86. **As a security architect, what would the "availability of security gateways" pose to the design and development for a secure architect when Voice over IP is used?**

A. Special consideration should be given to E-911 emergency services communications, because E-911 automatic location service is not available with VoIP in some cases.

B. SIP and H.323 may induce packet loss.

C. Stateful packet filters cannot track the state of connections, denying packets that are not part of an adequately originated call.

D. Some VoIP endpoints are not computationally powerful enough to perform encryption.

87. **Alice has decided to log onto a web-based application to check her email. The application she uses requires encryption standards that save her credentials to her computer hard drive for access. When the web application asks for Alice's authentication parameters, the browser accesses her information on the hard drive and performs the authentication on behalf of Alice. What authentication technology has configured for Alice?**

A. Remote Service authentication that uses certificates to encrypt data.

B. X.509, where SSL is used to tunnel information for Port 80.

C. Certificate-based authentication where SSL encrypts data for port 443.

D. Password authentication that has open access authentication is included within its algorithm.

88. Company ABC has decided to secure its perimeter defenses by hardening a webserver that will withstand external attacks. The system will also be placed in a configuration where public and private information is segmented with a screened subnet. The organization's external-facing services are exposed to a more extensive and untrusted network. Which of the following best describes the configuration?

    A. The company has installed a demilitarized zone while configuring the webservers as a bastion host.

    B. The company has installed a neutral zone configuration that filters traffic.

    C. A border router has been installed for just internal network protection.

    D. A bastion host has been installed with three layers of protection.

89. A security architect has decided to upgrade the company's infrastructure. The overall goal is to consolidate data traffic consisting of voice, data, and video into a convergence technology. Which of the following best provides an initial starting point to determine what media would be required?

    A. The level of crosstalk associated with servers should be assessed.

    B. The amount of signal strength, cross talk, and distortion for the media selected.

    C. The level attenuation and noise the datacenter will prevent.

    D. Whether the signal strength can carry the various form of data through VLAN configuration.

90. A security professional has decided to gather configuration data for a new firewall that was installed. After downloading the configuration data, the professional discovers that various protocols such as file transfer protocol (FTP), HTTP, and simple mail transfer protocol (SMTP) are not screened for security flaws and email messages for unauthorized attachments. Additionally, the security professional has discovered that the outbound IP Address for the gateway shows 123.1.1.1 instead of the assigned IP address. He further learns that the IP address-labeling scheme is standard for all network devices. What solution is required to resolve the issue with screening for flaws and labeling schemes?

    A. The organization needs to install the proxy-based firewall and change the addressing scheme for the IPs assigned.

    B. The organization needs to install an application-based firewall and update its configuration profile to indicate a NAT has been established to protect the organization from outside attacks.

    C. The organization needs to install a packet filtering firewall and update its configuration profile to indicate a NAT has been established to protect the organization from outside attacks.

    D. The organization needs to update its configuration profile to indicate a circuit proxy firewall is installed and update its configuration profile to indicate a proxy has been established to protect the organization from outside attacks.

91. A network has been established to support high availability and performance to stream media from internet-facing servers. Part of its features is that faster loading, file mirroring, and live streaming events are optimized. What type of network would this describe?

    A. A network designed to deliver content-based information

    B. Decentralized streaming architecture

    C. Data distribution network architecture

    D. Centralized streaming architecture

92. **The physical protection for a network can be best secured using the following type of physical devices or components?**

   A. Magnetic contact and vibration readers within the datacenter.

   B. Biometric readers within the entrance of the building and server rooms.

   C. Detection systems that alert for intrusive events for various entry points.

   D. Devices that separate a network from the rest of the world.

93. **A security management team has initiated a project to deploy endpoint software to 100,000 hosts within its architect. The management team wishes to gather further clarification on how the project will protect intrusions from reoccurring. Which answer would provide the best support for the management team?**

   A. Designing the system with a configured system with a host-based firewall will prevent unauthorized access

   B. Deploying a HIPS will help secure the endpoints and prevent authorized attacks

   C. Building a vulnerability management program that installs agents can prevent authentication errors.

   D. Build a virus infrastructure program to warn off malware.

94. **During a penetration test, the security team has discovered file-sharing programs that have installed malicious codes and implemented risks that could cause a denial of service attack. What security flaw and standard technology best describes the information discovered by the penetration team?**

   A. Exposure to sensitive information and traffic bypass have been identified for internal hosts.

   B. The team has discovered malware attacks that restrict data collaboration.

   C. Untrusted programs and peer-to-peer virus codes have caused data breaches to occur.

   D. P2P file-sharing technology and the installation of malicious codes are present within the organization.

95. **A network engineer has installed a packet sniffer to determine how traffic and protocols are configured for a remote logon session. The information gathered shows that the remote session has the following configuration: 1) The messages are encrypted, 2) Authentication and Integrity are achieved through a handshake series, and 3) The router and header information is not protected. Which of the following best describes the configuration settings?**

   A. The remote session is using IPSEC, which is configured for tunneling mode.

   B. The remote session uses Authentication Header (AH) and Encapsulating Security Payload (ESP), configured for tunnel mode.

   C. The remote session is using tunneling mode, which is configured for confidentiality.

   D. The remote session is using IPSec, which is configured for transport mode.

96. **A web interfacing application requires Layer 7 encryption using SSL 2.0. The vendor releases a bulletin stating that the current SSL 2.0 is incompatible with the web interfacing application. As a cost measure, what option should the organization consider as a solution?**

   A. Request the vendor to upgrade the application to the current version of TLS 1.2.

   B. Upgrade the web-based application to TLS/SSL.

C. Install separate VLANs that support TLS versions.

D. Acquire a new application that supports the current version of SSL.

97. **Organization ABC has upgraded its network to 8,000 nodes. The nodes have also induced changes for the firewall architecture, where 4,000 new firewall interfaces are required to balance the network traffic. The network has been recently upgraded to a VLAN architecture as well. What could additional technology help isolate and secure the environment?**

A. Separate the network through virtualized SAN circuits.

B. Install a Guess OS to integrate the Firewall OS from the external services.

C. Integrate a Private VLAN that will support network segregation.

D. Reconfigure a Secondary VLAN for additional firewalls to reside within the network virtualization platform.

98. **A network hacker has generated an attack on a system with the following characteristics: 1) The hacker watches a session open on a network, 2) Once authentication is complete, the hacker disables the client computer, 3) The attack is directed to a specific computer addressed as though it is from that same computer, and 4) The session is stolen, and the hacker distributes traffic to and from the computer. Which of the following best describes the attack for the organization?**

A. A transmission control protocol/synchronize (TCP/SYN) flood has occurred using IP spoofing to claim to be the authenticated client and prevent the attack from further occurring; two legitimate systems should be checked periodically during the session.

B. A man-in-the-middle attack has occurred using session attacks to claim to be the authenticated client. To prevent the attack from further occurring, two legitimate systems should be checked periodically during the session.

C. A Session Flood has occurred using man-in-the-middle attack methods to claim to be the authenticated client. To prevent the attack from further occurring, two legitimate systems should be checked periodically during the session.

D. A man-in-the-middle attack has occurred using IP spoofing to claim to be the authenticated client. To prevent the attack from further occurring, two legitimate systems should share a secret key that is checked periodically during the session.

99. **SEMAIS has integrated physical and logical access control settings to restrict users to only viewing data and using computers in LAB 1. LAB 2 has been limited to Administrators and testing groups during working hours. Which describes the best access and restriction used regarding working hours?**

A. Users have been restricted to write-only access for LAB 1, and mandatory access control has been implemented for LAB 2.

B. Users have been restricted to read-only access for LAB1, and role-based access control has been implemented for LAB 2.

C. Users have been restricted to read-only access for LAB 1, and role-based access control has been implemented for LAB 1.

D. Users have been restricted to Mandatory access control for Lab 1, and rule-based access has been implemented for LAB 2.

100. **Bob has been hired to work as a consultant at company ABC. Alice has been hired as well, and she has lower access than Bob for the database system and server room. Her role in the company is to produce metrics for all the data generated from various databases. Bob's role is to investigate logs and system accounts for intrusions. What fundamental access concept has the organization implemented for Alice and Bob within the database system?**

    A. Confidentiality as it relates to the physical security of the server room.

    B. Availability of resources for Bob to conduct his analysis.

    C. Physical and logical access based on least privilege principles.

    D. Separation of duties.

101. **Organization ABC has implemented control measures to restrict users from entering the datacenter without proper access. The restrictions have been implemented administratively, and logical access to the servers has been restricted to Administrators. What risk has company ABC forgot to address during its security measures?**

    A. Users are not having access to training programs on information security.

    B. The company has omitted physical security measures to restrict access to the datacenter by implementing card readers or biometric entry systems.

    C. Proper identification and authorization parameters for access control systems.

    D. System-level control measures to identify local profiles.

102. **Company ABC has decided to implement a Physical Access Control System (PACS) within its facility. The organization has a parking lot, authorization, entry monitoring, and external access control for vendors. Which of the following will be required under the PACS to support company ABC?**

    A. Visitor Management, Identification, Parking Permit Management, and Intrusion Detection Visitor.

    B. Management, Parking Permit Management, and Intrusion Detection.

    C. Identification, Parking Permit Management, and Intrusion Detection

    D. Visitor Management, Identification, and Intrusion Detection

103. **Company ABC has decided to upgrade its network to "single sign-on" technology. The security team has required that the company implement controls that would support data compromise and authentication to resources for authorized users. Which of the following combinations of technologies will provide the best security protection for users and the organization?**

    A. Use a directory service that prompts users for a password for each login session.

    B. Integrate a Kerberos ticket-granting ticket and a smart card-based authentication system with certificates.

    C. Integrate Kerberos and random key technologies to control session high jacking.

    D. Use a credential-based authentication system that integrates session control when authenticating.

104. After logging in to the bank's real site, account holders are being tricked by the offer of training in a new "upgraded security system." Moments later, money is moved from the user account without notice. After a preliminary investigation, it was discovered that a man-in-middle attack has occurred. What would not support the organization if the same attack occurred?

    A. Upgrading their sign-on technology to two-factor authentication.

    B. Authenticate the transaction session.

    C. Implement measures to prevent IP Spoofing from occurring

    D. Design technologies to control session high jacking.

105. A security engineer has decided to change the administrative account for a new SQL server that was installed. After changing the password, he then checks the logs to see what events have occurred. The events show that he was adequately authenticated as SQL Administrator and allowed access to all the services offered by the SQL server. What security principle was demonstrated for the events?

    A. The process of audit and accountability for logging activities.

    B. The process of identification and authentication for user events.

    C. The controls are associated with authorization to shared resources.

    D. The process of two-factor authentication and identity management.

106. Alice has decided to use a web-based application to check all the new IT developers' security awareness training at https:\\web.training. share01.com. After using the application, she decides to leave the screen available for additional tasks. After 10 minutes, her screen locks, and she must reenter her credentials for the web application. What fundamental attack could be prevented by the computer, and what was introduced as a control measure?

    A. The computer utilized a schedule limitation tool to secure session IDs and web traffic. This would prevent IP Spoofing.

    B. The computer utilized timeout as a tool to secure web traffic. This would prevent IP Spoofing.

    C. The computer utilized session management as a tool to secure session IDs and web traffic. This would prevent a Man-In-The-Middle Attack (MIM).

    D. The computer utilized access control as a tool to authenticate web traffic at port 80. This would prevent a Man-In-The-Middle Attack.

107. Bob has been approved to gain access to his company's network system. After he has submitted his information online via a web-based application, he noticed that there was a description block that stated, "If you are approved, the organization will have an assurance that through logon credentials and digital certificates you are the issued authority to use the assigned credentials and based on your profile you will only require a password and self-created pin for system access." Which one of the following explains the information presented in the description block for Bob?

    A. Bob will be verified via electronic authentication, and he was issued a "something you have" credential standard for system access.

    B. Bob will be verified via two-factor authentication, and he was issued a "something you have" credential standard for system access.

C. Bob will be verified via multi-factor authentication, and he was issued a "something you are" credential standard for system access.

D. Bob will be verified via multi-factor authentication, and he was issued a "something you know" credential standard for system access.

108. **A third-party corporation has issued access rights to its partnering company customers to use a collaborated website for financial transactions. The partnering company does the same for the third-party company. Bob has heard about the privileges and decides to use his single sign-on credentials to access web1 and web2, both affiliated sites. He will be making transactions for a supply line that requires webserver1 and webserver2 to process his authentication and access. What standard has been implemented to support business-to-business and business-to-consumer transactions?**

A. The organization has implemented an identity standard to address the assertion of data.

B. The technology standard used is Security Assertion Markup Language (SAML).

C. The organization has implemented a Kerberos standard for sign-on and authentication.

D. XML has been used along with trusted resource management to identify trusted transactions.

109. **A security architect has been tasked to develop a system that will support disaster recovery related to password management. The system is required to remain operable through configurable fail-over and redundancy for passwords during outages and emergency system recovery. What type of system would support the organization based on the scenario? What security methodology would it address? Choose the best answer.**

A. The organization will require a trusted recovery system to ensure password access is permanently restored, and through redundancy, the system is always available. The system supports the integrity of resources as outlined within the CIA triad.

B. The organization will require a credential management system to ensure password access and system redundancy is always available. The system supports the availability of resources as outlined within the CIA triad.

C. The organization will require an authentication system to ensure password access is always accessible. The system supports the availability of resources as outlined within the CIA triad.

D. The organization will require a credential management system to ensure password access or system redundancy is always available. The system supports the confidentiality of passwords as outlined within the CIA triad.

110. **A security architect has been tasked with developing cloud-based computing services that support access and authorization to services in the cloud. It must also target systems on customer's premises. The cloud service must reduce on-site servers and databases, provide easier management and a broader range of integration options for account management and access to corporate resources. What cloud solution is required for the organization, and what risks are involved for the service?**

A. The organization will require Software as a Service (SaaS) for its subscription services. Additional SaaS security risks involve software assurance and access privileges to software in the cloud.

B. The organization will require Infrastructure as a Service (IaaS) for its subscription services. Additional IaaS security risks involve firewall boundary rules that are not updated to support access in the cloud.

C. The organization will require Identity as a Service (IDaaS) for its subscription services. Additional IDaaS security risks involve data discovery, operational controls, access to customer data, and management of credentials.

D. The organization will require access control services for its subscription. Additional access control security risks involve data discovery, operational controls, access to customer data, and management of credentials.

111. **Organization ABC wants to purchase a cloud-based solution through a third-party provider. The organization requires Software as a Service for all its desktop applications. What security area should be considered before implementing the cloud solution for the corporation? Choose the best answer.**

    A. The organization should consider directory services and how the security features will support cloud identity management.

    B. The organization should consider subscription costs and how the security features will support cloud security.

    C. The organization should consider security services and how the security features will support cloud computing costs.

    D. The organization should consider federated identity services and how the security features will support cloud identity management.

112. **Organization ABC has implemented an identity management solution to separate users, accounts, and access resources for the developers and database administrators. The developers' accounts have been provisioned to restrict the use of the system after core working hours. The database administrators' access has been restricted to database functionalities and separated from the developers' access rights and duties. Which of the following defines the identity solution for the developers and database administrators?**

    A. The organization has implemented rule-based access control for the database administrators and role-based access control for the developers and database administrators.

    B. The organization has implemented mandatory access control for the database administrators and limited role-based access control for the developers.

    C. The organization has implemented discretionary access control for the database administrators and rule-based access control for the developers and database administrators.

    D. The organization has implemented rule-based access control for the developers and role-based access control for the developers and database administrators.

113. **A new firewall has been installed for company ABC. The Security Engineer has been tasked to draft a list of access restrictions based on IP range 123.34.45.234 to 134.45.56.234. What type of access control restriction will the Security Engineer implement?**

    A. Mandatory access control to restrict access between systems and owners within the IP range.

    B. Rule-based access control to restrict traffic for the IP ranges.

    C. Role-based access control to restrict traffic for the IP ranges.

    D. Limited Role-based access control for specific IP addresses.

114. **A multilayered security policy has been created to control system-level access. Each object will not have any control over policies due to the system invoking access control and restrictions. Particular objects have been identified as Top Secret and Secret. What has access control methodology been implemented for the system?**

    A. Discretionary Access Control where users are restricted from system-level resources.

    B. Bell-LaPadula model where system-level Secret objects cannot write to Top Secret objects.

C. Mandatory access control specifies system labels based on clearances and attributes.

D. Rule-based access control where subjects and objects are restricted from system-level resources based on their clearance.

115. Alice has a file stored on her computer that is accessible to the entire network. She decides to restrict the use of the file to Bob. To invoke the policy, she changes the file properties to the following:

Full Access - Alice and Bob

Read Access - Administrators, Alice, and Bob

Write Access – Alice

What access control method has Alice invoked?

A. Role-based access control for read-write properties.

B. Discretionary access control for read-write properties.

C. Discretionary access control for limited RBAC management.

D. Mandatory access control restrictions for different read/write classifications.

116. A web application has been experiencing authentication by-pass vulnerabilities based on audit findings and vulnerability scans. The Security Engineer has identified several issues with the web application that provides open access to several corporate web-based applications without proper authentication. What mitigation procedure should the organization implement to restrict authentication by-pass and control future occurrences with the vulnerability?

A. The organization should develop robust authentication algorithms within the application and check to ensure identity services are occurring. Implementing a stateful firewall will help with future occurrences and restricts access unless a user has been authenticated.

B. The organization should develop access control policies within the application and check to ensure identity services are occurring. Implementing a stateful firewall will help with future occurrences and restricts access unless a user has been authenticated.

C. The organization should develop access control policies within the application and check to ensure buffer overflows are not occurring. Implementing a web application firewall (WAF) will help with future occurrences and restricts access unless a user has been authenticated.

D. The organization should develop robust authentication algorithms within the application and check to ensure buffer overflows are not occurring. Implementing a web application firewall (WAF) will help with future occurrences and restricts access unless a user has been authenticated.

117. A web application has been experiencing authentication by-pass vulnerabilities based on audit findings and vulnerability scans. The Security Engineer has decided to implement a Web Application Firewall policy to restrict user traffic based on authentication bypass vulnerabilities. What identity and access provision area would provide ongoing efforts to monitor the firewall authentication by-pass security policy?

A. The organization should develop reviews and revocation lists that will identify authentication issues for the policy.

B. The organization should develop reviews that will identify authentication issues for the policy.

C. The organization should develop revocation lists that will identify authentication issues for the policy.

D. The organization should develop access control lists that will identify authentication issues for the policy.

118. **During security testing of a significant application, the test engineer discovers that the software product will not produce the intended requirements. What measures should the test engineer pursue based on his findings?**

    A. Recheck the verification data to ensure the specifications are accurately integrated into the testing plan.

    B. Recheck the validation data to ensure the solutions are accurately integrated into the testing plan.

    C. Continue to validate the solution for the product lifecycle.

    D. Continue to verify whether the product supports real-world solutions.

119. **A testing engineer has been tasked to evaluate whether software product risks have been mitigated after the initial design. The initial report demonstrated that the software product was 85 percent compliant based on the controls implemented during the software product design. To accurately determine the current compliance and remediation efforts, what security task should the organization perform?**

    A. The organization should pursue a penetration test to determine what controls are vulnerable; the test will also provide a current status of any vulnerable access points

    B. The organization should pursue a penetration test to determine what controls are vulnerable; the assessment will also provide a current remediation status.

    C. The organization should pursue a vulnerability assessment to determine what controls are vulnerable; the evaluation will also provide a current remediation status.

    D. The organization should pursue a verification assessment to determine what controls are vulnerable; the evaluation will also provide a current remediation status.

120. **A testing engineer has been tasked to evaluate whether a software product is vulnerable to buffer overflow attacks. The engineer decides to hire a penetration team to conduct the testing and analysis. What specific outcome will the organization not receive from the penetration test?**

    A. The organization will not receive a compliance review for vulnerable assets; instead, it will receive reports on vulnerable access points for buffer overflow conditions.

    B. The organization will not receive a business impact review for vulnerable assets; instead, it will receive compliance status for buffer overflow conditions.

    C. The organization will not receive additional data on countermeasures that could mitigate threats against the system; instead, they will receive reports on vulnerable access points for buffer overflow conditions.

    D. The organization will not receive additional data on defenders' ability to detect attacks and respond appropriately; instead, they will receive compliance status for buffer overflow conditions.

121. **Company ABC has decided to review the outcome of all accounts used for a recent assessment test. The overall goal is to determine operational tasks achieved from various servers and log onto the testing platform. After several requests, the organization receives a copy of dates, timestamps, and user activity. The information received shows information that was not consistent with the information required and old data for servers taken offline 2 years ago. What is the best solution that would support the organization to gain more accurate data for its test results?**

A. The organization should implement a log review and analysis program and perform a routine audit of its logs to identify risks associated with legacy data.

B. The organization should implement a log management program and perform a routine audit of its logs to identify risks associated with log data.

C. The organization should manage its security log data and perform a routine audit of its servers to identify risks associated with log data.

D. The organization should implement a vulnerability management program and perform a routine audit of its logs to identify risks associated with legacy data.

122. Company ABC has decided to test its local website to determine whether it can provide the requirements based on the test plan. The test will install agents on several web servers to actively monitor various transactions and emulate user experience. What technology has been described for the test plan?

A. The organization will use Agent monitoring to view the user's Real Use performance.

B. The organization will use Real Use performance monitoring to view the user's activity for alerts and notifications.

C. The organization will use Agent performance monitoring to view the user's activity for alerts and notifications.

D. The organization will use Synthetic Performance monitoring to view the user's activity for alerts and notifications.

123. A third-party security testing team has been directed to perform application testing for a new software product. The testing plan requires that the test involve the human intervention of selected tools while restricting the test team to have information concerning the network layout of IP Addresses and web servers. What testing strategy has been used for the test?

A. The organization has decided to use manual and automatic testing based on the test plan.

B. The organization has decided to use manual and black-box testing based on the test plan.

C. The organization has decided to use manual and white box testing based on the test plan.

D. The organization has decided to use automatic and white box testing based on the test plan.

124. During a software test, a testing engineer receives an error code that the input data is invalid. According to the test plan, the action performed should present an invalid input data request. What should the test engineer assume for the test step he or she had committed?

A. The test step was designed to demonstrate negative testing for an allowable number of characters.

B. The test step was designed to demonstrate negative testing for invalid data input.

C. The test step was designed to demonstrate positive testing for invalid data input.

D. The test step was designed to demonstrate interface testing for negative testing plans.

125. A testing engineer has decided to check the threshold for input data using negative testing. The range for the data is between -267,456,464 and 456,345,234. After inputting a value of 547,000,000, he receives an error code that the data selected exceeds the threshold value. What has the test engineer achieved as a result of the test?

A. The allowable number of characters has been tested and exceeded for the test.

B. The limitations for application coverage have been tested to determine session and buffer behaviors.

C. The test engineer has tested allowable data bounds based on the application coverage.

D. The test engineer has tested the application for buffer overflow conditions.

126. After a major application has been developed, the developers plan to use various test methods to determine whether the application meets specific security requirements. The first test is designed to determine whether the application components are in sync with each other. The test consists of nine application functions and will require users to interact with specific user tasks between application and web servers. The tasks are real-time in response to what users will encounter through routine use without using invalid data. What will the specific test be utilized?

A. The organization uses an interface testing strategy to determine whether the execution of specified functions is working properly.

B. The organization uses a system testing strategy to determine whether the execution of specified functions is working properly.

C. The organization is using an integrated testing strategy to determine whether software functions are working properly

D. The organization is using a negative testing strategy to determine whether errors are correctly handled.

127. A security architect performs annual data collection from logs and directory services to determine whether applicable controls are within compliance. He extracts information for several users whose accounts demonstrate they have privileges to three restricted database servers. Under the corporate policies, only DBAs should have access to the servers. To achieve compliance, the architect implements a control that restricts their privileges based on their job roles. Under what program has the security architect used to enforce compliance?

A. The security architect has used a compliance monitoring program to review continuous monitoring strategies and implement separation of duties.

B. The security architect has used a continuous monitoring program to review user accounts and account management practices for any escalated privileges.

C. The security architect has used privilege escalation programs as part of compliance reviews.

D. The security architect has used account metrics to review user accounts as part of an account management program.

128. The Security Manager for a large firm has asked his security team to gather metrics for all the security controls and monitoring activities over the past 60 days. After analyzing the collected data, the Security Manager finds three key areas failing outlined in the security policy. To gain further knowledge on the failing areas, the Security Manager requests a threat report. Which one of the following would least support the Security Manager after reviewing the threat report?

A. Ensure that deployed security controls are adequate and that monitoring operations are being followed.

B. Report incident activities from known threats and their impact on the organization.

C. Identifying material weaknesses and areas where controls and compliance are changing.

D. Provide reasonable detail on what areas need to be updated based on risk tolerances.

129. **Which one of the following would serve as a risk indicator when monitoring a system compliance status? Choose the best answer.**

    A. Management and operational controls are identified as Administrative controls.

    B. Metrics derived to show that a server has been causing 25 percent of all vulnerabilities over 90 days.

    C. Automated metrics that display data in real-time vs. delayed.

    D. Changes implemented within the configuration baseline and a risk assessment report contained a risk reduction above the organization trend.

130. **A system administrator has been tasked to check the daily logs for all backup occurrences using a log management application. The organization's policy is to review its data backup plan annually. After reviewing the records, he notices that DB-1 and DB-2 had critical backup failures for the past month. He further investigates the information and discovers that critical data for patient's health was not updated for the past month. He contacts the Senior DBA to remediate the issue, informing him that the DBA team is remediating the problem. As a control measure, what would the organization require to ensure the incident does not reoccur?**

    A. The organization should test backups annually to verify integrity and reliability, implement security controls, and document the date for the last test and who performed the testing.

    B. The organization should test backups semi-annually to verify controls, implement backup security controls, and document the date for the last test and who performed the testing.

    C. The organization should test all backup verification operations daily through its log management software, test backup controls annually, and document the test results.

    D. The organization should implement backup or verification operations daily through security control monitoring.

131. **Alice has checked on board with her new company. The organizational policy states that everyone must attend a security awareness course annually. Alice has completed the training with her previous company and has the information to show proof. The HR submits her name within the training management program, and it provides security awareness before accessing any IT system. The organization also discovered that 10 executive members had not taken the training as well. What action should HR take concerning the annual training requirements?**

    A. Since security awareness training for Alice is the most important, they should schedule the training for her and have closed session training for the executive staff later to discuss continuous monitoring and security controls.

    B. Since security awareness training must include contractors, executives, and anyone who has access to the system, they should schedule the activity for everyone.

    C. They should review their continuous monitoring program to determine why the executive staff never had training.

    D. They should develop better controls to track training as part of their continuous monitoring program and accept Alice's training as proof.

132. **As a continual effort in reducing risks, what fundamental practice should organizations consider concerning contingency planning? Choose the best answer.**

A. The organization should test and monitor contingency plans through tabletop exercises and review documentation as required.

B. The organization should verify that data collected through monitoring is accurate and provides the information required to make risk decisions concerning contingency operations.

C. The organization should gather and collect metrics to make risk decisions concerning contingency operations.

D. The organization must never realign contingency planning exercises based on metrics, trend analysis, vulnerabilities, and risk discovered.

133. **Which of the following represents automated test outputs concerning a robust Information System Continuous Monitoring program? Choose the best Answer.**

A. An organization has collected data from different teams showing risk data and metrics based on incidents, security status, and control failures.

B. An organization has various programs that print test data concerning control status.

C. An organization gathers test data via various programs such as a vulnerability scanner, a web-based firewall, and technical teams' paper logs.

D. An organization has dashboards and displays integrated test data and control status from various programs such as a vulnerability scanner, web-based firewall, and log management software.

134. **Which of the following represents a Statement on Auditing Standards (SAS)70 report that addresses users, auditors, and third parties or operational controls?**

A. A SOC2 report addresses service organizations relevant to security, availability, processing integrity, confidentiality, or privacy.

B. A SOC1 report addresses service organizations relevant to security, availability, processing integrity, confidentiality, or privacy for financial data.

C. A SOC1 and SOC2 audit report that addresses SAS70 operational requirements.

D. A Web Trust or Trust Service Report that addresses SOC3 requirements.

135. **Which one of the following is least likely to occur at a crime scene concerning digital investigations?**

A. The crime scene will have evidence collected by law enforcement agencies through digital media and should be recorded.

B. Once the scene has been secured, and the legal authority to seize the evidence has been confirmed, devices can be collected. Any passwords, codes, or PINs should be gathered from the individuals involved.

C. First, respondents need to take special care with digital devices in addition to normal evidence collection procedures to prevent exposure to things like extreme temperatures, static electricity, and moisture.

D. Suppose a computer is on but runs destructive software (formatting, deleting, removing, or wiping information). In that case, power to the computer should be disconnected immediately to preserve whatever is left on the machine.

136. **During a crime scene investigation, the forensic examiner collects data based on SHA-256. When the information is received in court, the evidence bit patterns are different from SHA-256. What fundamental issue will happen based on the differences in bit patterns collected?**

A. The information may be admissible in court if the signatures match previous information from other evidence collected using the same tool.

B. The information may be admissible in court if the interviewer asks a potential witness to provide a written statement on the data handling procedures.

C. The information may not be admissible in court if the signatures match previous information gathered between the two interviews.

D. The information may not be admissible in court due to the integrity of the data compromised, collected, and provided to the court.

137. **Which one of the following poses the most significant challenge for forensic teams when tasked with collecting data after an incident has occurred? Choose the best answer.**

A. The evidence must have privacy and collection rights approved for use.

B. The information collected for reports must have detailed metrics and statistical data specific to the organization, so trend analysis and risk-related areas can be hard to achieve.

C. All reports must be written in the same format to preserve the integrity of information.

D. The exact information collected must be authentic, accurate, complete, and have support from the courts.

138. **During an incident analysis, the security team has decided to use a hashing algorithm to obtain a cryptographic checksum for each designated file. The goal of the analysis is to determine whether checksum values have been altered by comparing previous values. What precursor or indicator has the analysis team used?**

A. The team is analyzing network behavior for file structures by viewing system profile changes.

B. The team is profiling attack vectors to determine whether changes have been made to important files.

C. The team is profiling the network through a file integrity software program to determine whether changes have been made to important files.

D. The team is using event correlation techniques to detect changes within the system files.

139. **A forensic team has decided to view the reports generated from other forensic experts to determine the purpose of a specified file. The report shows a file containing information about a file and possibly metadata that provides information about the file's structure. What information has the team reviewed?**

A. The examiners reviewed the file headers by using content analysis to determine the purpose of the file.

B. The examiners reviewed the context analysis to determine the impact of the file.

C. The examiners reviewed the file headers by using context analysis to determine the purpose of the file.

D. The team has identified the file structure and software analysis for the file structure.

140. **What are fundamental requirements every investigator should follow concerning computer investigations when combined with system operations? Choose the best answer.**

A. Maintain system, restore important operations without losing information related to the interruption, and preserve critical information that may be needed as evidence.

B. Understand evidence retention, system recovery stages, and cause identification.

C. Maintain a secure, provable, and evidence chain of custody for system state and user involvement.

D. Maintain maximum system, restore system operations without losing information related to the interruption, and preserve all information that may be needed as evidence.

141. An investigator has been called to a crime scene involving transferring a company's financial information to a third-party company. The computer used was seized, and the investigator notices that there are three CD-ROMs laid out on the desk that state "Critical Financial Files 1.8 GB." Based on the law of criminal investigations, what actions should the investigator take?

A. The crime scene should be seized, and the investigator should take no part in the forensic analysis due to the separation of duties required.

B. The investigator should use the chain of custody process to transfer evidence to a forensic laboratory since forensic analysis on-site can hamper the criminal case.

C. The investigator should use the chain of custody process to preserve the data and request additional support for onsite forensic analysis.

D. The investigator should develop admissible information and then submit the information to the lab experts for forensic analysis.

142. When a lawsuit has been filed concerning civil action among two organizations, the investigator must face many challenges due to the burden of proof. Which challenge poses the most constraints to the investigative process when civil investigations proceed?

A. The investigator must face legal limitations of gathering data to indicate that due diligence was not followed.

B. Computer fraud cases may require subject matter experts (SME) to explain technical terms.

C. Due diligence may not be a factor in every case.

D. Some trade secrets and private information may have to be withdrawn from court cases.

143. A forensic investigator for a company has been tasked to investigate email distribution outside of the company. The issue was reported by the IT Security team concerning two employees sending proprietary information to a third-party company. As a forensic investigator, what initial action should you not pursue?

A. Call the employees to a separate meeting to address the concern before starting the investigation.

B. Allow the appropriate party to gather all the required data and then review the company's email policies for discrepancies.

C. Review the company regulatory policy on email distribution.

D. Request the entire staff to remain clear of the investigation.

144. A forensic investigator for a company has been tasked to investigate electronic data transferred between two nations. The subject under investigation has been notified about the action. What fundamental practice should be imposed to gather data via ESI for the case?

A. Precaution to have clients maintain ESI should be investigated.

B. A litigation hold should be issued to prevent the forensic examiner from obtaining unrelated data.

C. A notice should be issued to preserve all data in a usable format for the forensic team.

D. A litigation hold should be issued to preserve the data under investigation.

145. **A forensic team has decided to view the reports generated from other forensic experts to determine the purpose of a specified file. The report shows a file containing information about a file and possibly metadata that provides information about the file's structure. What information has the team reviewed?**

A. The examiners reviewed the file headers by using content analysis to determine the purpose of the file.

B. The examiners reviewed the context analysis to determine the impact of the file.

C. The examiners reviewed the file headers by using context analysis to determine the purpose of the file.

D. The team has identified the file structure and software analysis for the file structure.

146. **What are fundamental requirements every investigator should follow concerning computer investigations when combined with system operations? Choose the best answer.**

A. Maintain system, restore important operations without losing information related to the interruption, and preserve critical information that may be needed as evidence.

B. Understand evidence retention, system recovery stages, and cause identification.

C. Maintain a secure, provable evidentiary chain of custody for system state and user involvement.

D. Maintain maximum system, restore system operations without losing information related to the interruption, and preserve all information that may be needed as evidence.

147. **An investigator has been called to a crime scene involving transferring a cloud customer's financial information to a third-party company. The data that was transferred resides within a storage location that hosted 100 customers' critical data. Based on the law of criminal investigations, what would not constitute a defined strategy once a digital investigation has initiated in a cloud environment?**

A. The cloud deployment model should be reviewed to determine the current data lines of responsibility.

B. The investigator should use the chain of custody process to transfer evidence to a forensic laboratory since forensic analysis in the cloud can hamper the criminal case.

C. The investigator should research the tenants and security zones to determine the data transfer features and privacy standards.

D. The CSP and the customer should develop a cloud-based SLA that addresses multi-tenant security and controls required to sustain privacy.

148. **When a lawsuit has been filed from a customer concerning their cloud service provider (CSP), what specific concern should the lawsuit address?**

A. Whether the SLA addressed the level of responsibility and how the cloud data should be managed.

B. Whether the multi-tenant environment required digital isolation between the CSP and its 3rd party affiliates.

C. Whether the SLA is a cloud-based or local system designed.

D. Whether trade secrets and private information were shared amongst the customers with other customers.

149. A forensic investigator for a company has been tasked to investigate email distribution outside of the company. The issue was reported by the IT Security team concerning two employees sending proprietary information to a third-party company. As a forensic investigator, what step would provide the most support for an ongoing case?

    A. Call the employees to a separate meeting to address the outcome after the investigation.

    B. Gather all the required data and then review the company's email policies for discrepancies.

    C. Review the company regulatory policy on email distribution.

    D. Disabling the employees' email account and ask the system administrators to backup all their email.

150. A forensic investigator for a company has been tasked to investigate a data breach between two cloud entities. The service provider under investigation has been notified about the action. What is the best practice in supporting the case?

    A. Develop a precaution plan to have the cloud entities in an agreement.

    B. Issue a cloud service agreement to preserve the digital data.

    C. An SLA notice should be issued to preserve all data in a usable format for the forensic team.

    D. A privacy impact assessment should be issued to preserve the data under investigation.

151. A new intrusion detection system has been implemented for SEMAIS. The security engineer has decided to configure the system to detect new threats and variants of known threats. The detection will monitor various states to determine whether the event is a false positive. Which one of the following would not support the configuration plan for the implemented intrusion detection system?

    A. Stateful protocol analysis that compares predetermined profiles of generally accepted definitions against observed events to identify deviations.

    B. Signature-based detection that compares created signatures against observed events to identify possible incidents.

    C. A profile for anomaly-based detection that can either be static or dynamic.

    D. Anomaly-based detection compares definitions of what activity is considered normal against observed events to identify significant deviations.

152. SEMAIS has decided to implement a continuous monitoring solution to capture network traffic for possible threats, determine vulnerability identification, generate log analysis, and consolidate logs for technical teams during audits. Which of the following systems will provide support for SEMAIS continuous monitoring efforts?

    A. Purchase a Log Management application to perform centralized aggregation and long-term retention of information.

    B. Develop an audit monitoring program and utilize organization security tools to filter traffic.

    C. Implement Security Information and Event Management tools to centralize logging that can facilitate aggregation and consolidation of logs from multiple information system components.

    D. Provide training to the technical teams on log analysis and event correlation.

153. A new server has been installed in a secured network zone. The organization wants to ensure that it can maintain visibility and compliance for vulnerability management, configuration control, and intrusive events for the server without affecting its security and operations. What tool would be appropriate to support the organization to maintain visibility and compliance for the server?

   A. The organization should use log analysis tools that automate events and provide real-time status for vulnerabilities.

   B. The organization should use continuous monitoring tools that automate events and provide real-time status for vulnerabilities.

   C. Includes metrics that provide meaningful indications of security status at all organizational.

   D. The organization should install a secure VLAN to isolate traffic from the server and a log manager to capture events.

154. A security organization has been consulted to help an organization control the transmission of information to external clients through email, restrict the use of stored data, and control archived data on the organization's network. The solution should also have leakage mechanisms that prevent the distribution of sensitive data. What solution should the security organization implement?

   A. A mitigation program to control leakage detection among different gateways.

   B. A data loss prevention program will incorporate data at rest, use, and transit for the organization to prevent—leakage of sensitive information.

   C. A data at rest program that will incorporate and prevent and leakage of sensitive information.

   D. Data solution that resides on file servers and DBs and needs to be monitored from being getting leaked.

155. SEMAIS has decided to use an automated program to build a collection of assets and their profiles. The information will be used to develop a patch and vulnerability management program for remediating software updates. What management program would help SEMAIS to achieve its goal?

   A. A configuration management program to distinguish asset identification and a centralized repository for all configurable items.

   B. Use an Information Technology Asset Management (ITAM) program for acquisition development and lifecycle resources for hardware and software.

   C. The organization should have an inventory management program to track all software and hardware profile for assets.

   D. Implement a configuration item (CI) tracking program in a controlled environment to change CIs and develop a report status for CIs.

156. SEMAIS has decided to update its SIEM application, security products, purchase new servers and printers for its network. As part of the upgrade, the company must ensure all documentation and associated information stay relevant; SIEM agents exist across every asset. What fundamental program can help SEMAIS establish its goals?

   A. Rename all artifacts under the jurisdiction of the CM.

   B. Develop a secure configuration management program to ensure relevant software controls are not changed.

   C. Establishing a CM program that would address hardware and software inventory, baseline compliance, configuration control for all configurable items, and artifacts are updated to reflect changes implemented.

D. Create a release baseline to track all changes, generate a configuration report for all artifacts, and implement a CM Plan that would support new artifacts.

157. **A security architect has been asked to design a new security framework for his organization. The products are mostly infrastructure devices such as servers, laptops, and tablets. After reviewing the requirements, he notices that the inventories are scattered across multiple artifacts, and different business units have their process. The organization has implemented a configuration management program to reduce any issues concerning artifacts and their locations. As a solution, what should the organization develop within the CM program?**

A. Develop a relational configuration management database (CMDB)-based repository to support a centralized collection of assets and inventory.

B. Implement an accurate inventory of installed hardware and software that forms the foundation of a solid ITAM program.

C. Institute standardized CM practices and means for selecting fewer hardware configuration and software titles.

D. Implement IT asset management that requires careful coordination between IT and process owners.

158. **Which of the following represents unique challenges for change management when integrated into a virtualization platform such as VSAN, virtual machine (VM), or Storage Defined Network (SDN)?**

A. Implementing a root cause analysis for items not found in a collection repository.

B. Storage capacity tracking for a relational CMDB-based repository to support a centralized collection of assets and their profiles.

C. Manually identifying physical and logical assets.

D. The traceability of data between different VM modules.

159. **When the organization ABC decides to implement virtual solutions, what fundamental challenges must be addressed for configuration management? Choose the best answer.**

A. Whether tracking and traceability areas of change and configuration control can be released from virtualization infrastructure.

B. Whether risk exposure defined under change management relates to the VM infrastructure.

C. Physical systems may be outdated and do not align with the VM solution.

D. Whether there exists a function to audit the configurations for the virtual assets continuously.

160. **When organization ABC decides to implement a cloud-based solution for its organization, what fundamental challenges must be addressed for configuration management? Choose the best answer.**

A. There may be limited visibility into the services and end-to-end status of physical systems.

B. Changes that occurred may not be updated adequately through tracking and traceability areas of change and configuration control.

C. Risks exposure defined under ITIL may not relate to the cloud infrastructure.

D. Physical systems maybe outdated and do not align with the cloud solution.

161. **Which security concept is appropriate for contractors and vendors required to have access to operational tasks but not the operational functions in a SOC?**

  A. Separation of duties for operational and non-operational tasks within the SOC for contractors.

  B. Access control parameters that describe the separation of duties for SOC teams and vendors.

  C. Least privilege of information that is proprietary and may cause a financial risk and public disclosur.

  D. Privilege escalation of system-level accounts for SOC personnel.

162. **A database developer has completed his code analysis and wishes to describe the results to the Database Administrators. He leaves his office, and a Senior Administrator tries to enter the development laboratory to see the code analysis. After inserting his biometric data, he receives a denied access error message. Why would the developer receive the error?**

  A. The concept of separation of duties has been implemented for the database administrator.

  B. The code analysis has not involved the database administrator, so his rights are not calculated.

  C. The code analysis has involved the database administrator, so his rights must be rejected.

  D. The access rights for receiving a described version of the code analysis have been rejected.

163. **A SOC team has been tasked to determine whether operators and administrators use a restricted system after working hours. The network has many tools and processes installed. Each has different data results, and the team wants to consolidate the information as much as possible to monitor the activities. Which application would support the team in its efforts?**

  A. The organization should monitor its IPS for traffic analysis.

  B. Installing a virtual platform will help with data consolidation and incident analysis.

  C. To investigate any policy violations, the organization should use a log management program.

  D. The organization should use computer logon activities, network traffic analyzers, and system alerts to gather the data.

164. **After an audit review, an organization has been tasked to implement an internal threat program to determine whether employees violate policies and create data breaches. What fundamental security concept would support the organization to determine the fraudulent activity of employees?**

  A. The organization should implement restricted access rights to detect fraudulent activity.

  B. The organization should use a log management program to view logon activities, network traffic, and system alerts to gather the data.

  C. The organization should implement a job-rotation policy to detect fraudulent activity.

  D. The organization should implement a separation of duties for database administrators and developers.

165. **When an organization decides to review and reclassify its security program based on annual assessments, the overall goal is to achieve what security objective?**

  A. Determine root cause analysis for different problem situations.

B. Manage its security lifecycle management program annually to determine whether control, policies, and processes are effective.

C. Analyze its security lifecycle management program based on financial budgets and metrics.

D. Implement new controls for the organization's security framework.

166. **An SLA agreement has been developed to support resource availability. The SLA states that the availability and response time. Which answer describes the overall requirements for the SLA?**

A. The uptime and mean time between failures (MTBF) must co-exist where MTBF exceeds uptime.

B. The serve availability and technical quality must be achieved within a prolonged duration.

C. The MTBF and meantime two repairs (MTTR) should be directly proportional.

D. The uptime and response time is in high demand for the organization to succeed.

167. **What is a fundamental concern that a security practitioner should consider with regards to cloud-based storage? Choose the best answer.**

A. Distributed data that is stored on physical servers throughout the enterprise.

B. Whether the encryption operates within the industry standard.

C. The number of people who only have authorized access to the data.

D. An extra consideration when using cloud computing concerns the handling of encryption keys - where are the keys stored, and how are they made available to application code.

168. **When organizations decide to use a disposal and reuse policy for data remanence, what fundamental technologies and policies will help without causing any damage?**

A. The use of object reuse assurance and degaussing media will ensure that any remanence of data is deleted permanently.

B. The use of coercively and object reuse assurance for media management.

C. The use of coercively and specialized hardware for media management.

D. Object reuse assurance and overwriting magnetic media will ensure that any remanence of data is deleted permanently.

169. **During an incident response activity, an unauthorized source has gained access to an organization's network. The team notices that the intruder was able to bypass its firewall and perimeter devices. The team detected the attack by utilizing an IDS, which provided a feed alert on the incident. What configuration should have been deployed to prevent the intrusion?**

A. Deploy an IPS within the IDS line of communication for Defense in Depth.

B. The organization should deploy an IPS in line with the communication path for the network.

C. Institute a network protection suite by deploying host-based security.

D. Deploy a separate IDS within the network boundary to filter outside attacks.

170. **When moving to containment during an incident response phase, what fundamental strategy should be instituted or deployed concerning DDoS attack?**

   A. The organization should plan for DDoS activities by viewing risks associated with system configurations and malware response procedures.

   B. Whether emergency system changes will affect the introduction of new DDoS attacks for remote networks.

   C. Organizations should define acceptable risks in dealing with incidents and develop strategies accordingly for DDoS.

   D. Institute a network protection suite for future DDoS attacks.

171. **After containing an attack, the SOC team has decided to mitigate any potential issues. The organization initially had an intruder that gains access through an authentication bypass vulnerability. Based on incident mitigation, what action should be taken for the intruder?**

   A. Mitigation is not necessary for this phase; administrators will move back to detection and analysis.

   B. Perform account audits on all users to determine whether exploits are contained.

   C. Mitigation is not necessary for this phase; considering no user account was compromised, it can be addressed during the recovery phase.

   D. Perform eradication and recovery in a phased approach so that reporting steps are prioritized.

172. **Organization ABC is required to make an incident report concerning a high-level attack. The SOC Manager has drafted the report and submitted his results to the CIO. As a CIO, what information on the report is important besides root cause analysis?**

   A. Service Level Agreements and shared information with external organizations that are considered trade secrets.

   B. The legal ramifications of a civil lawsuit that a hacker may pursue.

   C. Network isolation and loss for the organization.

   D. Timely metrics to recover incident and team-to-team relationships.

173. **After an incident has been mitigated, the SOC team decides to transition from a shutdown state and make changes required for hacked user accounts. What incident activity is the SOC team tasked to perform?**

   A. The team is gathering system-level data for metrics and reporting.

   B. The team is performing remediation of attack issues and preparing the system to recover.

   C. The team is making a recovery of operations and configuring compromised accounts with new passwords.

   D. The team is performing detection and analysis of potential intrusions through a system state.

174. **After an incident has been mitigated, the SOC team decides to transition from a shutdown state and make changes required for hacked user accounts. The account was hacked due to an authentication bypass vulnerability on a hosted server. What incident activity is the SOC team tasked to perform?**

   A. The team is gathering system-level data for recovery operations.

   B. Recovery and Remediation for the system and associated vulnerability induced by authentication bypass.

C. The team is performing system contingency operations to recover system states.

D. The team is performing a detection and analysis to remediate vulnerabilities.

175. On a Tuesday night, a database administrator performs off-hours maintenance on several production database servers. The administrator notices some unfamiliar and unusual directory names on one server. After reviewing the directory listings and viewing some files, the administrator concludes that the server has been attacked and calls the incident response team. The team's investigation determines that the attacker successfully gained root access to the server six weeks ago. When developing a lesson learned for the incident, which is least likely to occur?

A. Gathering a root-cause analysis and determine whether similar incidents may occur for the organization.

B. Evaluate the daily administration duties to determine where best practices would work or need to improve.

C. Examine information sharing with previous organizations to see what recovery strategies are in place.

D. Examine the database system configuration and decide whether the organization should implement a monitoring program or improve its reporting capability.

176. An attacker makes several attempts to gain access to a corporate network. The goal is to examine the network footprint to see how many servers and computers are online. After three failed attempts, the attacker session drops offline. What preventative solution was installed by the organization?

A. The organization has implemented ingress filtering and blocked ICMP incoming traffic.

B. The organization has implemented egress filtering to block ping traffic.

C. The organization has blocked incoming ICMP traffic to protect its network topology from being discovered and used concepts of ingress filtering to block ping traffic.

D. The organization has blocked all outgoing ping traffic and used ICMP to filter incoming traffic.

177. A NIDS has been deployed to help contain advanced attacks. While testing for the device, the security team notices that the NIDS has visibility into session information, ports, and protocols only for subnet 1. The information from subnet 2 has full filtering capability and monitoring. After several hours of researching the issue, the team notices that each subnet is hosted across different security zones. What is a probable cause for the NIDS unavailability?

A. The organization has implemented authentication bypass for subnet 2, which affects the availability for

   subnet 1.

B. The organization has implemented encrypted channels across subnet 1.

C. The organization has blocked all outgoing ping traffic and used ICMP to filter incoming traffic.

D. The organization has implemented ingress filtering and blocked ICMP incoming traffic.

178. An organization has decided to investigate recent spamming attacks on its network. The organization decides to block specific IP ranges and spamming malware going outbound for port 25. The information collected will be saved and submitted to a repository for controlling future spamming attacks. Which of the following describes the action the organization has developed to protect its network?

A. They have implemented SMTP port blocking for malware attacks and submitted information to a CERT team for blacklisting.

B. They have implemented SMTP port blocking to control spamming malware and submitted information to a blacklist.

C. The organization has blocked all outgoing ping traffic and used SMTP to filter incoming traffic.

D. They have implemented email bypass restrictions for malware attacks and submitted information to a white or greylisting.

179. **A vendor has released an advisory concern about a new software vulnerability, and they have not developed a patching solution or detection method. What solution could be utilized to test the software in its running state rather than source code analysis?**

A. Implement a dynamic application security testing tool for application testing.

B. Design a vulnerability tool that will detect the exploit on a production platform.

C. Implement a sandbox to detect zero-day malware using a virtualized platform.

D. Implement static application security testing (SAST) for application testing.

180. **A vendor has released an advisory that a new vulnerability has surfaced, and they have not developed a patching solution or detection method. The exposure is known to cause exploits that may damage organization databases. What explanation could the organization implement to control the exploit?**

A. Design a vulnerability tool that will detect the exploit on a production platform.

B. Implement a sandbox to detect zero-day malware using a virtualized platform and design a vulnerability tool to detect the exploit on a production platform.

C. Create a separate partition on the database hard drive to isolate exploits.

D. Implement a sandbox to detect zero-day malware using a virtualized platform.

181. **Which of the following describes the best configuration for a honeypot?**

A. They are designed within a server architect to detect exploits.

B. Implement a sandbox to detect zero-day malware using a virtualized platform.

C. Honeypots can be set up inside a DMZ of a firewall design.

D. Design a static application security testing (SAST) for detection through a firewall.

182. **Alice has been hired to define new malware and anti-virus solutions for SEMAIS and the IT industry. Part of her task is to develop new anti-malware testing procedures for desktop platforms. Which standard would support Alice in her new task?**

A. Review the National Institute of Standards and Technology (NIST) guidelines.

B. Use the Anti-Malware Testing Standard Organization (AMTSO) to detect new malware threats.

C. Implement a sandbox to detect zero-day malware using a virtualized platform such as Hypervisor.

D. Design a static application security testing (SAST) standard.

183. SEMAIS has decided to conduct its annual security assessment. One of the evaluators notices a device hosted with IP address 1.1.1.1 has an external IP address of 192.34.67.245, and the IPs are architected to conceal external traffic address information. What configuration has been designed for the architecture?

    A. Network Address Translator for all internal IPs.

    B. PAT for different labeling schemes.

    C. A proxy server to address IP address changes.

    D. A dynamic port translation device for IP address 1.1.1.1.

184. A company has just completed its impact assessment to determine its backup operations' restoration priority and scheme. The metrics indicate that the Recovery Time Objective must change from 15 minutes to 10 minutes. The impact has also shown that backups during the recovery period must be done for Day 1: 3 AM, Day 2: 3 AM, and minimal impact on the alternate site. Also, the company chooses to have the backups saved in continuous real-time at a remote location. Which strategy is appropriate for the organization to use?

    A. The organization can use remote journaling to backup the files in real-time. Use a differential backup strategy to support the RTO because you only need one backup data set and perform incremental backup on day one and Incremental on day 2.

    B. The organization can use remote journaling to backup the files in real-time, use a full backup strategy to support the RTO since you only need one backup data set, and perform a full backup on day 1 and Incremental on day 2.

    C. The organization can use electronic vaulting to backup the files in real-time, use a full backup strategy to support the RTO, and perform incremental backup on day 1 and full backup on day 2.

    D. The organization can use a full backup strategy for real-time synchronization, use a remote journaling strategy to support the RTO because you only need one backup data set, and perform a full backup on day 1 and Incremental on day 2.

185. A vendor has released a "hotfix" for a vulnerability classified as a "zero-day." Since the category for the vulnerability has changed, the organization decides to add the remediation task into its weekly maintenance schedule. The organization can classify this task under what remediation function?

    A. This can be classified as software removal since it will eliminate the vulnerability.

    B. This is considered a configuration adjustment since it will make changes to the registry.

    C. This can be classified as a high remediation effort since zero-day vulnerabilities have no fix.

    D. This can be classified as a security patch installation since it will repair the vulnerability.

186. What is a fundamental risk that organizations may encounter when using automated updates from vendor websites?

    A. Local network applications may induce coding errors from the automated updates.

    B. Automated updates can interfere with configuration management of assets and baseline compliance since changes are based on a vendors' recommendation.

    C. Manual updates can interfere with its configuration management of assets and baseline compliance since local changes are based on a vendors' recommendation.

D. Software tools may deploy automated updates and new configuration changes for "hotfix" and "zero-day" vulnerabilities.

187. Bob has been tasked to perform a patch and vulnerability remediation on servers located at Subnet 1. He was formally charged with doing subnet 2 and has never had any issues with the system owners. On Monday, he receives an email stating his access rights to scan subnet 1 has been restricted. The system owner tells him that he wants to hold off until he determines whether Bob needs to scan subnet 1. What action would cause the system owner to decide to restrict Bob's access rights for subnet 1?

A. The application may introduce manual reboots for production systems.

B. Subnet 1 may have embedded filtering capabilities that can cause ICMP failures.

C. The task may present new and additional risks that would cause network performance issues.

D. The scanning software utilized may not have been thoroughly tested for coding errors or malware infections.

188. Organization ABC has purchased a new software package that will be deployed to 500 hosts in subnet 1. The software is labeled as version 1.2, and the old version is labeled as version 1.1. The software for subnet 2 will not receive any of the updates since its configuration standard was different. The security team decides to update all documentation to reflect the changes and decides to enter the following table: Software Update v1.2 Subnet 1 updated. What information is missing from the table? Choose the "best" answer.

A. The organization has omitted the data that describes the previous baseline and software v1.2 reference or title.

B. The organization has omitted the baseline data that describes a subnet 2 configuration standard.

C. The organization has omitted the software reference or titles.

D. The organization has omitted software v1.1 and v1.2 references or titles.

189. SEMAIS has completed its first security assessment and discovers that the enterprise security architect has many inherent risks. The organization believes that continuous monitoring can reduce many of the risks. Additional risks can be resolved through routine administrative and technical tasks. In relationship to change and configuration management, what will SEMAIS achieve?

A. The organization will impose change and configuration management for operational issues.

B. The organization will impose change management under administrative tasks and configuration management for all technical implementations.

C. The organization will impose change management for operational assurance and configuration management for all administrative tasks.

D. The organization will impose change management and configuration management for all technical implementations.

190. A change control board has convened for SEMAIS. The board is meeting to determine whether new changes to its firewall have been implemented. As part of the change control process, SEMAIS must determine how changes to the information system may affect the security posture. What fundamental methodology must SEMAIS use to satisfy the change process? Choose the best answer.

A. SEMAIS will evaluate risks as part of a continuous monitoring strategy

B. A baseline compliance review is required to ensure that changes have been implemented.

C.   SEMAIS will have to perform a threat analysis to determine the changing status.

D.   SEMAIS will have to perform a security impact analysis to determine whether risks exist.

191. **When a security engineer evaluates a baseline change control task, which is least likely to occur?**

A.   The task may present new and additional risks that would cause the baseline to change discrepancies.

B.   The change control board will be the approval authority before implementing changes.

C.   The organization will maintain clear traceability for all changes to the approved baseline.

D.   Changes will be incorporated in a disciplined and timely manner.

192. **SEMAIS wishes to back up its data to an offsite location. The site is a shared facility with a partnering company. The partnering company has been a trusted source for SEMAIS for 10 years. As a good business practice, what should SEMAIS consider for the offsite storage location?**

A.   Whether testing was conducted by the partnering company onsite and what security measures exist.

B.   Whether the partnering company has the same security requirements and whether the reciprocal agreement has been executed.

C.   Whether onsite testing has been completed and the agreements such as SLAs and MOU are updated.

D.   SEMAIS should rely on its partnership and trusted relationship since the partnering company has been a trusted source.

193. **SEMAIS decides to develop its contingency plan for emergency operations. After reviewing the impact assessment, the organization discovers that the recovery time objective is 30 minutes after a disaster strikes. This data indicates they require a redundant system that is immediately available for business operations. What is the recovery site strategy required for SEMAIS?**

A.   SEMAIS needs a warm site combined with a mobile site to support its operations.

B.   SEMAIS needs a cold site or a mirrored site to support its operations.

C.   SEMAIS needs a mobile site combined with a friendly site to support its operations.

D.   SEMAIS needs a hot site or a mirrored site to support its operations.

194. **After an impact assessment, organization ABC has determined that they need a system to write an exact duplicate to an additional disk. What technology and disk type would the organization require?**

A.   The organization will require a redundant system that uses a random array of independent disks (RAID) 0 for disk striping.

B.   The organization will require a mirrored system that uses parity bits and disk striping.

C.   The organization will require a redundant system that uses RAID 1 for disk mirroring.

D.   The organization will require a mirrored system that uses RAID 1 for disk parity.

195. **SEMAIS decides to develop its contingency plan for emergency operations. After reviewing the impact assessment, the organization discovers that the power for the building must remain available through emergency periods that exceed 24-hours. What type of system and what resources would help SEMAIS?**

A. SEMAIS needs an offsite facility combined with a mobile site to support its operations.

B. SEMAIS needs a mobile system that would require a hot site to remain online.

C. SEMAIS needs a High Availability (HA) system that would require the use of a UPS.

D. SEMAIS needs a HA system that would require a diesel-powered generator.

196. **Once the impact assessment has been completed, an organization can perform what fundamental task for the recovery strategies?**

    A. Begin to start the activation and notification of the disaster to the recovery team

    B. Start activities to test and validate system capability and functionality.

    C. Begin to start the activation and notification of the continuity plan.

    D. Assemble the recovery team to perform recovery and restoration of operations at an alternate site.

197. **During the business impact assessment, the recovery team has identified key areas that involve personal information required to facilitate disaster recovery. Who should be included to develop the impact assessment and other related functions for role assignments?**

    A. The human resource department should be available to help update contact list information.

    B. All employees should help with the impact assessments to resolve the issue.

    C. The DRP coordinator should be involved to help coordinate personnel assignments.

    D. The BCP coordinator should be involved to help coordinate personnel assignments.

198. **A major database fails during the recovery of a backup solution, which supports about 35% of business operations. The recovery team decides to manually build the database before the CIO returns. The CIO arrives and asks why he was not notified. Based on the scenario, what solution is available for the incident?**

    A. All employees should help with the impact assessments to resolve the issue.

    B. The organization should implement disaster action plans for the CIO within the impact assessment.

    C. The organization should implement communication plans that involve the CIO within the impact assessment.

    D. All High Availability systems should have individual communication action plans developed.

199. **After an outage assessment, the team delivers the final report to the executive team with the following:**

    System – Loss of an entire facility.

    Mission – Unable to perform business operations.

    Downtime – Estimated to be 30 Days.

    Facility - Locate to a primary facility.

    What assessment category or tier has been reported?

    A. The report has described an incident where the entire facility will be inoperative for a specific period.

B. The report has described a non-incident, and the entire facility will be inoperative for a specific period.

C. The report has described a notification where the DRP will activate.

D. The report has described a severe incident where the DRP will activate.

200. During recovery, the team performed a functional test for a high-impact system by logging into the system and running a series of operations to ensure that the entire system operates correctly; afterward, the DRP was deactivated. What recovery effort has the team performed?

A. The team has performed a reconstitution of operations through a series of validation tests.

B. The team has performed activation and recovery strategies through a series of functional tests.

C. The team has performed notification strategies to resume normal operations through a series of validation tests.

D. The team has performed a high availability of resources by implementing deactivation strategies.

201. SEMAIS has updated its DRP and wants to ensure it is effective and supports the company's vision. What key area can SEMAIS institute to determine the effectiveness of its DRP? Choose the best answer.

A. The company can validate its effectiveness by testing employee's knowledge by using the DRP strategies.

B. The organization can complete training and awareness for roles and responsibilities outlined within the DRP.

C. The company can validate its effectiveness by monitoring employee knowledge using DRP strategies.

D. The company can validate its effectiveness by performing a trial-and-error test.

202. After a DRP has been created, SEMAIS distributes copies to all business units for review. What type of test has SEMAIS implemented?

A. The organization has performed a simulation test to measure the responses of all team members.

B. The organization has performed a structured walkthrough test to measure the responses of all team members.

C. The organization has performed a simulation test to test the system operations after a disaster occurs.

D. The organization has performed a checklist review so functional managers can identify any omitted areas.

203. After a DRP has been created, SEMAIS decides to verify the accuracy by having its organization perform a test by doing the following: 1) Describing the plan activation criteria and whether the plan is activated under the described circumstances, 2) Requesting the team leader to provide direction to the team customers as they describe their responses and actions to the situation, 3) Monitoring the various team activities, noting the performance of the team customers to the disaster scenario, 4) Providing additional events, clarifications to the situation, and simulate responses from other recovery teams, as appropriate, to keep the simulation active, and 5) Identifying enhancements needed to the plan. What type of test has been performed? Choose the best answer.

A. The organization has performed a simulation test to measure the responses of all team members.

B. The organization has performed a structured walkthrough test to measure the responses of all team members.

C. The organization has performed a structured walkthrough test to test all participants' knowledge of the disaster recovery plan.

D. The organization has performed a simulation test to test the system operations after a disaster occurs.

204. **Organization ABC wants to create scenarios where the backup and restoration of a critical database are tested for functionality. The test will involve operational and support functions practicing the disaster scenario to the extent of an offsite facility. What disaster recovery exercise will they perform?**

    A. The organization will perform a simulation test to verify that specific steps are realistic.

    B. The organization will perform a structured walkthrough test to measure the responses of all team members.

    C. The organization will perform a checklist review so functional managers can identify any omitted areas.

    D. The organization will perform a simulation test to test the system operations after a disaster occurs.

205. **What outcome should an organization expect after conducting a parallel test for its DRP?**

    A. The staff allocated for the primary and alternate sites will have different skill sets.

    B. The alternate and primary site will produce identical results, and a period to adjust any system performance issues at the alternate location will exist.

    C. The alternate and primary sites will produce different results.

    D. Operations at the main site will be at risk due to the overlap in operations.

206. **When performing a full-scale test for the DRP, what is a fundamental risk that may not invoke changes to the DRP?**

    A. The recovery procedures for the alternate site may have functional areas that were not addressed.

    B. Through the system shutdown sequence, the primary site may have to contact business partners.

    C. The testing method may not work for the alternate site, and communication channels will probably fail.

    D. Communications with the executive team on public relations may need improvements.

207. **After conducting an annual review of the BCP, an organization has decided to ensure the change control board and executive staff are aware of any changes; and the BCP expectation and IS capabilities are matched based on a review by the system owners. What administrative document and role would be assigned for this task?**

    A. A crisis management plan would be assigned, and the team coordinator would be required to coordinate BCP for their organization or system.

    B. A change management plan and a configuration control manager must coordinate BCP for their organization or system.

    C. A business continuity plan would be assigned, and the business continuity planner would be required to coordinate BCP for their organization or system.

    D. A Disaster Recovery Plan would be assigned, and the business continuity planner would be required to coordinate BCP for their organization or system.

208. **After conducting an annual review of the BCP, an organization has found several weaknesses in its physical security measures. These failures may allow an attacker to overpower a security guard. As a defensive measure to maintain the continuation of physical security services, what should the organization implement?**

A. The organization should implement a new BCP Plan that focuses on defense in depth.

B. A change management plan and a configuration control strategy for their organization or system.

C. A Disaster Recovery Plan to coordinate BCP for their organization or system.

D. The organization can implement automated door locks and mechanisms that are bulletproof.

209. **Which one of the following is not considered good practice for visitor control?**

A. Maintain logs to record the entry and departure of all visitors. The IT staff should retain the logs.

B. All visitors must sign in/out, obtain a visitors' sticker, and be escorted.

C. An after-hours log must be maintained at the visitors' desk. All employees and visitors who are in the facility after regular business hours must sign the after-hours log.

D. In restricted areas, all computer monitors should be located to prevent viewing by unauthorized persons.

210. **During a physical risk assessment, the team has noticed that duress testing was not performed for the organization. To identify potential risks for duress situations, what would be a possible solution? Choose the best answer.**

A. Perform an isolated tabletop exercise to identify risks associated with duress situations.

B. Implement scenario analysis to determine what risks exist and alternatives to reduce the risks.

C. Implement employee monitoring programs to determine what risks exist and alternatives to reduce the risks associated with duress situations.

D. Take a survey from all employees to identify hazards and their impact during duress situations.

211. **An organization has decided to develop five steps for its software and security development platform. Each stage has a quality assurance task to determine whether the phase has been completed. What model has been selected?**

A. An Agile method has been selected because there are five steps for developing the software application, and developers cannot make changes after completing a step.

B. A waterfall method has been selected for an incremental approach to software development.

C. A waterfall model has been selected to support a sequential process.

D. An agile method has been selected to address testing at the end of each phase.

212. **When utilizing a development lifecycle, an organization must ensure what practice is instituted to reduce any potential risks associated with software development?**

A. Security must be integrated into requirement analysis and validation early to identify and mitigate security vulnerabilities and misconfigurations.

B. The security framework for the software specifications has to align with all the functional requirements for software lifecycle assurance.

C. Security must be integrated into software development early to identify and mitigate security vulnerabilities and misconfigurations from system inception.

D. The testing and evaluation stage must have implementation steps designed to support different security assurance models.

213. **SEMAIS decides to review its software lifecycle assurance strategies to identify points of weakness during a risk assessment. The outcome will include a continuous improvement methodology to track the software project process through the development stages. Which of the following is least likely to occur based on the assessment of SEMAIS lifecycle strategies?**

A. The software maturity process will designate a common language and framework for prioritizing actions towards effective continuous improvement strategies.

B. The Capability Model will express repeatable, managed, defined, and optimized facts to express a system development status.

C. The continuous improvement strategy will incorporate an initial level that will first be identified as unrepeatable due to disorganized software assurance practices.

D. The system lifecycle will experience Software Capability Model areas of improvements based on the software change control process.

214. **A software developed has been reviewed and classified as Top Secret. The system owner has decided to recertify the software to satisfy higher classification requirements and implement the required changes. What phase of the SDLC addresses the change?**

A. The operation and maintenance phase has been addressed to cover any data sensitivity changes for the software security architect.

B. The system design and specifications have been identified and integrated to address configuration changes for the data sensitivity blueprints.

C. The testing and evaluation stages have been identified to address coding for the sensitivity of data.

D. The development stage has been identified and integrated to address configuration changes for the data sensitivity requirements.

215. **SEMAIS has decided to implement change management into its SDLC process. What outcome or benefit will be achieved through the integration?**

A. The application for change control during patch installation will help vendors discover zero days.

B. A rigorous process that addresses quality assurance for change management through a submittal approved, tested, and recorded with a back-out plan.

C. The testing and evaluation stage for the SDLC can control and user interface issues during acceptance testing.

D. A rigorous process that addresses the integrity of applications will ensure configuration changes are tested for coding errors during patch cycles.

216. **A small firm has experienced significant planning and budgeting issues for its software development platform. The different teams are testing codes without any formal standard against the production system. Various operational units and software engineers are working to achieve other software delivery goals, and project monitoring for repeatable and reliable processes is not integrated into development tasks. What strategy is appropriate to help the organization succeed?**

A. The organization needs an Integrated Product Team for team delivery of software products.

B. The organization could commit to having an Integrated Product Team and Software Capability Maturity process to deliver software products.

C. The organization could commit to having an Integrated Product Team and DevOps deliver software with a business-to-customer strategy.

D. The organization could commit to having a Capability Maturity Model Integration (CMMI) approach and Development Operations to deliver software with a business-to-customer strategy.

217. **Alice has access to an administrator database location that details the alias used to develop passwords for all new users. Since she has not been assigned a User ID, she deduces the information and finds Bob's password. What type of database attack has occurred?**

A. Alice has performed an inference attack and used data analysis to determine the passwords.

B. Alice has performed an aggregation attack and used inference of data to determine the passwords.

C. Alice has performed a covert analysis attack and used the inference of data to determine the passwords.

D. Alice has performed an inference attack and used data aggregation of data to determine the passwords.

218. **Which one of the following can be used to prevent java applets from causing system attacks?**

A. Generalizing that involves adding random values to the values already in the java database.

B. Performing scan code analysis on a different system and JAVA virtual machines during production.

C. Creating a virtual sandbox that would limit applets to any of the system resources.

D. URL validation with a separate open-source tool.

219. **What is a safe practice to use concerning HTTP sessions?**

A. Configure proxy firewalls to detect buffer overflows.

B. Decrypt all cookies and use random and unique indicators.

C. Do not store session identifiers in local storage as the data is always accessible by JavaScript Cookies.

D. Validate all input codes to deter buffer overruns through memory.

220. **A database administrator has opened a file called update. Db. Simultaneously, another database administrator has attempted to do the same and receives an error that the file is locked for editing. The security policies are configured to restrict concurrent access to files. What condition and vulnerability have been prevented for the shared location?**

A. A race condition has been restricted while preventing an open access vulnerability.

B. An excess privilege condition has been restricted while preventing an open access vulnerability.

C. A race condition has been restricted while preventing time of check to time of use vulnerability.

D. A restricted privilege condition has been created while preventing an authentication bypass vulnerability.

221. **Which one of the following can be used to prevent inference attacks?**

A. Noise Addiction, which involves removing some of the cells of the database before it is made public.

B. Cell Suppression by using some values in the database replaced more general ones before it is made public.

C. Polyinstantiation when a database contains public data, and data collection should be kept secret.

D. Generalizing that involves adding random values to the values already in the database. For example, a random number between -5 and 5 is added to an individual's age.

222. **Alice has decided to change her web browser and notices that her appearance and possible personal identity may be at risk. She further investigates by evaluating the website data collection fields and sees that the links have changed. What can be concluded about Alice's web browser?**

A. Web database content on the private interface can be vulnerable to SQL injection and needs proper validation and parameterization.

B. The website is prone to HTML injection attacks.

C. Do not store session identifiers in local storage as the data is accessible by JavaScript Cookies.

D. HTML settings are configured for user interface changes vs. code.

223. **When reviewing the potential risk and security impact for software delivery, a developer can have greater confidence that iterative development will minimize any coding risks compared to the waterfall method based on what philosophy?**

A. Developing a software product using the Waterfall Model can be a long process that does not yield a working version of all software security issues until late in the process.

B. The Waterfall Model allows the development team to demonstrate coding and security risks earlier on in the process and obtain valuable feedback from system users due to the separation of projects.

C. The iterative approach combines security into phases where changes cannot be designed after each stage of development.

D. The Waterfall Model uses a prototype development strategy where security issues are duplicated between production and development systems.

224. **A web application has been experiencing malformed errors with invalid codes. A software developer has decided to investigate the issue and discovers parameter codes designed by the vendor producing various memory overload issues. What vulnerability has been induced by coding errors?**

A. The application has experienced improper parameter validation as a result of coding errors.

B. The application has experienced buffer overflows, which resulted from improper input validation.

C. The application has experienced buffer underflow errors, which resulted from improper input validation of codes.

D. The application is experiencing coding errors from different memory locations.

225. **A software developer has completed the coding updates for a program. After testing the program, he discovers that the software has security issues and codes that were not documented during the last code review. He further learns that the version and release dates for the program were inaccurate. What tool would be appropriate to solve the issue?**

A. A consistent model that integrates configuration control and releases management should be used for security analysis toolsets.

B. The organization should have a secure configuration management tool that addresses software versions and release policies to help streamline quality checks.

C. The organization should have a secure configuration management tool that addresses software versions and release policies to help streamline security code reviews.

D. The organization should have a secure configuration management tool that addresses software versions and release policies to help code.

226. Alice has completed new coding for a major software program. She has decided to save the results in a restricted repository for code reviews and analysis. She has been designated as the Lead Developer for the project and has been granted full administrative rights to all repositories. She has several developers that work in different time zones. To ensure the codes are available and safe, what additional actions could Alice pursue?

A. Create a role-based access policy for her team to have physical and logical access to codes without restricting periods and integrate all the secure logging under a continuous monitoring task.

B. Create a rule-based access policy for her team to have physical and logical access to codes during specific periods and integrate all the secure logging under a continuous monitoring task.

C. Design a group access control policy for her team to have logical access to codes during specific periods and integrate secure logging as a separate task.

D. Design a secure code repository policy for her team to have physical and logical access to codes 24 X 7 and integrate all the secure logging under a continuous monitoring task.

227. Which of the following represents a security control feature for Application Program Interfaces (API)?

A. Encrypt all static keys by use of SSH as a primary encrypted channel.

B. Employ a standard security mechanism for all web-based applications using Representational State Transfer (REST).

C. Design an open security mechanism for all web-based applications using REST - API.

D. Utilize internal security solutions to help deter risks associated with frameworks.

228. A software control has been implemented for a large enterprise. The organization would like to integrate a management strategy to capture software issues, failing interfaces, and interoperability for different applications. What would system-level features be appropriate to integrate?

A. Integrate Auditing, Configuration Management, Continuous Monitoring, and Change Management principles to capture, remediate, and document software variations and versions based on software changes.

B. Integrate Forensic Analysis, Auditing, Configuration Management, Continuous Monitoring, and Change Management principles to document software variations and versions based on software changes.

C. Integrate Intrusion Analysis, Configuration Management, Continuous Monitoring, and Change Management principles to capture, remediate, and document software variations and versions based on software changes.

D. Integrate Change Management principles to capture, remediate, and document software variations and versions based on software changes.

229. What is a fundamental relationship between Risk Analysis and Software Development Lifecycle?

A. Corrective actions for the SDLC can address risk during the requirement stage, preventing future dangers from occurring.

B. Assessment and remediation of coding errors, vulnerabilities, and threats are coupled to minimize impacts through every phase of the software development platform.

C. Risks inherited through change control can be prevented using software development models such as the Waterfall over the Agile method.

D. The risk analysis stage should be integrated within the SDLC during pre-and post-assessment for security effectiveness.

230. **A developer receives an email with an attachment that states, "Tested and Verified." After he opens the file, he notices that several codes are not correct. The company must provide a demonstration once the code has been entirely acceptable to the corporate managers. As a security measure, what action should the developer consider?**

A. Before indicating the acceptance for the code, he should identify the error and assign a unique identifier for the code. As a security practice, he should hand carry the file on a disc to the development team.

B. Assign a unique identifier for the code. He should digitally sign the file as a security practice before emailing it out to the development team.

C. Before indicating the acceptance for the code, he should fix the error, perform regressive testing, and assign a unique identifier for the code. He should digitally sign the file as a security practice before emailing it out to the development team.

D. Before indicating the acceptance of the code, he should fix the error. He should digitally sign the file as a security practice before emailing it out to the development team.

231. **Which of the following constitutes proper software assurance strategies when software services are required for an organization? Choose the best answer.**

A. Work statements should include contracting rules and budget constraints for contractors.

B. Applicable risks should be discussed and determined whether they can be monitored through contract management.

C. Sustainment for services should include risks, budgets, and manpower.

D. The planning phase should implement risk factors associated with decisions that address evaluation and assessment for software services.

232. **A security engineer has noticed that a secure connection for its VPN uses IP, point-to-point protocol (PPP), and L2TP to protect the company's gateway. The engineer has decided to add another layer of protection for encrypting the traffic. What technology would support the security engineer?**

A. IPSec because it is considered a great protocol for maintaining confidentiality.

B. PPTP to help extend PPP connections by providing a tunnel through networks that do not understand PPP.

C. SSL Tunnel VPNs to securely access multiple network services, including applications and protocols that are not web-based.

D. SSL Portal VPN is a single standard SSL connection to a website to access multiple network services securely.

233. A cloud provider has been provided an SLA that requires data auditing every sixty days. What other agreement should be included that may directly comply with the requirements. Choose the best answer.

    A. Work statements should include contracting rules and budget constraints for contractors.

    B. Data Rights Management (DRM) that bridges ownership and cloud responsibility across all platforms.

    C. Sustainment for services should include risks, budgets, and manpower.

    D. A Privacy Level Agreement that focuses on data privacy between the customer and the CSP.

234. A cloud architect receives a project requirement list for a potential customer. The outlines that the customer needs to secure many endpoints such as mobile devices, tablets, and laptops. The current cloud architect focused on multitenancy models for the client. What cloud do characteristics describe the client's need?

    A. The security requirements will provide end-to-end protection.

    B. Data Rights Management (DRM) that bridges ownership and cloud responsibility across all platforms.

    C. Building On-demand self-service can provision more endpoints.

    D. The integrating of thin and thick clients that require broader network access can support the enterprise.

235. Which of the following best describes a SaaS application for a cloud environment?

    A. SaaS applications are usually deployed as non-hosted services and are accessed via an IaaS architect.

    B. The cloud consumer use application/service for business process operations.

    C. The consumer installs, manages, maintains, and supports the software application on a cloud infrastructure.

    D. The cloud consumer is the secondary stakeholder that the cloud computing service is created to support.

236. A security engineer has noticed that a secure connection for its VPN uses IP, PPP, and L2TP to protect the company's gateway. The engineer has decided to add another layer of protection for encrypting the traffic. What technology would support the security engineer?

    A. IPSec because it is considered a great protocol for maintaining confidentiality.

    B. PPTP to help extend PPP connections by providing a tunnel through networks that do not understand PPP.

    C. SSL Tunnel VPNs to securely access multiple network services, including applications and protocols that are not web-based.

    D. SSL Portal VPN is a single standard SSL connection to a website to access multiple network services securely.

237. SEMAIS has decided to update its organization's security standards to include remote authentication and different encryption standards. The current security architect uses standard usernames and passwords to authenticate across another web, network, and system boundaries. There are 15 database servers, IP Range 123.45.23.234 to 123.45.23.218, requiring system-level authentication to access the centralized database repository located in a remote region. The company also decides to integrate protocols and standards to offset legacy technology utilized by the organization. What technology is appropriate for the organization to implement?

A. Implement a packet filtering and web application firewall and appropriate ACLs for the remote repository, develop a solution that encrypts across port 80 and 443 by using SSL VPN, integrate user-based authentication by use of smart card technology for different roles, services, and authentication requirements, and use a certificate management strategy to reduce any compromise of system and services encryption.

B. Implement a packet filtering firewall and appropriate ACLs for the remote repository, develop a solution that encrypts across port 80 by using SSL VPN, integrate two-factor authentications by use of smart card technology for different roles, services, and authentication requirements, and use a key management strategy to reduce any compromise of system and services encryption.

C. Implement a packet filtering and web application firewall and appropriate ACLs for the remote repository, develop a solution that encrypts across port 443 by using SSL VPN; integrate two-factor authentications by use of smart card technology for different roles, services, and authentication requirements; and use a key management strategy to reduce any compromise of system and services encryption.

D. Implement a signature-based IDS and appropriate ACLs for the remote repository, develop a solution that encrypts across port 443 using SSL, integrate token-based authentication for different roles, services, and authentication requirements, and use an assurance strategy reduce any compromise of system and services encryption

238. **An organization has a user base of 45 employees who will need symmetric keys for accessing the network. A new security engineer has posed a solution to use PKI as a solution for the organization. After a week of debating, the company decides to halt the process until further research is done. The original proposal team chooses to draft a review of their findings to demonstrate how effective symmetric keys would support the organization. Which of the following should be submitted by the proposal team?**

A. The organization will require 990 symmetric key pairs to support the implementation of symmetric encryption, and RSA, Diffie-Hellman, and Digital Signature Algorithm (DSA) are standard algorithms that can be used. In addition, Symmetric-key cryptosystems are suitable for digital signatures and key exchange.

B. The organization will require 90 symmetric key pairs to support the implementation of symmetric encryption, and RSA, Diffie-Hellman, and Digital Signature Algorithm are standard algorithms that can be used. In addition, Symmetric-key cryptosystems are suitable for digital signatures and key exchange.

C. The organization will require 90 symmetric key pairs to support symmetric encryption, and AES, DES, Blowfish, and Skipjack are standard algorithms that can be used. In addition, Symmetric-key cryptosystems are Keys for symmetric-key cryptosystems are shorter compared to public key algorithms.

D. The organization will require 990 symmetric key pairs to support the implementation of symmetric encryption, and AES, DES, Blowfish, and Skipjack are standard algorithms that can be used. In addition, Symmetric-key cryptosystems are more efficient and can handle high rates of data.

239. **Company A has discovered that users with different roles can view the same data via data mining techniques during a recent audit. The roles for the database were designed to accommodate a supervisor and administrator account for data integrity. The structure for the database was audited as well, and the auditors discovered that controls designed to filter unauthorized database statements and modification privileges were not configured. Based on the information provided, what security-related areas should be addressed?**

A. The company should address the need for a Biba security architect to prevent unauthorized modifications; the threats addressed should define how an inference attack can occur through data aggregation and buffer attacks due to the schema. The controls should be reassessed to determine whether the schema for the database was accurate to support data manipulation requirements.

B. The company should address the need for a Clark-Wilson security architect for well-formed transactions, the threats addressed should define how an inference attack can occur through data aggregation and SQL injection attacks due to the schema, and the controls should be reassessed to determine whether the schema for the database was accurate to support transaction management requirements.

C. The company should address the need for a Clark-Wilson security architect for improper modifications, the threats addressed should define how an inference attack can occur through data aggregation and SQL injection attacks due to the schema, and the controls should be reassessed to determine whether the schema for the database was accurate to support data manipulation requirements.

D. The company should address the need for a Biba security architect for well-formed transactions, the threats addressed should define how an inference attack can occur through data aggregation and SQL attacks due to the schema, and the controls should be reassessed to determine whether the schema for the database was accurate to support transaction management requirements.

23. Comprehensive Examination - Answers and Explanations

1. **D.** In network security, endpoint security refers to a methodology of protecting the corporate network when accessed via remote devices such as laptops or other wireless and mobile devices. Each device with a remote connecting to the network creates a potential entry point for security threats. Endpoint security is designed to secure each endpoint on the network created by these devices. Usually, endpoint security is a security system that consists of security software located on a centrally managed and accessible server or gateway within the network, and client software is installed on each of the endpoints (or devices). The server authenticates logins from the endpoints and updates the device software when needed. While endpoint security software differs by vendor, you can expect most software offerings to provide antivirus, anti-spyware, firewall, and a host intrusion prevention system (HIPS).

2. **C.** A security architect can implement control measures such as ring protection, virtualization, firewalls, and intrusion systems to secure a plan. Logging of data is a function within network intrusion systems.

3. **C.** The appropriate action is to have training for all employees and counsel the employee to violate the privacy regulations. Since no action was stipulated about employee disciplining for a privacy violation, the company can counsel the employee. Using OECD would not support the issue since OECD is guidance and not an internal policy for the organization.

4. **C.** Open System Authentication is the default authentication protocol for the 802.11 standards. It consists of a simple authentication request containing the station ID and an authentication response containing success or failure data. Upon successful authentication, both stations are considered mutually authenticated. It can be used with WEP (Wired Equivalent Privacy) protocol to provide better communication security. However, it is important to note that the authentication management frames are still sent in clear text during the authentication process. WEP is used only for encrypting data once the client is authenticated and associated. Any client can send its station ID in an attempt to associate with the AP. In effect, no authentication is done. Shared Key Authentication (SKA) is a standard challenge and response mechanism that uses WEP and a shared secret key to provide authentication. Upon encrypting the challenge text with WEP using the shared secret key, the authenticating client will return the encrypted challenge text to the access point for verification. Authentication succeeds if the access point decrypts the same challenge text.

5. **B.** Users use end-to-end encryption, but only the data payload is encrypted. Service providers use link encryption, and it provides encryption to headers, trailers, addresses, and routing data.

6. **B.** During an asymmetric key exchange, the sender, must encrypt with their private key, and the receiver must decrypt with the sender's public key. Rule: private keys are held and encrypted by the owner. In this case, Alice must encrypt with her private key.

7. **D.** There should be limits to collecting personal data, and any such data should be obtained by lawful and fair means, where appropriate, with the knowledge or consent of the data subject. http://oecdprivacy.org/#collection

8. **D.** The deployment of baselines is designed to meet safeguard requirements for a system's relevant controls.

9. **D.** The data subject must have proper and legal knowledge of personal data and its use. http://oecdprivacy.org/#collection

10. **B.** The data owner has full responsibility for updating controls. The privacy officer's role is to enforce the policies and procedures for privacy.

11. **D.** Classifying data according to availability needs: Supportive Data is necessary for day-to-day operations but is not critical to the business mission or core functions (examples - meeting minutes, workstation images, etc.). High-priority data - availability of data is necessary for a business function, and destruction or temporary loss of data may have an adverse effect on mission, but would not affect the enterprise-wide process. Critical data has the highest

need for availability. If the information is not available due to system downtime, modification, destruction, etc., the business functions and mission would be impacted. The availability of this information must be rigorously protected. http://eits.uga.edu/access_and_security/infosec/pols_regs/policies/dcps/.

12. C. Traffic confidentiality hides addressing information when transmitting data, which prevents an inference attack. An inference attack is a data mining technique performed by analyzing data to gain knowledge about a subject or database illegitimately.

13. A. Data can be classified either in terms of its need for protection (e.g., Sensitive Data) or its need for availability (e.g., Critical Data). http://eits.uga.edu/access_and_security/infosec/pols_regs/policies/dcps/ Classifying Data According to Protection Needs: The four categories are Public, Internal, Sensitive, and Restricted. Public Data - Data can be disclosed without restriction (Directories, Maps, Syllabi and Course Materials, de-identified data sets, etc.). Internal Data - confidentiality of data is preferred, but the information in data may be subject to open records disclosure (email correspondence, budget plans, etc.). Sensitive Data - data confidentiality required by law, policy, or contractual obligation. Restricted Data involves privacy and security protections.

14. A. A baseline security standard should address the following: Enterprise assets to be protected by the baseline, deployment of one or more baselines, security level of baseline, and control determination for the baseline.

15. A. Firewall and routers contain Access Control Lists (ACL) to restrict traffic. They are both Layer 3 devices, and an IDS can only provide alerts. A router is sometimes referred to as a gateway device.

16. C. Part Risk Analysis determines Qualitative (Value) and Quantitative (Cost) for a risk-based decision. The SLE is derived by examining the EF (Exposure Factor) and AV (Asset Value). The CIO only needs the calculation for the SLE. The ALE is derived later in the risk analysis process (SLE * ARO = ALE)

17. B. The CIO dictates through policies on risk responsibility. Some organizations address a shared responsibility which is outlined in their approach and procedures.

18. C. For an effective relationship with external partners, agreements need to be established on how their employees will perform tasks, and access to background data should also be discussed. Background data consist of employee identification, work agreements, and period of performance.

19. D. When a risk determination has to be made, an organization can transfer (buy insurance), mitigate (decrease or reduce the risk exposure), accept (a risk that is low in impact does not cause much harm), or avoid (remove the activity that is causing the risk).

20. D. As a good practice through Information Risk Management, it is best to access threats and vulnerabilities for potential issues. Based on this scenario, the assessment report must address vulnerabilities and threat exploitation for proper reporting. The process of vulnerability scans is not required since the assessment is within its reporting stage. Vulnerability scans are conducted in the evaluation. All human considerations and impacts are considered within the threat analysis.

21. B. Any technology used should screen traffic, block unwanted traffic, and offer increased security for system access. An intrusion detection system will generate alerts but will not block traffic like an intrusion prevention system. Opening firewall and ports are much more of a security risk. Combining an IDS and IPS will help lower many threats and risks.

22. C. Phishing attacks use email or malicious websites to solicit personal information by posing as a trustworthy organization. For example, an attacker may send an email seemingly from a reputable credit card company or financial institution that requests account information, often suggesting a problem. When users respond with the requested information, attackers can use it to gain access to the accounts.

23. B. A tangible asset is anything that can be seen and has a physical presence, such as cash, property, plant, and machinery or investments. On the other hand, intangible assets cannot be seen, such as the goodwill of a company, trademark, and intellectual property rights.

24. D. Preventative is intended to avoid an incident occurring while corrective fixes components or systems after an incident has occurred.

25. B. To achieve compliance within personnel security, an organization must consider whether policies are designed to address background checks and investigations. The policies are intended to standardize practices for maintaining compliance.

26. D. Countermeasures should always support the CIA triad. The CIA triad should be audited and derived from a trusted source such as the NIST 800-53 control selection.

27. C. Security threat modeling, or threat modeling, is a process of assessing and documenting a system's security risks. Security threat modeling enables you to understand a system's threat profile by examining it through the eyes of your potential foes. With techniques such as entry point identification, privilege boundaries, and threat trees, you can identify strategies to mitigate potential threats to your system. Your security threat modeling efforts also enable your team to justify security features within a system or security practices for using the system to protect your corporate asset.

28. A. An organization's privacy can exist beyond regular working hours if information sharing has been used. The company's privacy objectives should be well developed and addressed within its policy and procedures.

29. A. To reduce a threat's ability to exploit a system, an organization must ensure controls are implemented and regularly access employees, systems, and operations for weaknesses. Making system changes can induce threats, especially after the system has been tuned and evaluated for weaknesses. New standards are sometimes not the best solution.

30. D. The implementation of controls requires sound knowledge of how the changes will affect the network environment. The changes will require new policy updates and configuration changes that may cause the security architect to change. A security framework is established before any control implementation. Auditing standards are not a significant factor unless an audit is performed.

31. A. Deterrent control is intended to discourage a potential attacker. A directive control is a mandatory control that has been placed due to regulations. Preventative access control is deployed to stop unwanted or unauthorized activity from occurring. http://cisspstudy.blogspot.com/2007/05/types-of-access-control.html

32. A. When an employee has been terminated, an organization needs to review their account and disable the account access. This procedure ensures that proprietary information and any wrongdoings are viewed for criminal action. If an account is deleted too early, any evidence will be removed as well. This is not a good security practice.

33. A. Before acquiring shared service, it is important to understand the state of an organization's system audits and baseline status. Risks and security issues can affect your organization as well. Human and personnel security issues are evaluated through audits.

34. D. This serves as industry best practices for holistically managing security controls within organizations around the world. ISO follows the Plan – Do – Check – Act (PDCA) cycle, an iterative process commonly used in business process quality control programs. The Plan component pertains to establishing objectives and making plans. The Do component deals with the implementation of the plans. The Check component pertains to measuring results to understand if objectives are me. The Act component provides direction on how to correct and improve plans to achieve success better.

35. C. Securities and vulnerabilities assessments are aimed at finding vulnerabilities, often without regard to exploitation and access. Thus, penetration testing usually goes more profound, seeking to take over systems and steal data. At the same time, security and vulnerability assessments are broader, involving discovering security flaws. These assessments likewise involve policy and procedure reviews, which are usually not included in penetration testing.

36. A. Security control assessments provide a line of defense in knowing the strengths and weaknesses of an organization's information system. Security controls assessment determines whether security controls in an information system are operating as intended.

37. A. ALE (Annualized Loss Expectancy) calculations are a component of every risk analysis process. ALE calculations, when appropriately done, portray risk accurately. ALE calculations provide meaningful cost/benefit analysis. ALE calculations are used to:
* Identify risks
* Plan budgets for information risk management
* Calculate loss expectancy in annualized terms SLE x ARO = ALE

38. D. A configuration control program supports the unauthorized changing for controls from an unauthorized source. When it is used properly, privileged escalation can be controlled and monitored without formal approval. Tuning an IDS would only help with false positives. A risk analysis has no purpose at this stage because the overall goal is to achieve compliance. Risk analysis = threat identification Risk assessment = control identification and implementation.

39. A. A Multi-level Security Policy-Systems must have both sensitivity labels for both subjects and objects; also, it must use mandatory access control. Classification and clearances represent multiple layers of security.

40. A. Non-Interference Model is related to the information flow model with restrictions on the information flow. Multi-level security properties can be expressed in many ways, one being noninterference. This concept is implemented to ensure any actions at a higher security level do not affect or interfere with actions at a lower level. This type of model does not concern itself with data flow but instead with what a subject knows about the system's state. If an entity at a higher security level acts, it cannot change the state for the entity at the lower level.

41. A. Multi-level Security Policy-Systems must have both sensitivity labels for both subjects and objects; also, it must use mandatory access control. The Bell-LaPadula model defines a secure state through 3 multilevel properties. The first two properties implement mandatory access control, and the third one permits discretionary access control. 1) SSP states that reading of information by a subject at a lower sensitivity level from an object at a higher sensitivity level is not permitted (no read up). 2) Security Property (star*) states that writing of info by a subject at a higher level of sensitivity to an object at a lower level of sensitivity is not permitted (no write down). 3) Discretionary Security Property uses an access matrix to specify DAC.

42. C. When a computer or network component fails, and the computer or the network continues to function, it is called a fault-tolerant system. For fault tolerance to operate, the system must be capable of detecting that a fault has occurred, and the system must then correct the fault or operate around it. In a fail-safe system, program execution is terminated, and the system is protected from being compromised when a hardware or software failure occurs and is detected.

43. C. When a computer or network component fails, and the computer or the network continues to function, it is called a fault-tolerant system. For fault tolerance to operate, the system must be capable of detecting that a fault has occurred, and the system must then correct the fault or operate around it. In a fail-safe system, program execution is terminated, and the system is protected from being compromised when a hardware or software failure occurs and is detected.

44. C. A security label is assigned to a resource to denote a type of classification or designation. This label can then indicate special security handling, or it can be used for access control. Once labels are assigned, they usually cannot be altered and are an effective access control mechanism.

45. D. Bell-LaPadula (BLP) is built on the state machine concepts. Focuses on confidentiality. This concept defines a set of allowable states in a system. Transition functions define the transition from one state to another upon receipt of an input. The objective of this model is to ensure that the initial state is secure and that the transitions always result in a secure state. BLP defines a secure state through three multi-level properties: 1) SSP states that reading of information by a subject at a lower level from an object at a higher level is not permitted (no read up). 2)

Security Property (Star*) states that writing of information by a subject at a higher level to an object at a lower level is not permitted (no write down). Discretionary Security Property (DS) uses an access matrix to specify discretionary access controls. The model prevents users and processes from reading above their security level. In addition, it prevents processes with any given classification from writing data associated with a lower classification. The "no write down" prevents placing data that is not sensitive but contained in a sensitive document into less sensitive files.

46. **A.** Whenever a hardware or software component of a trusted system fails, it is essential that the failure does not compromise the security policy requirements of that system. In addition, the recovery procedures should not also provide an opportunity for violation of the systems security policy. Trusted recovery also means that if a system fails, security remains intact when it is restored and does not allow any security breaches.

47. **A.** Since we want to maintain the backups offsite, it is always better to send Full Backups (Entire) because they contain a consistent base of the system. We perform the beginning of restoring a full backup. Remember that the backups stored offsite are, in most cases, in a secure place. Therefore, a full backup is the best practice for any network administrator. We do not have all we need to restore a system to a consistent state with incremental or differential backups. We need to start from the full backup. Offsite backup is not a valid backup method name.

48. **A.** Operational goals are daily activities that are reoccurring and provide continuous operation for an organization.

49. **A.** This is an absolute best practice in the software testing field, and you should always have to keep all your testing approaches with the results as part of the product documentation. This can help you if you have problems with some tasks or components of the software in the future; you can re-check your testing and results and see if the system was doing the jobs correctly and if anything changed from that environment.

50. **C.** With a separation of the two environments (test and development), we can get a more stable and more controlled environment. Since we are making test in the development environment, we do not want our production processes there; we also do not want to experiment things in our production processes. With a separation of the environments, we can get a more risk-free production environment and more control and flexibility over the test environment for the developers.

51. **A.** A Risk Management Framework provides a disciplined and structured process that integrates information security and risk management activities through design, implementation, and continuous monitoring for improvement. For risk management to succeed at all levels of the organization, the organization must have a consistent and practical approach to risk management applied to all risk management processes and procedures - which is the goal of a risk management framework.

52. **A.** The certification process assures that a system has passed a security assessment that qualifies the plan to deploy. The functionality and assurance evaluation method under ITSEC is F5 + E5, aligning with the TCSEC B3 rating of evaluation. Verified protection (A1) is aligned to F5 + E6 of ITSEC. The target of assessment describes how the security target is evaluated under the standard criteria model. The question addresses ITSEC and TCSEC evaluation models.

53. **A.** To filter web-based traffic, the organization needs to have a web-based firewall. The web-based firewall operates at Layer 7 of the open systems interconnection (OSI) model. A layer three device will only filter IP traffic. Answers A and C do not relate to the question. WAF is an intermediary device sitting between a web client and a web server. The web application firewall also analyzes the OSI Layer-7 messages for violations in the programmed security policy and is used as a security device protecting the web server from attack.

54. **A.** Strong authentication or Multi-factor authentication requires two levels of credentials. This feature prevents hackers from gaining access to servers with just a username and password. Adding a level of authentication enforces strong authentication. Key loggers can record keystrokes and save the information for a hacker to decipher a password. Configuration control supports change management principles. Shared services share information on servers between users and groups; this does not affect authentication. Session controls are used to terminate a session after a period of inactivity.

55. D. Inference is a database system technique used to attack databases where malicious users infer sensitive information from complex databases at a high level. The inference is a data mining technique used to find information hidden from regular users in basic terms. It is the intended result of aggregation. Data mining involves the running of queries within data warehouses.

56. C. Distributed and parallel DBMSs provide the same functionality as centralized DBMSs except in an environment where data is distributed across the sites on a computer network or across the nodes of a multiprocessor system. When databases are clustered together to perform and distribute data upon node failures, it is called a parallel database management system. All the clusters cooperate to keep data operating and distributed within the enterprise or organization.

57. C. In the traditional security model, all the data stored in the database and the users who access that data belong to the same security level. A multilevel secure database system assigns security levels to each transaction and data. The clearance level of a transaction is represented by the security level assigned to it, and the classification level gives the classification level of data. A multilevel secure database management system (MLS/DBMS) restricts database operations based on the security levels.

58. A. There are many other common cryptographic mistakes: implementations that repeat "unique" random values, digital-signature algorithms that do not properly verify parameters, or hash functions altered to defeat the very properties they are being used for. Cryptographic protocols are often used in ways unintended by the protocols' designers. For example, they are "optimized" in seemingly trivial ways that completely break their security—in this example, altering and design address a design flaw for crypto systems. Answer "D" can be omitted because it addresses a data exchange policy, not a design factor. Registering and tampering are not design factors for a crypto system.

59. A. The vulnerabilities associated with Industrial Control Systems are no different from regular systems. ICS that lack access control policies and standard use of insecure COTS products can impose risks. The most common vulnerabilities are Buffer overflow, Cross-Site Scripting, lack of proper access control policy, lack of password policy, poor patch management, lack of data protection policy, no maintenance of OS and security patches, outdated software utilization, lack of testing facilities, dual NIC usage, lack of remote access security, DoS and DDoS vulnerabilities, clear text utilization, lack of Intrusion Detection System (IDS) and Intrusion Prevention System (IPS), poor log maintenance, and lack of proper AV or Malware Protection software.

60. B. A buffer overflow condition exists when a program attempts to put more data in a buffer than it can hold or when a web program tries to put data in a memory area past a buffer size. Attackers use buffer overflows to corrupt the execution stack of a web application. By sending carefully crafted input to a web application, an attacker can cause the web application to execute arbitrary code – effectively taking over the machine. Injection flaws occur based on SQL commands.

61. D. Bluejacking is initiated by an attacker sending unsolicited messages to a user of a Bluetooth-enabled device. The actual messages do not cause harm to the user's device, but they are used to entice the user to respond in some fashion or add the new contact to the device's address book. This message-sending attack resembles spam and phishing attacks conducted against e-mail users. Bluejacking can cause harm when a user initiates a response to a bluejacking message sent with harmful intent. A countermeasure to bluejacking is to place the device in non-discoverable mode.

62. C. As a countermeasure, using a TCP/IP protocol would support the ping sweep task vs. a proprietary protocol that does not support ICMP commands. A ping sweep (also known as an ICMP sweep) is a basic network scanning technique used to determine which range of IP addresses map to live hosts (computers). Whereas a single ping will tell you whether one specified host computer exists on the network, a ping sweep consists of ICMP (Internet Control Message Protocol) ECHO requests sent to multiple hosts. If a given address is live, it will return an ICMP ECHO reply. Internet Control Message Protocol (ICMP) is a required TCP/IP standard defined in RFC 792, "Internet Control Message Protocol (ICMP)." With ICMP, hosts and routers that use IP communication can report errors and exchange limited control and status information.

63. A. The generation of key exchange and registration. Once keys have reached the end of their life cycle or become compromised, tickets need to be properly destroyed (and, if necessary, formally deactivated or deregistered) so the key will not continue to be used. In addition, some cryptographic keys may need to be archived to ensure access to data that has been encrypted and to verify digital signatures. Once a key has become deprecated, restricted, or defined as a legacy, the life cycle has ended for the key.

64. B. The equation used to calculate the number of symmetric keys needs is $N(N-1)/2$ = Number Keys $10(10-1)/2$ = 45 keys Symmetric encryption: 1) Speed is fast; 2) Size of cipher text is usually the same or less than that of the plain text; Number of keys used is the square of the number of participants; 4) Key exchange is a significant problem (hence, algorithms like the Diffie-Hellman Key Exchange algorithm are used), and 5) More storage space is required. Asymmetric encryption: 1) Slower in speed, 2) Cipher text size is usually more significant than that of the plain text; 3) Number of keys used is same as the number of participants; 4) Key exchange is no problem, and 5) Less storage space is required.

65. C. PKI binds public keys to entities, enables other entities to verify general key bindings, and provides the services needed for ongoing management of keys in a distributed system using X.509 protocol suite. Asymmetric key cryptography, also known as public-key cryptography, uses a class of algorithms in which Alice has a private key, and Bob (and others) have her public key. The public and private keys are generated at the same time. Data encrypted with one key can be decrypted with the other key.

66. B. The proper management of cryptographic keys is essential to the effective use of cryptography for security. Keys are analogous to the combination of a safe. If an adversary knows the combination, the strongest safe provides no security against penetration. Similarly, poor key management may easily compromise strong algorithms. Ultimately, the security of information protected by cryptography directly depends on the strength of the keys, the effectiveness of mechanisms and protocols associated with the keys, and the protection afforded the keys. Cryptography can be rendered ineffective through weak products, inappropriate algorithm pairing, poor physical security, and the use of vulnerable protocols.

67. A. A digital signature algorithm allows an entity to authenticate the integrity of signed data and the signatory identity. The recipient of a signed message can use a digital signature to validate claimed signatory. This is known as non-repudiation since the signatory cannot repudiate their signature. A digital signature algorithm is intended for electronic mail, electronic funds transfer, electronic data interchange, software distribution, data storage, and other applications that require data integrity assurance and data origin authentication. A digitally signed message will provide authentication (authentic), non-repudiation, and integrity. A message can be encrypted and digitally signed, which provides confidentiality, authentication, non- repudiation, and integrity.

68. D. DRM is any of several technologies used by publishers to control access to digital data (such as software, music, movies) and hardware, handling usage restrictions associated with a specific instance of digital work. A USB key has a proprietary "software key" on it. Some business software manufacturers use them to make sure the software is only on one machine. Instead of typing in a software key, the software requires that the USB Key be plugged in.

69. A. A digital signature results from completing a digital signature algorithm operating on data (e.g., a message) to be signed. When used appropriately, a digital signature can provide assurance of data integrity, origin authentication, and signatory non-repudiation. This includes data insertion, deletion, and modification. To ensure data integrity, a system must be able to detect unauthorized data modification. The goal is for the receiver of the data to verify that the data has not been altered. Confidentiality services restrict access to the content of sensitive data to only those individuals who are authorized to view the data. Confidentiality measures prevent the unauthorized disclosure of information to unauthorized individuals or processes. Identification and authentication services establish the validity of a transmission, message, and its originator. The goal is for the receiver of the data to determine its origin. Non-repudiation services prevent an individual from denying that previous actions had been performed. The goal is to ensure that the recipient of the data is assured of the sender's identity.

70. C. A secure hash function is a collision-resistant, one-way function. Collision resistance means that it is extremely difficult to find two different messages that will produce the same hash value. One way means that it is easy to compute the hash value from the input, but it is extremely difficult to reproduce the input from the hash value or to find another information that will produce the same hash value. Hash functions are often used to determine whether data has changed. Many algorithms and processes that provide a security service use a hash function as a component of the algorithm or process, including Keyed-hash message authentication code (HMAC), Digital signatures, Key derivation functions (KDFs), and random number generators (RNGs). Example A is an algorithm, while B is a secure hash standard.

71. **A.** A chosen-plaintext attack (CPA) is an attack model for cryptanalysis that presumes that the attacker can choose arbitrary plaintexts to be encrypted and obtain the corresponding cipher-texts. The goal of the attack is to gain some further information that reduces the encryption scheme's security. In the worst case, a chosen-plaintext attack could reveal the scheme's secret key.

72. **D.** When a building is designed, a threat assessment is conducted to see potential threats and vulnerabilities. The overall outcome of both will determine the level of risk when designing a building. The risks can be of any factors such as people, weather, disasters, and building access. In areas where crime exists, it is important to mitigate and prevent unauthorized access by installing fences, bollards, security guards, or any prevention method to counter and deter crime.

73. **C.** The situation produces a vulnerability for the environment. Since the control (policy) was not implemented, a weakness is produced within the physical environment. A threat exists when someone exploits the physical vulnerability. Risk is just the probability or likely hood that a threat will exploit a vulnerability. In this case, a threat can be some unauthorized person entering the datacenter.

74. **C.** Datacenters should be located within the core location of a building. This helps to reduce loss if a storm hits the building. The outside structure can absorb the level of impact.

75. **B.** Media must be protected from environmental and access control within an organization. Fire and natural weather disasters can destroy backup media, so having controls in place will prevent the destruction of the media material. Temperature, security access, and core locations are physical controls.

76. **D.** Evidence should be maintained in a secure (locked) location and in a manner that will not alter the physical properties of the evidence (temperature, light, moisture, cross-contamination, etc.). The Chain-of-Custody Form should capture the identity (name & signature) of the person removing the evidence from the evidence storage facility, as well as the time, date, and purpose of the removal. Everyone who has legitimate access to the evidence does not have to sign the Chain-of-Custody Form, only the person who removes it from the evidence storage facility.

77. **C.** Access control list provides the most detailed information for physical access and space zones. Color markings can be used, but the layer of physical controls and defense can be the best choice. The first layer is always the access control list, with the rest to follow.

78. **A.** The best choice is to have key cards installed. A biometric system should have one cross-over error rate. Security awareness training and security guards are a good choice, but they are more of administrative control. The organization needs physical and technical controls implemented.

79. **C.** Most generators have specifications on how long they will last based on fuel consumption. Having a backup plan to refuel is a good choice. Purchasing another generator with the same or lower specifications will not work. Users and their computers mostly control power restrictions. HVAC must always stay online.

80. **B.** When moisture occurs in a building, the cause can be directed towards the ventilation system. The airflow and heat dissipation must balance for the datacenter to become cool. If there is not enough air, heat will form, and condensation will build. The condensation can evolve into large water deposits around electrical equipment. When these issues occur, we must look at the entire datacenter and not individual server racks. The fire suppression system has no direct effect on the ventilation system.

81. **C.** Water sprinklers may be one of the most common means of fire suppression, but they are far from the best choice for extinguishing flames in a server room. Because water can cause irreparable damage to computer equipment and other critical electronics, it should be passed up in favor of gas-based (also known as the clean agent) fire suppression methods. While halon was the flame-smothering agent of choice in early gas fire suppression systems, it has since been replaced by non-toxic, non-corrosive, environmentally friendly gases that fight fire without harming server room equipment, fixtures, or personnel. FM-200 is a fire chemical agent replacement. Designed to flood an enclosure, FM-200 should be used where agents such as water, dry chemical, and carbon dioxide are unacceptable because they cause damage to electronic equipment or present a safety risk to people.

82. **C.** The third-lowest layer of the OSI Reference Model is the network layer. Suppose the data link layer is the one that defines the boundaries of what is considered a network. In that case, the network layer is the one that defines how internetworks (interconnected networks) function. The network layer is concerned with transmitting data between computers locally and remotely. In contrast, the data link layer only deals with devices that are local to each other. Layer 3 also filters IP addresses within Routers and Firewall. Layer 2 Filters MAC Addresses and uses switches at this level.

83. **D.** The IP Address 134.56.34.234 is a Class B address. 127.0.0.1 is a reserved IP address corresponding to the host computer. Known as the loopback address, 127.0.0.1 is used whenever a program needs to access a network service running on the same computer as itself. Although used as a testing and development address, the loopback address can access local services, such as web servers, that are usually only accessed over a network and have no local interface. Additionally, most modern operating systems that implement TCP/IP regard the name "localhost" equivalent to 127.0.0.1. The loopback address can also be used to troubleshoot Network Interface issues for hosts. Any IP Address designated with a socket such as this case should state 134.56.34.234: Port Number (i.e., 134.56.34.234:23 for Telnet). The format for Answer C is incorrect.

84. **A.** The process of protecting data in the cleartext and implementing authentication involves encapsulation (VPN) of the data transmitted. The point-to-point Modbus protocol has become a virtual standard for Remote Terminal Unit communications. During communication on a Modbus network, the protocol determines how each controller will know the device address, recognize a message addressed to it, determine the action to be taken and extract any information/data attached to it. A typical RTU in the field contains a central processor, set of Input /Output modules, and communication devices to connect to field devices. The RTUs are similar to Programmable Logic Controllers (PLCs - a small computer that controls relays, switches, coils, counters, and other devices.). PLCs are used within a local area and connected by a local area network, as RTUs are used in remote locations and connected by a Wide Area Network. Otherwise, both have CPU, I/O units, and communication ports. https://www.isa.org/standards-and-publications/isa-publications/intech-magazine/intech-whitepapers/SCADA/protocols/and-communication-trends/

85. **D.** Network convergence is the efficient coexistence of telephone, video, and data communication within a single network. Multiple communication modes in a single network offer convenience and flexibility not possible with separate infrastructures. Network convergence is also called media convergence. The technology uses various converged protocols such as Fiber Channel over Ethernet (FCoE), which encapsulates FC frames inside Ethernet frames and uses the Fiber Channel security model.

86. **A.** Unlike traditional telephone connections, which are tied to a physical location, VoIPs packet-switched technology allows remote numbers to be anywhere. This is convenient for users because calls can be automatically forwarded to their locations. This flexibility severely complicates the provision of E-911 service, which normally provides the caller's location to the 911 dispatch office. This means that an IP-based system has a longitude and latitude different from the user's location. For example, you are in New York, but your VoIP is in Miami.

87. **C.** The certificate-based authentication is based on the premise that you and only you have access to the secret information associated with your certificate. The website never sees your secret information, so your identity is secure (unlike password authentication). Unlike passwords, certificates are too big to remember, and the mathematical operations to prove that you have the associated secret information are too involved in performing manually. Therefore, certificate-based authentication must be performed by a computer. Fortunately, all popular browsers handle certificates and the associated math. The certificate and secret information are usually held on the

computer's hard drive, smart card (a portable device the size of a credit card), or a USB token (a portable device plugs into a USB port). When a website asks for user authentication, the browser accesses the certificate and secret information and performs the authentication on behalf of the user. The browser can automatically authenticate the user, so the user is unaware that the authentication took place.

88. **A.** DMZ (Demilitarized Zone) refers to a part of the network that is neither part of the internal network nor directly part of the Internet. Normally, DMZ is the area between your Internet access router and your bastion host (A bastion host is a computer on a network which is configured to withstand attacks). Bastion is another term to mean "locked down." DMZ is also known as Perimeter Network. DMZ adds a layer of security to an organization's internal network, and an external attacker has only had access to network devices and servers in the DMZ. An outside user needs one hop in the DMZ by creating a DMZ before accessing sensitive information inside the trusted network. DMZ typically holds web servers, FTP servers, Name servers (DNS), E-mail Servers, Honeypots.

89. **B.** When selecting cable or media, an organization must ensure that the attenuation, crosstalk, and noise ratio are specified. These factors determine if the media can withstand EMI and data loss based on its length and overall rating. Attenuation addresses the signal strength, crosstalk occurs when signal channels are crossed with another signaling channel, and noise produces distortion.

90. **B.** Firewalls reside at layers three and seven of the OSI model. Layer 7 checks applications, and layer 3 filters packets. In this scenario, FTP and the other protocols require an application-based firewall for screening. The purpose of the NAT is to perform as stated in the question, and the organization needs to update its configuration data. http://www.excitingip.com/205/what-are-packet-filtering-circuit-level-application-level-and-stateful-multilayer-inspection-firewalls/

91. **A.** Content delivery network (CDN) uses multiple servers in many geographic locations that improve deliveries of static and streaming content. Global content requests automatically get routed to the closest servers, speeding up page loads, maximizing bandwidth, and providing identical content regardless of site traffic spikes. Depending on traffic and the number of nodes, the network's algorithms select the best routing options to deliver optimum performance and avoid bottlenecks. The goal of a CDN is to serve content to end-users with high availability and high performance. CDNs serve a significant fraction of the Internet content today, including web objects (text, graphics, and scripts), downloadable objects (media files, software, documents), applications (e-commerce, portals), live streaming media, on-demand streaming media, and social network.

92. **C.** The physical types of network security protect from fire, unauthorized access, and natural disasters. Restrict physical access to systems, routers, firewalls, etc., by combining high-quality locks with secondary verification systems, such as biometric scanners. Security guards, IDS systems, video monitoring, and alarms are other ways to help keep areas secure. Password-protect and monitor physical access to all systems to ensure that only authorized users access data. Invest in fire detection and waterless fire suppression systems to protect data and equipment from damage.

93. **A.** Secure endpoints consist of firewalls, vulnerability management, anti-virus, and host-based intrusion software. Endpoints can be a server, mobile device, laptop, or printer. Since the management team needs to understand avenues to prevent intrusions, a host-based firewall would provide the best support.

94. **D.** File sharing involves using technology that allows internet users to share files housed on their individual computers. Peer-to-peer (P2P) applications, such as those used to share music files, are some of the most common forms of file-sharing technology. However, P2P applications introduce security risks that may put your information or your computer in jeopardy. Installation of malicious code - When you use P2P applications, it is difficult, if not impossible, to verify that the source of the files is trustworthy. Attackers often use these applications to transmit malicious code. Attackers may incorporate spyware, viruses, Trojan horses, or worms into the files. When you download the files, your computer becomes infected (see Recognizing and Avoiding Spyware and Recovering from Viruses, Worms, and Trojan Horses for more information). https://www.us-cert.gov/ncas/tips/ST05-007

95. D. The primary protocol indicated was IPSEC. IPSEC is a collection of protocols that assist in protecting communications over IP networks. IPsec protocols work together in various combinations to protect communications. AH is one of the IPsec security protocols that provide integrity protection for packet headers and data and user authentication. ESP is the second core IPsec security protocol. In the initial version of IPsec, ESP provided only encryption for packet payload data. When IPSEC is configured within the transport mode, only the payload is encrypted. The tunnel mode encrypts the headers, payload, and routing data. Since the routing information was not protected, the VPN is configured for the transport mode of operation.

96. A. It would cost more to purchase a new application by using the organization's budget. Requesting the vendor to upgrade the application to TLS reduces costs for the organization. Upgrading the application to TLS/SSL poses risks considering TLS/SSL offers backward compatibility. This means a TLS/SSL configuration can support older SSL connections and reduce the security protection provided by TLS. Installing a separate VLAN will not resolve the issue.

97. C. Private VLANs are used for network segregation when: Moving from a flat network to a segregated network without changing the IP addressing of the hosts. A firewall can replace a router, and then hosts can be slowly moved to their secondary VLAN assignment without changing their IP addresses. There is a need for a firewall with many tens, hundreds, or even thousands of interfaces. Using Private VLANs, the firewall can have only one interface for all the segregated networks. https://en.wikipedia.org/wiki/Private_VLAN

98. D. A MIM requires an attacker to monitor an open network session. Once authentication is complete, they may attack the client's computer to disable it and use IP spoofing to claim the client who was authenticated and steal the session. This attack can be prevented if the two legitimate systems share a secret key which is checked periodically. IP spoofing - an attacker may fake their IP address, so the receiver thinks they are the destination access. There are various forms and results to this attack. The attack may be directed to a specific computer addressed as though it is from that same computer. This may make the computer think that it is talking to itself. This may cause some operating systems such as Windows to crash or lock up. If the attack used half-open connections, a TCP/SYN Ack or Flood would occur. Session flooding and session attacks do not relate to this question since the session was not flooded with data packets.

99. B. Since the users can only view the data; they are restricted to read-only access. In LAB 2, the concept of role-based access control has been implemented. Role-based access control defines access for groups and roles. In this case, the role of an administrator or tester would have access to LAB 2 during working hours. Rule-based access control would apply if we were concerned with time, but MAC does not relate to the question.

100. C. Physical and logical access to any system will be granted based on least privilege. When establishing accounts, standard security principles of "least privilege" to perform a function must always be used, where administratively feasible. Access privileges should be limited to those with a genuine need to complete job responsibilities and procedures. For example, a root or privileged administrative account must not be used when a non-privileged account will do. Privileges must never be granted "in case" a user might need them.

101. B. The facility needs to address physical security devices as well. Under the defense-in-depth model, security occurs at different boundaries. In this case, protection exists at the door entry, so the company should assess physical entry systems for risks.

102. A. PACS operates access control and intrusion detection functions and comprises a suite of applications that serve as a mechanism for managing electronic access points and alarms. PACS produces automated transactional reports, documenting what activity took place. https://www.dhs.gov/xlibrary/assets/privacy/privacy_pia_dhs_pacs.pdf

103. B. Single sign-on (SSO) is a mechanism whereby a single action of user authentication and authorization can permit a user to access all computers and systems where he has access permission, without the need to enter multiple passwords. Single sign-on reduces human error, a significant component of systems failure and is therefore highly desirable but challenging to implement. Lightweight Directory Access Protocol (LDAP), Kerberos, and Smart Cards support SSO technologies. Kerberos can handle session authentication, and LDAP provides access to directory services. Credential-based authentication occurs with Kerberos and smart cards.

104. A. Authentication occurs at login and sessions. Two-factor authentication supports users' ability to log onto a system, and session authentication supports secure transmission. In this scenario, we are concerned about the user session where a man-in-the-middle attack (session high jacking) has occurred; this depends on IP Spoofing.

105. A. The process of auditing events or logging falls under accountability within the Identification, Authentication, Authorization, and Accountability (IAAA) scheme of operation. IAAA defines the scheme of the process: Identification - User Identity; Authentication - Validate identity; Authorization – Grant Access to Resources; Accounting – Maintains Audit.

106. C. The session ID or token binds the user authentication credentials (in the form of a user session) to the user HTTP traffic and the appropriate access controls enforced by the web application. The complexity of these three components (authentication, session management, and access control) in modern web applications, plus the fact that its implementation and binding resides on the web developer's hands (as web development framework do not provide strict relationships between these modules), makes the performance of a secure session management module very challenging. In this scenario, session management was used as a control measure. The web application session was closed after 10 minutes, an excellent control measure for having open sessions hijacked through MIM attacks. The website operates at port 443, not port 80.

107. D. Electronic authentication (e-authentication) is the process of establishing confidence in user identities electronically presented to an information system. The three forms of authentication are: 1) Something you know (pin and password); 2) Something you have (an ID badge or a cryptographic key); and 3) Something you are (a voice print or other biometric).

108. A. Security Access Markup Language (SAML) specifies three components: assertions, protocol, and binding. There are three assertions: authentication, attribute, and authorization. Authentication assertion validates the user's identity. Attribute assertion contains specific information about the user. Authorization assertion identifies what the user is authorized to do. The single most important requirement that SAML addresses are web browser single sign-on (SSO). SAML for Web browser SSO involves three parties. A user, an identity provider (IdP), and a Service provider (SP). The IdP stores information about the user in a database like Active Directory. The user connects to the SP and attempts to authenticate. If the SP recognizes the username, it delegates authentication to the IdP. The IdP validates the user against its identity database and then sends a SAML assertion about that user to the service provider. The SP then gives the user access to the application.

109. B. A credential management system is designed to ensure passwords and user logon information is protected, updated, aligns with the enterprise security standards. It provides a mechanism to ensure passwords are available. This is achieved via different system requirements and configurations and redundancy methods imposed for secure fail-over and recovery systems. When a system is to remain operable or available, it supports resources based on the CIA triad.

110. A. Identity-as-Service (IDaaS) is a cloud-based service that provides a set of identity and access management functions to target systems on customers' premises and in the cloud. IDaaS functionality includes: Identity governance and administration (IGA) consists of the ability to provision identities held by the service to target applications. Access provides user authentication, single sign-on (SSO), and authorization enforcement. Intelligence includes logging events and providing reporting to answer questions such as "who accessed what and when?"

111. A. One of the most daunting tasks for cloud solutions is to provide directory services and what security features are implemented. Cloud identity, federated identity, and directory synchronization are part of directory services offered through cloud-based computing. Cost is calculated after the requirements are developed.

112. A. In RBAC, access decisions are based on individual users' roles as part of an organization. Users take on assigned roles (such as a doctor, nurse, teller, or manager). Access rights are grouped by role name, and the use of resources is restricted to individuals authorized to assume the associated role. For example, within a hospital system, the doctor's part can include operations to perform a diagnosis, prescribe medication, and order laboratory tests; the role of the researcher can be limited to gathering anonymous clinical information for studies. The use of functions to control access can be an effective means of developing and enforcing enterprise-specific security policies and streamlining the security management process. Rule-based access control can be combined with role-based access control, such that the role of a user is one of the attributes in the ruleset. Some provisions of access control systems have rule-based policy engines in addition to a role-based policy engine.

113. **A.** Rule Bases Access Control (RuBAC) (as opposed to RBAC, role-based access control) allow users to access systems and information based on predetermined and configured rules. It is important to note that there is no commonly understood definition or formally defined standard for rule-based access control as there is for DAC, MAC, and RuBAC. Rule-based access is a generic term applied to systems that allow some form of organization-defined rules; therefore, rule-based access control encompasses a broad range of systems. RuBAC may, in fact be combined with other models, particularly RuBAC or DAC. A RuBAC system intercepts every access request and compares the rules with the user's rights to make an access decision. Most rule-based access control relies on a security label system, which dynamically composes a set of rules defined by a security policy. Security labels are attached to all objects, including files, directories, and devices. Sometimes roles to subjects (based on their attributes) are assigned as well. RuBAC meets the business needs as well as the technical needs of controlling service access. It allows business rules to be applied to access control. For example, customers who have overdue balances may be denied service access.

114. **A.** Mandatory access control (MAC) is used in environments where different levels of security are classified. It is defined as a sensitivity-based restriction, formal authorization subject to sensitivity. In MAC, the owner or user cannot determine whether access is granted or not. i.e., Operating system rights. Security mechanism controls access to all objects, and individuals cannot change that access. Mandatory access control (MAC) policy means that access control policy decisions are made by a central authority, not by the individual owner of an object. The owner cannot change access rights. An example of MAC occurs in military security. An individual data owner does not decide who has a Top Secret clearance, nor can the owner change the classification of an object from Top Secret to Secret.

115. **A.** Discretionary Access Control (DAC) defines the basic access controls for objects in a file system. This is the typical access control provided by file permissions, sharing, etc. Such access is generally at the discretion of the object's owner (file, directory, device, etc.). DAC provides a means of restricting access to objects based on the identity of the users or groups (subjects) that try to access those objects. Depending on a subject's access permissions, they may also pass permissions to other subjects. ACLs and owner/group/other access control mechanisms are the most common mechanism for implementing DAC policies. Even though not designed with DAC in mind, other mechanisms may have the capabilities to implement a DAC policy.

116. **D.** Authentication bypass vulnerabilities, like buffer overflows, are generally caused by programmers assuming that users will behave in a certain way and failing to foresee the consequences of users doing the unexpected. The safest method is to ensure applications apply correct coding and algorithms, and use a web application firewall to restrict traffic based on rule sets. When an application or device checks that the user has previously been authenticated, it is important that this check is effective. Authentication bypass vulnerabilities will occur if this is not the case. A simple example of this is when a simple parameter is appended to the end of a URL. For example, imagine a system that uses a parameter "auth" to signify if a user has been authenticated and prompts the login procedure if auth=0, switching it to auth=1 once a successful login occurs. As long as auth=1, the user remains authenticated and able to access restricted pages.

117. **A.** The IaM life cycle addresses account management from creation to deletion. When an account is first created, it is provisioned with appropriate privileges. During the useful lifetime of an account, these privileges are often modified, and the account is periodically reviewed to ensure that it has not been granted excessive privileges. When the account is no longer being used, such as when an employee leaves the company, it should be disabled as soon as possible. The three function areas for the important lifecycle are: Understand issues related to the provisioning of an account - For example, what is permission creep? Understand review - For example, which accounts are the most important to review during the identity and access provisioning life cycle? Understand the importance of revocation - For example, what should be done to a user account when an employee leaves the company?

118. A. Verification is the confirmation that a product meets identified specifications or requirements. Validation is the confirmation that a product appropriately meets its design function or the solution. http://softwaretestingfundamentals.com/verification-vs-validation/

119. A. Vulnerability Assessments include identifying key assets and resources, prioritization, quantifying the value of these assets and resources, identifying the vulnerabilities of these assets, and systematically eliminating or mitigating the risks for the most critical assets or resources. A vulnerability assessment usually includes mapping the network and systems connected to it, identifying the services and versions of services running, and creating a catalog of the vulnerable systems. Once the plans and vulnerabilities are identified, the organization can re-mediate the findings. A vulnerability assessment forms the first part of a penetration test typically. The additional step in a penetration test exploits any detected vulnerabilities to confirm their existence and determine the damage that might result from the vulnerability being exploited and its resulting impact on the organization. A vulnerability assessment is not intrusive and does not always require the same technical capabilities compared to a penetration test.

120. A. Pentesting is security testing in which assessors mimic real-world attacks to identify methods for circumventing the security features of an application, system, or network. Businesses conduct pentesting to determine how vulnerable and what impact does the organization faces based on attacks. They are not concerned about compliance status, just vulnerable points and exploitation. It often involves launching real attacks on real systems and data that use tools and techniques commonly used by attackers. Most pentesting involve looking for combinations of vulnerabilities on one or more systems that can be used to gain more access than could be achieved through a single vulnerability. Pentesting can also help determine: How well the system tolerates real-world-style attack patterns, the likely level of sophistication an attacker needs to compromise the system successfully, additional countermeasures that could mitigate threats against the system, and defenders' ability to detect attacks and respond appropriately.

121. A. Log management can benefit an organization in many ways. It helps to ensure that computer security records are stored for a while. Routine log reviews and analyses are beneficial for identifying security incidents, policy violations, fraudulent activity, and operational problems shortly after they have occurred and provide valuable information for resolving such issues. Logs can also help perform auditing and forensic analysis, support the organization's internal investigations, establish baselines, and identify operational trends and long-term problems.

122. D. Synthetic performance monitoring, sometimes called proactive monitoring, involves having external agents run scripted transactions against a web application. These scripts are meant to follow a typical user's steps–search, view product, log in, check out–to assess a user's experience. Traditionally, synthetic monitoring has been done with lightweight, low-level agents. Still, increasingly, these agents must run full web browsers to process JavaScript, CSS, and Asynchronous JavaScript and XML (AJAX) calls on page load. Unlike RUM, synthetics do not track real user sessions. This has a couple of important implications. First, because the script executes a known set of steps at regular intervals from a known location, its performance is predictable. That means it is more helpful in alerting than often noisy RUM data. Second, it is better for assessing site availability and network problems than RUM because it occurs predictably and externally, particularly if your synthetic monitoring has integrated network insight. For example, you can create a synthetic transaction that performs a customer's actions connecting to the site and browsing through its pages for a website. For databases, you can create transactions that connect to the database. You can then schedule these actions to occur at regular intervals to see how the database or website reacts and see whether your monitoring settings, such as alerts and notifications, react as expected.

123. B. The plan involves a black box where teams do not have access to IP and Webservers. Manual Testing requires human intervention to use the tools. Automated Testing is a testing technique that uses automation testing tools to control the environment set-up, test execution, and results reporting. It is performed by a computer and is used inside the testing teams. Manual-Support Testing involves testing all the functions performed by the people while preparing the data and using these data from an automated system. Testing teams conduct it. A software testing method verifies an application's functionality without having specific knowledge of the application's code/internal structure. Tests are based on requirements and functionality. Quality Assurance (QA) teams perform it. White Box Testing is a testing technique based on knowledge of the internal logic of an application's code and includes tests like coverage of code statements, branches, paths, conditions. Software developers perform it.

124. **B.** Negative testing is the process of applying as much creativity as possible and validating the application against invalid data. The intended purpose is to check errors and determine whether a bad request exists. Positive testing, often referred to as "happy path testing," is generally the first form of testing that a tester would perform on an application. It is the process of running test scenarios that an end-user would run for his use. Hence as implied, positive testing entails running a test scenario with only correct and valid data. If a test scenario does not require data, positive testing would require running the test according to application specifications.

125. **A.** Allowed data bounds and limits – Applications can use input fields that accept data in a certain range. For example, there can be an edit box into which you enter an integer number from 10 to 50 or an edit box that accepts the text of a specific length. To check the application's behavior, create a negative test that enters a value smaller than the lower bound or greater than the upper bound of the specified field. Another example of this negative test case is entering data that exceeds the data type limits. For instance, an integer value can normally contain values in the range of 10,000 – 50,000 (the number of bytes in memory limits the size). To check the application's behavior, you can create a negative test that enters a value exceeding the bounds. For instance, the test can enter a large number (100,000,000,000) into an integer field.
https://support.smartbear.com/articles/testcomplete/negative-testing-with-testcomplete/

126. **A.** Integration testing involves testing the different components of an application, e.g., software and hardware, in combination. This kind of combination testing ensures that they are working correctly and conforming to the requirements based on which they were designed and developed. Interface testing is different from integration testing in that interface testing is done to check that the various components of the application or system being developed are in sync with each other. In technical terms, interface testing helps determine that different functions like data transfer between the different elements in the system are happening according to how they were designed to happen. Negative testing is the process of applying as much creativity as possible and validating the application against invalid data.

127. **A.** It is a good practice to perform an annual review and re-certification of user accounts to verify if the account holder required continued access and whether the account has the level of privileges required. This can be achieved by implementing a continuous monitoring program to collect the data required for the defined measures and report on findings, automate the collection, analysis, and reporting of data where possible.

128. **B.** It is a sound control measure; every manager must review and update the monitoring program, revise the continuous monitoring strategy, and mature measurement capabilities to increase visibility into assets and awareness of vulnerabilities. This is to ensure security controls are effective and areas of risk tolerance are addressed. The idea of reporting incident activities from known threats and their impact on the organization is the least concern for the Security Manager.

129. **B.** When monitoring a network environment, it is important to stay abreast of trends and metrics. These can serve as key performance indicators of risk. If one device is causing 25 percent of all known issues, the organization is at risk. Any trend that is above the organization average for risk reduction is positive. Compliance status is mainly achieved through metrics and percentages. Administrative, Technical, and Management are references for controls.

130. **A.** One of the most important functions of continuous monitoring is to maintain the integrity of the data. This is important because servers and databases are often some of the most exposed and vital hosts on an organization's network. A server or database could fail due to a malicious or unintentional act or a hardware or software failure. Data should also be backed up regularly for legal and financial reasons. Security controls developed to indicate daily operational tasks and annual reviews should be implemented as well. Data Verification using log management software supports daily monitoring of failed and successful backups. Documentation is required to establish a trend analysis and metrics for backup activities and status (i.e., date, time, status, etc..). A backup verification operation is a combined task that should never be separated.

131. **B.** Organizations should regularly monitor training for all employees to determine when training is required by analyzing trends and metrics. Software programs can provide metrics that determine expiration or upcoming training. The training awareness should focus on the exact scheduling requirements for all personnel to include executive personnel. Acceptance of previous training may not support the organization since security awareness training is designed for organization-specific needs. D Organizations should analyze metrics related to awareness and exercise (e.g., percentage of users completing required awareness session or exposure, percentage of users with significant security responsibilities who have been trained in role-specific material).

132. **B.** When data is collected via continuous monitoring, it must be validated to determine its accuracy and purpose. The information gathered can be used for risk decisions, and changes are required for contingency plans. When tabletop exercises are conducted, it requires the updating of documentation as well. Documentation should constantly be reviewed when tabletop exercises are performed. Contingency plans are realigned based on metrics, trend analysis, vulnerabilities, and risks.

133. **D.** An automated test output will use programs to collect, analyze, sort, and display data. Manual output requires humans to determine status and metrics based on record keeping and various reports. Automated provides more accurate data and does not introduce human data collection. Manual data requires more time and collection from multiple feeds; it's best to use automation as continuous monitoring. Automated can provide data in real-time, while manual can be offset and latent.

134. **A.** SOC 1 is a report on controls at a service organization relevant to a user entity's internal control over financial reporting. A type 1 report focuses on a description of a service organization's system and on the suitability of the design of its controls to achieve the related control objectives included in the description as of a specified date. A type 2 report contains the same opinions as a type 1 report with an opinion on the operating effectiveness of the controls to achieve the related control objectives included in the description throughout a specified period. A type 2 report also includes a detailed description of the service auditor's tests of controls and results. The use of the report is restricted to the management of the service organization, user entities, and user auditors. SOC 2 reports on controls at a service organization relevant to security, availability, processing integrity, confidentiality, or privacy. SOC 3 is a trust service report for service organizations. Covers the same subject matter as SOC 2. Does not include a description of the service auditor's tests of controls and results. Also, the description of the system is less detailed than the description in a SOC 2 report. A seal can be issued on a service organization's website. The Canadian Institute of Chartered Accountants (CICA) administers a seal program for these engagements (if the CPA is licensed for the seal by the CICA). The use and distribution of the report are NOT restricted.

135. **A.** There are general best practices, developed by organizations like Scientific Working Group on Digital Evidence (SWGDE) and NIJ, to properly seize devices and computers. Once the scene has been secured and legal authority to take the evidence has been confirmed, devices can be collected. Any passwords, codes, or PINs should be gathered from the individuals involved, if possible, and associated chargers, cables, peripherals, and manuals should be collected. Thumb drives, cell phones, hard drives, and the like are examined using different tools and techniques, most often done in a specialized laboratory. First, respondents need to take special care with digital devices in addition to normal evidence collection procedures to prevent exposure to things like extreme temperatures, static electricity, and moisture.

136. **D.** For evidence to be admissible in court, the chain of custody and collection process must be done correctly. When the evidence at a crime scene is collected, a collection profile will help identify the information and help with transfer and storage policies. Since the data collected and the information presented to the court are different, it shows that the law of integrity has not been followed. A witness statement cannot support the mishandling of evidence, nor can an interview.

137. **A.** The challenge organizations face when collecting evidence after an incident is the metrics and trends used for future analysis. The information collected will help identify risks for the organization if it's correct. Privacy and style of written reports are the least concern. The most important feature is accurate data analysis. The courts will never support evidence since it is a mediator in the process of digital crimes.

138. **A.** Profiling measures the characteristics of everyday activity so that changes to it can be more easily identified. Examples of profiling are running file integrity, checking software on hosts to derive checksums for critical files,

and monitoring network bandwidth usage to determine the average and peak usage levels on different days and times. In practice, it is challenging to detect incidents accurately using most profiling techniques; organizations should use profiling as one of several detection and analysis techniques.

139. **A.** Content analysis involves the analysis of the purpose of the file. Context analysis is used to develop an impact for the file. Analysts can more accurately identify the data stored in many files by looking at their file headers. A file header contains identifying information about a file and possibly metadata that provides information about the file's contents. A file header could be in a file separate from the actual file data. Another effective technique for identifying the type of data in a file is a simple histogram showing the distribution of ASCII values as a percentage of total characters in a file. For example, a spike in the "space" A and E lines generally indicates a text file, while consistency across the histogram shows a compressed file. Other patterns are indicative of files that are encrypted or that were modified through stenography.

140. **A.** The business objectives of implementing an operational investigative program are threefold: 1). Maintain maximum system availability (99.999 percent or five-nines "uptime;" 2). Quickly restore system operations without losing information related to the interruption; 3). Preserve all required information as evidence should court action be warranted in an acceptable legal form. Definition of the process to prioritize the three key actions when an event occurs: 1) evidence retention, 2) system recovery, and 3) cause identification.

141. **A.** Computer storage devices (like hard disks or CD-ROMs) can store the equivalent of millions of pages of information. Additionally, a suspect may try to conceal criminal evidence; he or she might store it in random order with deceptive file names. This may require searching authorities to peruse all the stored data to determine which files are evidence. This sorting process can take weeks or months, depending on the volume of data stored, and it would be impractical and invasive to attempt this kind of data search on-site. Separation of duties can exist, but it is directed to the investigator who must participate in the investigation.

142. **A.** Legal limitations can cause many challenges in a civil case due to the rights to review and obtain data. In these cases, civil investigators can use due diligence investigations and computer investigations to uncover the complicated details of company management. These investigations can be a big help for companies facing due diligence, fraud, or other digital cases. Businesses affected by the theft of trade secrets or trademark infringement can also benefit from civil investigators, who can find the evidence needed to start a lawsuit that can mean compensation for businesses.

143. **A.** The initial action is to review the company's policies on email distribution before taking part in the forensic case. Due to the separation of duties, the System Administrators should disable the accounts and provide the data to the forensic examiner. The forensic examiner under separation of duties cannot address the employees about the case.

144. **D.** Electronic discovery (also known as e-Discovery or eDiscovery) is a type of investigation that works to discover information that is presented in an electronic format with the intent of using as evidence in litigation. In some ways, it is similar to many computer forensic investigations where evidence is analyzed, and then reviewed using a document review platform. Documents are reviewed as to their native file or as a portable document format (PDF) or tagged image file format (TIFF) after conversion. The platform provides investigators with the ability to search large amounts of electronically stored information (ESI) at one time. As a rule, when a client learns that it is a subject of an investigation, it is advisable to issue a litigation hold and document-preservation notice. Federal law provides severe criminal penalties for anyone who knowingly alters, destroys, mutilates, conceals, covers up, falsifies, or makes a false entry in any record, document, or tangible object with the intent to impede, obstruct, or influence the investigation.

145. **A.** Content analysis involves the analysis of the purpose of the file. Context analysis is used to develop an impact for the file. Analysts can more accurately identify the data stored in many files by looking at their file headers. A file header contains identifying information about a file and possibly metadata that provides information about the file's contents. A file header data could exist in separate versus an actual file. Another effective technique for identifying the type of data in a file is a simple histogram showing the distribution of ASCII values as a percentage of total characters in a file. For example, a spike in the "space" A and E lines generally indicates a text file, while consistency across the histogram indicates a compressed file.

146. D. The business objectives of implementing an operational investigative program are threefold: 1) Maintain maximum system availability (99.999 percent or five-nines "uptime"); 2) Quickly restore system operations without losing information related to the interruption; 3) Preserve all information that may be needed as evidence, in an acceptable legal form, should court action be warranted. Definition of the process to prioritize the three key actions when an event occurs: Evidence retention, system recovery, and cause identification.

147. D. Cloud computing provides several benefits to organizations, such as increased flexibility, scalability, and reduced cost. However, it offers several challenges for digital forensics and criminal investigation. Some of these challenges are the dependence of forensically valuable data on the deployment model, multiple virtual machines running on a single physical machine, and multiple tenancies of clients. When investigations occur, the chain of custody should have adhered to; and the cloud architect should be reviewed before removing data since IaaS, SaaS, and PaaS include different data protection responsibilities. SLAs should be developed before engaging cloud operations. Once the business relationship starts, the development of an SLA may cause additional risks for the investigation.

148. A. A cloud SLA should specify the security performance requirements that the service provider is to meet. This would include describing security performance metrics for protecting data, such as data reliability, data preservation, and data privacy. Cleary defines the access rights of the cloud service provider and the customer and their respective responsibilities for securing the data, applications, and processes to meet all business requirements. Describe what would constitute a breach of security and how and when the service provider is to notify the agency when the requirements are not met.

149. D. The initial action is to review the company's policies on email distribution before taking part in the forensic case. Due to the separation of duties, the System Administrators should disable the accounts and provide the data to the forensic examiner – which would provide the most support.

150. C. An SLA serves as the official source in determining the liability in the cloud. The SLA should be developed and approved before investigations. An SLA notice is executed once the investigation starts.

151. A. Signature-based detection is highly effective at detecting known threats, but largely ineffective at detecting previously unknown threats, threats disguised by evasion techniques, and many variants of known threats. For example, if an attacker modified the malware in the previous example to use a file name of "freepics2.exe," a signature looking for "freepics.exe" would not match it.

152. A. To enhance the ability to identify inappropriate or unusual activity, organizations may integrate the analysis of vulnerability scanning information, performance data, network monitoring, and system audit record (log) information using SIEM tools. SIEM tools are a type of centralized logging software that can facilitate the aggregation and consolidation of logs from multiple information system components. SIEM tools can also facilitate audit record correlation and analysis. The correlation of audit record information with vulnerability scanning information is important in determining the veracity of the vulnerability scans and correlating attack detection events with scanning results. Log management is integrated into SIEM tools.

153. B. Continuous monitoring is an ongoing effort within daily operations that helps to monitor a system or an organization's assets for events and changes. A well-implemented continuous monitoring program will: 1) verify compliance with information security requirements derived from organizational missions and business functions, federal legislation, directives, regulations, policies, and standards and guidelines, 2) help to maintain visibility into the security of the assets, 3) offer interoperability with other products such as help desk, inventory management, configuration management, and incident response solutions, and 4) allow for data consolidation into SIEM tools and dashboard products.

154. B. Data loss is the exposure of proprietary, sensitive, or classified information through either data theft or data leakage. Data theft occurs when data is intentionally stolen or exposed, such as espionage or employee disgruntlement. Data leakage is the inadvertent exposure of data, such as a lost or stolen laptop, an employee storing files using an Internet storage application, or an employee saving files on a USB drive to take home. An effective data loss prevention (DLP) strategy includes data inventory and classification; metric data collection; policy development for data creation, use, storage, transmission, and disposal; and tools to monitor data at rest, in use, and in transit(motion). There are a variety of tools available for DLP. Typical network and security tools such as network analysis software, application firewalls, and intrusion detection and prevention systems can be used to monitor data and its contents as it is transmitted. Specially purposed DLP software also exists with port and endpoint control, disk and file encryption, and database transaction monitoring. These tools may be specialized network traffic monitors or software agents installed on desktops, laptops, and servers. DLP tools have built-in detection and mitigation measures such as alerting via email, logging activities, and blocking transmissions. Data in motion is data that needs to be protected when in transit, i.e., data on the wire. This includes channels like HTTP/S, FTP, IM, P2P, SMTP, and email. Data in use is data that resides on the end-user workstation and needs to be protected from being leaked through removable media devices like USB, DVD, CD's, etc. will fall under this category. Data at rest is data that resides on file servers and DBs and needs to be monitored from being getting leaked will fall under this category.

155. **C.** The goal of inventory management is to have a complete, up-to-date, and accurate view of all network components, including PCs, servers, printers, hubs, routers, switches, and software—everything that comprises the IT infrastructure. At a minimum, inventory management should tell you the device class and installed on the device (profiles). Thus, inventory management provides the "actual" state of all infrastructure components for any given time frame. This means that you know what you have and where it is located—across the entire enterprise. Implementing automated inventory management is foundational—and critical—to configuration management, IT asset management, and all service management disciplines. By delivering a clear view into network assets, it provides a host of direct (as well as indirect) benefits. Inventory management is about capturing the basics—what assets are on hand, where they reside, and who owns them. It is about maintaining an accurate, up-to-date view of owned hardware and software assets so that at any time, you can see an "actual state" of the components that comprise your infrastructure. Configuration management adds a relationship dynamic, such that you can associate each item with other items in the inventory. In configuration management, classes and components, upstream and downstream, and parent/child relationships establish relationships between each CI (configuration item). Furthermore, it involves processes around planning and identifying CI structures, having a controlled environment for changing CIs, and reporting on the status of CIs. IT asset management (ITAM) is a much broader discipline, adds several management dimensions, and involves a much broader base on stakeholders. First, it introduces the financial aspects of assets, including cost, value, and contractual status. ITAM also refers to the full lifecycle management of IT assets, from the point of acquisition or procurement through disposition, which together accounts for a comprehensive "expected state." Taken together, ITAM is designed to manage the physical, contractual, and financial aspects of those assets.

156. **D.** Configuration Management (CM) refers to a discipline for evaluating, coordinating, approving, or disapproving, and implementing changes in artifacts used to construct and maintain software systems. An artifact may be a piece of hardware or software or documentation. CM enables the management of artifacts from the initial concept through design, implementation, testing, baselining, building, release, and maintenance. CM is intended to eliminate the confusion and error brought about by different versions of artifacts at its heart. Artifact change is a fact of life: plan for it or plan to be overwhelmed by it. Changes are made to correct errors, provide enhancements, or simply change control.

157. **B.** Set up a centralized, relational CMDB-based repository: Ensure that there is a centralized repository—one that is capable of serving as a CMDB—to hold inventory items and, eventually, financial and lifecycle aspects of those assets with ITAM processes. It is a good practice for organizations to centralize their inventory. When different divisions have their list, it creates more risks.

158. **B.** Storage capacity is vital for many VMs with a SAN environment. A configuration management profile that is traceable can provide data on a VSAN storage setting. Having a CMBD will better enable an organization to manage and foresee issues with storage capacity and plan for changes.

159. **D.** Configuration management imposes many issues to implement and develop cloud and virtual solutions. The challenges are: 1) Flexibility - maintaining flexibility enabling a swift response to ever-changing market dynamics? You might need to sway outside of set IT management processes and workflows, taking shortcuts to accelerate

changes while you still must stay in control. 2) Visibility (Traceability) - It is tremendously challenging to analyze the overwhelming amount of configuration information separating the critical from non-critical. 3) Multiple Environments - multiple IT environments typically serve different teams and might be managed by different groups. 4) Change Validation (Auditing) - what is requested to be changed and what comprises the change typically is not captured (files to be touched, parameters to be updated).

160. **B.** Configuration management imposes many issues to implement and develop cloud and virtual solutions. The challenges are: 1) Flexibility - maintaining flexibility enabling a swift response to ever-changing market dynamics? You might need to sway outside of set IT management processes and workflows, taking shortcuts to accelerate changes while you still must stay in control. 2) Visibility (Traceability) - It is tremendously challenging to analyze the overwhelming amount of configuration information separating the critical from non-critical. 3) Multiple Environments - multiple IT environments typically serve different teams and might be managed by different groups. 4) Change Validation (Auditing) - what is requested to be changed and what comprises the change typically is not captured (files to be touched, parameters to be updated).

161. **C.** Least privilege refers to the security objective of granting users only those accesses they need to perform their official duties. Data entry clerks, for example, may not have any need to run analysis reports of their database.

162. **A.** Separation of duties refers to dividing roles and responsibilities so that a single individual cannot subvert a critical process. For example, in financial systems, one person should issue checks. Rather, one person initiates a payment request, and another authorizes that same payment.

163. **C.** Log management can benefit an organization in many ways. It helps to ensure that computer security records are stored in sufficient detail for an appropriate period. Routine log reviews and analyses are beneficial for identifying security incidents, policy violations, fraudulent activity, and operational problems and providing helpful information. Logs can also help perform auditing and forensic analysis, support the organization's internal investigations, establish baselines, and identify operating trends and long-term problems.

164. **C.** The organization's first line of defense is an effective information protection program. To meet this need, adequate internal controls must be implemented. These controls include adequate separation of duties for sensitive job functions or transactions and required vacation time or job rotation schedules. A surprising number of fraudulent occurrences are discovered when employees cannot report to work due to some unexpected event such as illness. A major financial institution uncovered a scheme that drained as much as $5 million through fraudulent wire transfers in a recent case. The breach was discovered only after a cashier, one of the perpetrators, died suddenly.

165. **B.** Providing adequate computer security requires a comprehensive approach that considers various areas both within and outside the computer security field. This comprehensive approach extends throughout the entire information life cycle. Like other IT systems, security is best managed if planned for throughout the IT system's life cycle failure. Classification and categorization are two of the most important aspects of the information lifecycle. Classification ensures that the appropriate clearance exists, while categorization evaluates the level of impact based on the CIA Triad. There are many models for the IT system lifecycle, but most contain five primary phases: initiation, development/acquisition, implementation, operation, and disposal. Not following a life cycle usually results in written policies and procedures that are not mapped to and supported by security activities. Severe disconnect and confusion between the different individuals throughout the organization attempting to protect company assets. No way of assessing the progress and ROI of spending and resource allocation. No way of fully understanding the security program deficiencies and having a standardized way of improving the deficiencies. No assurance of compliance to regulations, laws, or policies. Relying fully on technology as all security solutions. A patchwork of point solutions and no holistic enterprise solution.

166. **D.** Typically, a service level agreement covers Uptime which applies to important equipment, software, or services that your business needs. The uptime applies to servers, cloud services (like email or web hosting), or other vital parts of your IT system. This should be reviewed whenever the environment changes. For example, your IT

supplier might guarantee 99.9% uptime for your cloud backup system. Response times measure how long it takes your IT supplier to respond when you raise a support request. Usually, support requests must be raised in a specific way (often through an online system), making sure you have a good IT support process in place. This should be reviewed whenever the environment changes. For example, your IT supplier might promise to respond to critical problems within 15 minutes. SLA's are designed to be quick and effective. The MTBF should never exceed uptime. This means the MTBF is occurring so often, and it has a longer duration than uptime. MTBF and MTTR should be indirectly proportional. This means that the time between repairs should take less time, and the time between failures should be increasing. For example, MTBF is 1 hour, and MTTR is 10 minutes.

167. **D.** Data is at the core of IT security concerns for any organization. Cloud computing does not change the concept, but cloud computing does bring an added focus because of the distributed nature of its infrastructure and the shared responsibilities. Security considerations apply to data at rest (held on some form of storage system) and data in motion (being transferred over some form of communication link), which may need consideration when using cloud computing services. An extra consideration is when cloud computing handles encryption keys or key storage.

168. **D.** Object reuse means that an object is provided, such as a file, no data from its previous use is accessible. Assurance requires testing for obvious flaws and obvious bypass. When a software program overwrites data, it is injecting object reuse assurance to ensure that any residual data does not remain. A degausser does not assure that object reuse will be safe because it can destroy a drive. Coercively - reducing the magnetic field to zero - works with degaussing.

169. **B.** During the detection phase of incident management, the goal is to detect and block intrusive activity. An IDS will send alerts based on intrusive activity. An IPS will do the same and block an attack. The organization needed an IPS which must be in-band with the communication path. The issue is that the network perimeter needed to be protected. The host-based protection will not work in this case.

170. **D.** Containment is important before an incident overwhelms resources or increases damage. Most incidents require containment, so that is an important consideration early in the course of handling each incident. Containment provides time for developing a tailored remediation strategy. An essential part of containment is decision-making (e.g., shut down a system, disconnect it from a network, disable certain functions). Such decisions are much easier to make if there are predetermined strategies and procedures for containing the incident. Organizations should define acceptable risks in dealing with incidents and develop strategies accordingly. Containment strategies vary based on the type of incident. For example, the strategy for containing an email-borne malware infection is quite different from that of a network-based DDoS attack. Organizations should create separate containment strategies for each major incident type, with criteria documented clearly to facilitate decision-making.

171. **C.** After an incident has been contained; eradication may be necessary to eliminate components of the incident, such as deleting malware and disabling breached user accounts, and identifying and mitigating all exploited vulnerabilities. During eradication, it is important to identify all affected hosts within the organization to be remediated. For some incidents, eradication is either not necessary or is performed during recovery.

172. **A.** Organizations trying to share information with external organizations should consult with their legal department before initiating coordination efforts. There may be contracts or other agreements that need to be put into place before discussions occur. An example is a nondisclosure agreement (NDA) to protect the confidentiality of the organization's most sensitive information. Organizations should also consider any existing requirements for reporting, such as sharing incident information with an ISAC or reporting incidents to a higher-level computer incident response team (CIRT).

173. **C.** In recovery, administrators restore systems to regular operation, confirm that the systems are functioning normally, and (if applicable) remediate vulnerabilities to prevent similar incidents. Recovery may involve such actions as restoring systems from clean backups, rebuilding systems from scratch, replacing compromised files

with clean versions, installing patches, changing passwords, and tightening network perimeter security (e.g., firewall rule sets, boundary router access control lists). Higher levels of system logging or network monitoring are often part of the recovery process. Once a resource is successfully attacked, it is often attacked again, or other resources within the organization are attacked similarly.

174. **B.** In recovery, system administrators restore systems to normal operations and remediate vulnerabilities to prevent similar attacks from occurring again. This may include rebuilding systems, installing patches, and implementing tighter network perimeter security controls.

175. **C.** We are not concerned about previous organizations. One of the most important parts of incident response is the most often omitted learning and improvement. Each incident response team should evolve to reflect new threats, improved technology, and lessons learned. Holding a "lessons learned" meeting with all involved parties after a major incident, and optionally periodically after lesser incidents as resources permit, can be extremely helpful in improving security measures and the incident handling process itself. Multiple incidents can be covered in a single lesson learned meeting. This meeting provides a chance to achieve closure with respect to an incident by reviewing what occurred, what was done to intervene, and how well the intervention worked.

176. **C.** Attackers can use various ICMP types and codes to perform reconnaissance or manipulate network traffic flow. However, ICMP is needed for many valuable things, such as getting reasonable performance across the Internet. Some firewall policies block all ICMP traffic, but this often leads to problems with diagnostics and performance. Other common policies allow all outgoing ICMP traffic but limit incoming ICMP to those types and codes needed for Path Maximum Transmission Unit (PMTU) discovery (ICMP code 3) and destination reachability. The ping command (ICMP code 8) is an important network diagnostic. Still, incoming pings are often blocked by firewall policies to prevent attackers from learning more about the internal topology of the organization's network. The session failed because there were no echo replies from the web. ICMP allowed incoming and blocked outbound ping commands.

177. **B.** Another common problem with encryption over the wire is that network security devices cannot perform stateful application layer inspection on the contents of the encrypted data stream. This is a major problem in the firewall world, where modern firewalls, such as the ISA Server 2004 firewall, can perform both stateful packet and application layer inspection. The problem is that advanced firewalls can only perform stateful packet inspection (not application layer inspection) on encrypted communications because the firewall does not have access to the encrypted application layer contents; thus, attackers can easily hide their exploits from the firewall's application layer inspection mechanisms by using encrypted tunnels. As it is with firewalls, so it is with NIDS. The NIDS needs to listen to all traffic moving past its interface and compare that traffic with its rules for legitimate and illegitimate communications.

178. **B.** Domain Name System Blacklists, also known as DNSBLs or DNS Blacklists, are spam blocking lists that allow a website administrator to block messages from specific systems with a history of sending spam. As their name implies, the lists are based on the Internet's Domain Name System, which converts complicated, numerical IP addresses such as 66.171.248.182 into domain names like example.net, making the lists much easier to read use, and search. If the maintainer of a DNS Blacklist has in the past received spam of any kind from a specific domain name, that server would be "blacklisted," and all messages sent from it would be either flagged or rejected from all sites that use that specific list. A whitelist is a list or register of entities provided a particular privilege, service, mobility, access, or recognition. Entities on the list will be accepted, approved, and recognized. Greylisting is a method of defending e-mail users against spam. A mail transfer agent (MTA) using greylisting will "temporarily reject" any email from a sender it does not recognize. If the mail is legitimate, the originating server will try again after a delay, and if sufficient time has elapsed, the email will be accepted. Blocking outbound SMTP traffic will not stop malware or user indiscretions, but it will stop spamming malware using your Internet connection as a conduit for SPAM.

179. **B.** When the NIDS encounters encrypted traffic, it can only perform a packet-level analysis since the application layer contents are inaccessible. Given that exploits against today's networks are primarily targeted against network services (application layer entities), the packet-level analysis ends up doing very little to protect our core business assets.

180. **A.** Dynamic application security testing (DAST) is a process of testing an application or software product in an operating state. It is helpful for industry-standard compliance and general security protections for evolving projects. IT professionals contrast dynamic application security testing (DAST) with another type of testing, static application security testing (SAST). Whereas DAST involves operational testing, SAST consists of looking at the source code and theorizing about security vulnerabilities or spotting design and construction flaws with potential vulnerability.

181. **D.** Zero-day exploits pose some of the most serious risks to users everywhere. The absence of a patch means that it is up to users (and whatever security products they use) to protect against these attacks. One of the tools used in mitigating these attacks is a virtual sandbox (signature-based malware defense) that allows for on-the-fly analysis of various threats entering an organization's network. This allows an organization to detect attacks that use zero-day exploits without any necessary updates, providing immediate protection to users. Virtualizing a server can provide some security benefits. Running a server within a hypervisor provides a sandbox, limiting the impact of a compromise, and the hypervisor might provide a smaller attack surface than a host operating system would, reducing the possibility of expanding a successful compromise outside the guest OS.

182. **C.** Honeypots can be setup inside or outside a DMZ. Honeypots are hosts with no authorized users other than the honeypot administrators because they serve no business function; all activity directed at them is considered suspicious. Attackers will scan and attack honeypots, giving administrators data on new trends and attack tools, particularly malware. However, honeypots are a supplement to, not a replacement for, other security controls such as intrusion detection and prevention systems. If an organization uses honeypots, qualified incident handlers and intrusion detection analysts should manage them. The legality of honeypots has not been established; therefore, organizations should carefully study the legal ramifications before planning any honeypot deployments.

183. **B.** Anti-Malware Testing Standards Organization (AMTSO) is an international non-profit organization set up in 2008[1] to address a perceived need for improvement in the quality, relevance, and objectivity of anti-malware testing methodologies. According to the AMTSO web site, the organization's charter currently lists the following objectives: 1) Providing a forum for discussions related to the testing of anti-malware and related products, 2) Developing and publicizing objective standards and best practices for testing of anti-malware and related products, 3) Promoting education and awareness of issues related to the testing of anti-malware and related products, and 4) Providing tools and resources to aid standards-based testing methodologies.

184. **A.** The primary function of NAT is to assign a private host a public address to access the Internet. The private host uses a private IP address for communication within the internal network. Upon receiving a packet destined to the Internet, the NAT device translates the source IP address in the header into a valid public network address and records the entry. While NAT alters the Local IP of end systems to Public IPs for communication over the Internet, Proxy provides application-level security to end systems. It mitigates vulnerabilities that may directly affect the end systems. PAT is a type of NAT where the multiple private IP addresses are mapped into a single public IP (many-to-one) by using ports.

185. **B.** A full backup provides the fastest restoration process for a recovery strategy. When doing backups, it is essential to perform a full first, then incremental afterward. Remote journaling is the best method to support real-time synchronization. Reference the following link for additional information for this question: http://www.semais.net/Backup%20and%20Recovery.pdf

186. **D.** Organizations should deploy vulnerability remediation to all systems with the vulnerability, even for systems that are not at immediate risk of exploitation. Vulnerability remediation should also be incorporated into the organization's standard builds and configurations for hosts. There are three primary methods of remediation that can be applied to an affected system: installing a software patch, adjusting a configuration setting, and removing the affected software. Security Patch Installation is applying a security patch (also called a "fix" or "hotfix") to repair the vulnerability since patches contain code that modifies the software application to address and eliminate the problem. Patches downloaded from vendor websites are typically the most up-to-date and are likely free of malicious code.

186. B. Whenever possible and appropriate, many newer applications provide a feature that checks the vendor's website for updates. This feature can be handy in minimizing the level of effort required to identify, distribute, and install patches. However, some organizations may not wish to implement this feature because it might interfere with their configuration management process. A recommended option would be a locally distributed automated update process, where the patches are made available from the organization's network. Applications can then be updated from the local network instead of from the Internet.

187. C. While non-standard systems and legacy computers can hamper a widespread deployment, personnel issues can be an even more significant challenge. System owners (and computer users) may have some initial qualms about giving administrators access to their computers to another group and having that group regularly install and update software. Their concerns include the following issues: 1) the agent software may decrease computer performance or stability, 2) the patches being installed may cause unexpected problems with existing software, 3) a user may lose data when the enterprise patching application reboots the computer to install a patch, 4) the enterprise patching application may present a new security risk in and of itself, and 5) a mobile user may become frustrated and confused when the enterprise patching application attempts to install a broad set of patches as soon as the mobile user connects to the network. These concerns should be discussed with system owners and computer users. All of them can be addressed by good communication, a carefully phased roll-out, and the selection of a robust and secure enterprise patch management tool.

188. A. As changes are made to baseline configurations, the new baseline becomes the current version, and the previous baseline is no longer valid but is retained for historical purposes. All documentation should host the appropriate references and titles for the software or hardware. If there are issues with a production release, retention of previous versions allows for a rollback or restoration to a previous secure and functional version of the baseline configuration. Additionally, archiving previous baseline configurations is helpful for incident response and traceability support during formal audits.

189. B. The configuration management (technical) focuses on how any change to the "product" should be done. Configuration management documents how changes will be monitored and controlled. It is a process of defining configurable items (product, service, result, component) and managing changes to such things. It can be considered as a version control system for the product. The change management (administrative) focuses on how any "process" should be done. It is relevant to many kinds of changes to the project. For this process, a change management plan should be prepared to manage how the changes will be handled, evaluated, documented, and collected throughout the project's life cycle.

190. D. Security impact analysis is the analysis conducted by qualified staff within an organization to determine how changes to the information system affect the system's security posture. Because information systems are typically in a constant state of change, it is essential to understand the impact of changes on the functionality of existing security controls and in the context of organizational risk tolerance. Security impact analysis is incorporated into the documented configuration change control process. The analysis of the security impact of a change occurs when changes are analyzed and evaluated for adverse effects on security; preferably before they are approved and implemented, but also in the case of emergency/unscheduled changes. Once the changes are implemented and tested, a security impact analysis (and/or assessment) is performed to ensure that the changes have been implemented as approved and determine any unanticipated effects of the change on existing security controls.

191. A. The primary objectives of the Baseline Change Control Procedure are to describe the change process. It supports incorporating changes in a disciplined and timely manner, maintaining clear traceability for all changes to the approved baseline, and obtaining appropriate approval authority before implementing changes.

192. B. Two or more organizations with similar or identical system configurations and backup technologies may enter into a formal agreement to serve as alternate sites for each other or enter a joint contract for an alternate site. This type of site is set up via a reciprocal arrangement or memorandum of understanding (MOU). A reciprocal agreement should be entered into carefully because each site must be able to support the other, in addition to its own workload, in the event of a disaster. This type of agreement requires the recovery sequence for the systems from both organizations to be prioritized from a joint perspective, favorable to both parties. Testing should be conducted at the partnering sites to evaluate the different processing thresholds, compatible system and backup configurations, sufficient telecommunications connections, compatible security measures, and the sensitivity of data that might be accessible by other privileged users, in addition to the functionality of the recovery strategy.

193. **D.** Regardless of the type of alternate site chosen, the facility must support system operations defined in the contingency plan. The three alternate site types commonly categorized in their operational readiness are cold sites, warm sites, or host sites. Other variations or combinations can be found, but generally, all variations retain similar core features found in one of these three site types. Progressing from basic to advanced, the sites are described as follows: Cold Sites (not immediately available) are typically facilities with adequate space and infrastructure (electric power, telecommunications connections, and environmental controls) to support information system recovery activities. Warm Sites are partially equipped office spaces that contain some or the entire system hardware, software, telecommunications, and power sources. Hot Sites (expensive) are appropriately sized to support system requirements and configured with the necessary system hardware, supporting infrastructure, and support personnel. As discussed above, these three alternate site types are the most common. There are also variations and hybrid mixtures of features from any one of the three. Each organization should evaluate its core requirements to establish the most effective solution. Two examples of variations to the site types are: 1) Mobile Sites are self-contained, transportable shells custom-fitted with specific telecommunications and system equipment necessary to meet system requirement; 2) Mirrored Sites are fully redundant facilities with automated real-time information mirroring. Mirrored sites are identical to the primary site in all technical respects.

194. **C.** The most common example of this in-built redundancy is systems or devices which have redundant onboard power in the event of a power supply failure. In addition to redundant power, it is also common to find redundant network interface cards (NICs) and redundant disk controllers. Some applications and systems are so critical that they have more stringent up-time requirements than can be met by redundant standby systems or spare hardware. These systems and applications typically require what is commonly referred to as a high-availability (HA) or failover cluster. A high-availability cluster employs multiple systems that are already installed, configured, and plugged in. If a failure causes one of the systems to fail, then the other can be seamlessly leveraged to maintain the service's availability or application. RAID 0: Striped Set As is suggested by the title, RAID 0 employs striping to increase reading and writing performance. By itself, striping offers no data redundancy, so RAID 0 is a poor choice if data recovery is the reason for leveraging RAID. RAID 1: Mirrored Set This RAID level is perhaps the simplest of all RAID levels to understand. RAID 1 creates/writes an exact duplicate of all data to an additional disk. The write performance is decreased, though the read performance can see an increase. Mirroring is the most obvious and basic of the fundamental RAID concepts and is simply used to complete data redundancy by writing the same data to multiple hard disks. Striping is a RAID concept focused on increasing the read and write performance by spreading data across multiple hard disks. With data being spread among multiple disk drives, reads and writes can be performed parallel across multiple disks rather than serially on one disk.

195. **D.** A UPS usually provides 30 to 60 minutes of temporary backup power to permit a graceful shutdown. A UPS can also protect against power fluctuations by filtering incoming administration and providing a steady power source. If high availability is required, a gas- or diesel-powered generator may be needed. The generator can be wired directly into the site's power system and configured to start automatically when a power interruption is detected. A combination UPS/generator system can provide clean, secure power for a system, provided fuel is available for the generator. Fuel availability should be considered for those who opt for a UPS/generator to support their system environment. HA is a process where redundancy and failover processes are built into a system to maximize uptime and availability. The concept of HA is to achieve an uptime of 99.999 percent or higher, which equates to just a few minutes per year of downtime. Several vendors offer HA products and services designed to minimize downtime by building redundancy and resiliency into the architecture. HA can be an expensive option for systems, with the same hardware and special failover software to eliminate any single point of failure. Normally, there are higher cost maintenance and support requirements associated with HA systems. Therefore, HA is not a viable option for many systems and should be considered only for those systems that cannot tolerate downtime. Examples of this may be air traffic systems and financial systems. Also, HA systems cannot replace a solid backup strategy, as a corruption of data on a system may propagate through an HA system, making the system unusable. Without a backup of the system separate from the system itself, recovery may not be possible.

196. **A.** The Activation/Notification Phase describes activating the plan based on outage impacts and notifying recovery personnel. The Recovery Phase details a suggested course of action for recovery teams to restore system operations at an alternate site or use contingency capabilities. The final phase, Reconstitution, includes activities to test and validate system capability and functionality and outlines actions that can be taken to return the system to normal operating conditions and prepare the plan against future outages. The DRP should be activated if one or more of the activation criteria for that system are met. If an activation criterion is completed, the designated authority should start the plan. Activation criteria for system outages or disruptions are unique for each organization and should be stated in the contingency planning policy. Criteria may be based on: Extent of any damage to the system (e.g., physical, operational, or cost), the criticality of the system to the organization's mission (e.g., critical infrastructure protection asset), and the expected duration of the outage lasting longer than the RTO.

197. **B.** Human Resources is responsible for the "human" aspects of the disaster, including post-event counseling and next-of-kin notification, answer questions related current roster of personnel. The DRP and BCP coordinator should be involved as well – which satisfies the need for all employees.

198. **C.** Protocols for when to notify management should be clearly understood and documented. Consider events that occur on a holiday weekend or in the middle of the night. It should be clear to staff what situations require immediate notification of management regardless of the time of day. Similar protocols and procedures should be established to notify directors, investors, and other important stakeholders. Management does not want to learn about a problem from the news media.

199. **D.** After an assessment has been completed; the team can classify the event as non-incident, incident, or severe. Non- incident is caused by system malfunctions that result in a short downtime. Incidents can cause an entire facility or service to be inoperative for a significant amount of time. A severe incident is the destruction of a facility where a primary site must be created.

200. **A.** The Activation/Notification Phase describes activating the plan based on outage impacts and notifying recovery personnel. The Recovery Phase details a suggested course of action for recovery teams to restore system operations at an alternate site or using contingency capabilities. The final phase, Reconstitution, includes activities to test and validate system capability and functionality and outlines actions that can be taken to return the system to normal operating condition and prepare the plan against future outages; and steps taken to test and validate system capability and functionality at the original or new permanent location. This phase consists of two major activities: Validating successful Reconstitution and deactivation of the plan. During validation, the system is tested and validated as operational before returning it to its normal state. Validation procedures may include functionality or regression testing,
concurrent processing, and data validation. The system is declared recovered and operational by system owners upon successful completion of validation testing. Deactivation includes activities to notify users of system operating status. This phase also addresses recovery effort documentation, activity log finalization, incorporation of lessons learned into plan updates, and readying resources for future events.

201. **B.** Organizations should conduct training events periodically, following organizational or system changes, issuing new training guidance, or as otherwise needed. Execution of training events assists organizations in determining the plan's effectiveness and that all personnel knows what their roles are in the conduct of each information system plan. Training event schedules are often dictated in part by organizational requirements.

202. **D.** A checklist review is distributed to all members of a disaster recovery team. The members are asked to review the checklist. This ensures that the checklist is still current and that the assigned members of disaster recovery teams are still working for the company.

203. **C.** A structured walkthrough is a test in which employees review and discuss the processes to be followed during specific contingency scenarios. Generally, these exercises are conducted with all participants in the same room. Key decision-makers may be placed in role-playing situations to follow certain steps in the disaster recovery plan. The objective is to test the participant's knowledge of the procedures, identify any potential gaps in the program, and evaluate the plans to respond to various events. Simulation testing involves creating small real-life situations on the existing system to observe how team members react and how effective are the solutions outlined in the recovery plan. The simulation should be carried out so that the scenarios created do not disrupt system performance.

204. A. Simulation testing involves creating small real-life situations on the existing system to observe how team members react and how effective are the solutions outlined in the recovery plan. The simulation should be carried out so that the scenarios created do not disrupt system performance.

205. B. A parallel test involves bringing the recovery site to a state of operational readiness but maintaining operations at the primary site. The staff is relocated, backup tapes transferred, and operational readiness established by the disaster recovery plan while operations at the primary site usually continue.

206. B. Full-interruption/full-scale test is the most comprehensive type of test. In a full-scale test, a real-life emergency is simulated as closely as possible. Therefore, comprehensive planning should be a prerequisite to this type of test to ensure that business operations are not negatively affected. The institution implements all or portions by processing data and transactions using backup media at the recovery site that involves: 1) Enterprise-wide participation and interaction of internal and external management response teams with full involvement of external organizations; 2) Validation of crisis response functions; 3) Demonstration of knowledge and skills as well as management response and decision-making capability; 4) On-the- scene execution of coordination and decision-making roles; 5) Actual, as opposed to simulated, notifications, mobilization of resources, and communication of decisions; 6) Activities conducted at actual response locations or facilities; 7) Actual processing of data using backup media, and 8) Exercises generally extending over a longer period to allow issues to fully evolve as they would in a crisis and to allow realistic role-playing of all the involved groups.

207. C. A business continuity plan is a plan to continue operations if a place of business is affected by different levels of disaster, which can be localized short-term disasters, to days long building wide problems, to a permanent loss of a building. Such a plan typically explains how the business would recover its operations or move operations to another location after damage by events like natural disasters, theft, or flooding. For example, if a fire destroys an office building or datacenter, the people and business or datacenter operations would relocate to a recovery site. Because mission/business processes use information systems (ISs), the business continuity planner must coordinate with information system owners to ensure that the BCP expectations and IS capabilities are matched.

208. D. The organization can use the current defense in depth model without creating a new one. They would have to reexamine all the physical barriers and reallocate automated mechanisms within the chain of physical security. This means that after the security protection offered by the guard, computerized systems should be available.

209. A. Logs should be obtained and safeguarded by a physical security officer. 1) All visitors to the facility should be required to sign in when they come to the facility and sign out when they leave. The receptionist or security officer, not the visitor, should enter information into the visitor log for best security. 2) The visitor log should include the following information at a minimum: date, time visitor arrived/departed, visitor name, visitor company affiliation, name of company sponsor, and sponsor's telephone number. 3) All visitors should be issued a visitor badge. The visitor badge should include the date, visitor name, and name of the company sponsor. You may wish to consider the use of a "self-expiring" type of visitor badge. These badges automatically expire after a certain number of hours, preventing the badge from being reused on another day.

210. B. Scenario analysis is a process of analyzing possible future events by considering possible alternative outcomes (sometimes called "alternative worlds"). Thus, scenario analysis, a primary method of projections, does not try to show one exact picture of the future. A scenario analysis attempts to play out all the possible outcomes for a duress situation by measuring employee actions and responses to potential risks.

211. C. Much like construction and manufacturing workflows, waterfall methodology is a sequential design process. This means that as each of the eight stages (conception, initiation, analysis, design, construction, testing, implementation, and maintenance) are completed, the developers move on to the next step. As this process is sequential, developers cannot go back to a previous step once an effort has been completed – not without scratching the whole project and starting from the beginning. There is no room for change or error, so a project outcome and an extensive plan must be set initially and followed carefully. Agile came about as a "solution" to the disadvantages of the waterfall methodology. Instead of a sequential design process, the Agile methodology follows an incremental approach. Developers start with simplistic project design and then begin to work on small modules. The work on these modules is done weekly or monthly sprints, and at the end of each sprint, project priorities are evaluated, and tests are run. These sprints allow bugs to be discovered and customer feedback incorporated into the design before the next sprint is run.

212. C. To be most effective, information security must be integrated into the SDLC from system inception. Early integration of security in the SDLC enables organizations to maximize return on investment in their security programs. Early identification and mitigation of security vulnerabilities and misconfigurations result In a lower cost of security control implementation and vulnerability mitigation, awareness of potential engineering challenges; identification of shared security services; and reuse of security strategies and tools to reduce development cost.

213. D. Change management and configuration controls are operational assurance practices. A maturity model provides a place to start, the benefit of a community's prior experiences, a common language and a shared vision, a framework for prioritizing actions, and a way to define what improvement means for an organization. At the initial level, processes are disorganized, even chaotic. Success is likely to depend on individual efforts and is not considered repeatable because processes would not be sufficiently defined and documented to be replicated. Basic project management techniques are established at the repeatable level, and successes could be repeated because the requisite processes would have been established, defined, and documented. An organization has developed its standard software process at the specified level through greater attention to documentation, standardization, and integration. At the managed level, an organization monitors and controls its operations through data collection and analysis. At the optimizing level, processes are continually being improved by monitoring current operations' feedback and introducing innovative approaches to better serve the organization's needs.

214. A. In the Operations and Maintenance Phase, systems and products are in place, and operating enhancements and modifications to the system are developed and tested. The organization should continuously monitor the system's performance to ensure that it is consistent with pre-established user and security requirements and that needed system modifications are incorporated. Configuration management (CM) and control activities should be conducted to document any proposed or actual changes in the system's security plan. Information systems constantly evolve with upgrades to hardware, software, firmware, and possible modifications in the surrounding environment.

215. B. When using change management for application development, a team must review the outcome for the change for different version controls and documentation. Under a strict change management program, newer software versions are not released until thoroughly tested and approved for production. Any changes should be documented and archived as records for back-out plans and future changes.

216. C. The use of CMMI supports continuous improvement strategies. The question relates to team development and the production of software delivery through the integration of project and development teams. IPPD is a management technique that integrates all acquisition activities, starting with requirements definition through production, fielding/deployment, and operational support to optimize the design, manufacturing, business, and supportability processes. IPPD, as a multidisciplinary management technique, uses design tools such as modeling and simulation, teams, and best commercial practices to develop products and their related processes concurrently. Integrated Product Teams (IPT) is a multidisciplinary group of collectively responsible people delivering a defined product or process. The IPT comprises people who plan, execute, and implement lifecycle decisions for the system being acquired. DevOps is a set of practices that automate and integrate the processes between software development and IT teams to build, test, and release software faster and more reliably. DevOps was formed by combining the words "development" and "operations" and signifies a cultural shift that bridges the gap between development and operation teams, which historically functioned in siloes.

217. D. Aggregation happens when a user does not have the clearance or permission to access specific information, but they can access the components. The inference is the result of aggregation. The inference problem happens when a subject deduces the full story from the pieces he or she learned via collection. This is seen when data at a lower security level portrays data at a higher level. The inference is a database system technique used to attack databases where malicious users infer sensitive information from complex databases at a high level. The inference is a data mining technique used to find information hidden from regular users in basic terms. An inference attack may endanger the integrity of an entire database. The more complex the database, the greater the security implemented in association with it should be. If inference problems are not solved efficiently, sensitive information may be leaked to outsiders. Two inference vulnerabilities in databases are data association and data aggregation (inference is a result aggregation). When two values taken together are classified at a higher level than one of every value involved, this becomes a data association. When a set of information is classified at a higher level than the individual level of data, it is a clear case of data aggregation. The sensitive data leaked through inference involves bound data. An attacker finds a range of data holding expected data or harmful data obtained because of specific innocent queries. An attacker might try to access sensitive information through a direct attack, indirect attack, or tracking.

218. **C.** Virtualization is the simulation of the software and hardware upon which other software runs. This simulated environment is called a virtual machine (VM). There are many forms of virtualization, distinguished primarily by the computing architecture layer. For example, application virtualization provides a virtual implementation of the application programming interface (API) that a running application expects to use, allowing applications developed for one platform to run on another without modifying the application itself. The Java Virtual Machine (JVM) is an example of application virtualization; it acts as an intermediary between the Java application and operating systems (OS). Another form of virtualization, known as operating system virtualization, provides a virtual implementation of the OS interface used to run applications written for the same OS as the host, with each application in a separate VM container. A sandbox will isolate the virtual machine to carry out applets.

219. **B.** It is essential to follow all the steps except for the decryption of cookies. Cookies need to be encrypted due to the stale states that HTTP sessions employ. Input validation is a critical tool.

220. **C.** Race conditions in the software are when two concurrent threads of execution access a shared resource that unintentionally produces different results depending on how the code is executed. For example, a multi-threaded program may spawn two threads with access to the exact location in memory. Thread #1 might store the value 300 in this location and expect 300 still a few instructions later. Since thread #2 is executing simultaneously as thread #1, thread #2 may overwrite the memory location with another value, while thread #1 still expects it to be 300. Sometimes it will happen; sometimes, it will not. It depends on if thread #2 is "lucky enough" to execute just after thread #1 wrote the value 300. TOCTOU states that race conditions can occur if the system changed when a process checked some condition and when the action was taken based on that condition by the same process. This can be prevented via a file locking process.

221. **C.** The Polyinstantiation technique is used when a database contains a set of data that can be made public and data that should be kept secret. It allows the database owner to set security levels on data, so a person viewing the database would only see the data he is authorized to see. The cell Suppression technique involves removing some of the cells of the database before it is made public. The goal is to suppress the critical cells that can be used to carry out an inference attack. Generalization - using this technique, some values in the database are replaced with more general ones before it is made public. For example, "1967" becomes "1960-1970" or "597-4080" becomes "597-XXXX". The goal is to generalize values, mix them, and make it less feasible to carry out an inference attack. The Noise Addition technique involves adding random values to the values already in the database. For example, a random number between -5 and 5 is added to an individual's age. The goal is to obscure the individual value while leaving the average value unchanged.

222. **B.** Changing a website's appearance is not the only risk that this type of attack brings. It is similar to the XSS attack, where the malicious user steals another person's identities. Therefore, stealing another person's identity may also happen during this injection attack. The essence of this type of injection attack is injecting HTML code through the vulnerable parts of the website. The Malicious user sends HTML code through any weak field to change the website's design or any information displayed to the user. As a result, the user may see the data that the malicious user sent. Therefore, in general, HTML Injection is just the injection of markup language code to the page's document.

223. A. The Waterfall Model is the earliest method of structured system development. Although it has come under attack in recent years for being too rigid and unrealistic, when it comes to meet customer's needs quickly, the Waterfall Model is still widely used. It is attributed to providing the theoretical basis for other Process Models because it most closely resembles a "generic" model for software development. The problems with the Waterfall Model created a demand for a new method of developing systems that could provide faster results, require less up-front information, and offer greater flexibility. With Iterative Development, the project is divided into small parts. This allows the development team to demonstrate results earlier on and obtain valuable feedback from system users. Often, each iteration is a mini-Waterfall process, with the input from one phase providing vital information for the design of the next stage. In a variation of this model, the software products produced at the end of each step (or series of steps) can go into production immediately as incremental releases.

224. B. When the input data is more extended than it will fit in the reserved space, it will overwrite other data in memory if you do not truncate it. When this happens, it is called a buffer overflow. If the memory is overwritten contained data essential to the program's operation, this overflow causes a bug that, being intermittent, might be very hard to find. Suppose the overwritten data includes the address of other code to be executed, and the user has done this deliberately. In that case, the user can point to malicious code that your program will run. Input validation is performed to minimize malformed data from entering the system. Input Validation is not the primary method of preventing XSS SQL Injection. These are covered in output encoding and related cheat sheets. Similarly, when the input data is or appears to be shorter than the reserved space (due to erroneous assumptions, incorrect length values, or copying raw data as a C string), this is called a buffer underflow.

225. C. Traditionally, when performing code reviews, a reviewer receives a list of files and versions of these files to review. The trick is determining which version to compare against when doing the review. Should you compare the latest performance against the immediate predecessor, the last baseline, or some other arrangement? With the changeset information, the Security Configuration Management (SCM) tool can provide the developer with the predecessor version of the changeset automatically. This makes performing code reviews easier and reduces risks. Version control is the maintenance of a history of revisions to be compared to each other, and a copy from an arbitrary modification can be exported at any time. Release management is when source code is converted to a final product (e.g., a website or an executable application). Version control is usually involved and is recommended but is not a requirement.

226. A. Particular attention should be placed upon code repositories, emphasizing systems that support distributed code contributions with check-in/check-out functionality (continuous monitoring). Role-based access should apply to access the code repository, and logs should be reviewed regularly as part of the secure development process. Standard practices should develop the code. Developers should have full access (physical and logical) to the principles 24/7 unless rule-based access control methods are utilized.

227. B. REST is an architectural style and an approach to communications that is often used in Web services development. REST is often preferred over the more heavyweight SOAP (Simple Object Access Protocol) style because REST does not leverage as much bandwidth, making it a better fit for use over the Internet. The SOAP approach requires writing or using a provided server program (to serve data) and a client program (to request data).

228. A. Change Management and Configuration Control are the essential features of software change. If an organization wants to track previous changes, tasks auditing and continuous monitoring are appropriate. Intrusion and forensic analysis are used when incidents are involved.

229. B. The most effective way to protect information and information systems is to integrate security into every step of the software development process. Early identification and mitigation of security vulnerabilities and problems with systems configuration, resulting in lower costs to implement security controls and ease of vulnerabilities. Awareness of potential engineering challenges caused by mandatory security controls. Identification of shared security services and reuse of security strategies and tools will reduce development costs and improve the system's security posture by applying proven methods and techniques. Facilitation of informed executive decision-making through the application of a comprehensive risk management process on time.

230. C. Regression testing is the act of retesting a product around an area where a bug was fixed. If a data access component is changed, the code directly affected by that change will be regression tested to improve security. A good team will also test-related code, such as UI-based functions, which leverage the methods and class impacted by the fix. For proper identification, each code file should have unique identifiers to distinguish changes, and digitally signing email messages can validate the file and allow non-repudiation to exist.

231. D. Planning, contracting, monitoring, and follow-on are phases for software assurance. The overall approach evaluates its services and requirements early on to determine risks associated with acquiring software services. The risks can be related to management, work statements, budget, and contracting capabilities. A failure can result in software packages that have errors and lost software codes. This is important, considering some companies may disestablish themselves. Now! Who has the code?

232. A. SSL Portal VPNs as a single standard SSL connection to a website to securely access multiple network services. PPTP extends PPP connections by providing a tunnel through networks that do not understand PPP – no confidentiality. IPsec provides encryption, data integrity, and system-based authentication. When something is encrypted, it creates confidentiality due to encapsulation. SSL Tunnel and Portals are web-based technologies. 1) SSL Portal VPNs - An individual uses a single standard SSL connection to a website to securely access multiple network services. The website accessed is typically called a portal because it is a single location that provides access to other resources. The remote user accesses the SSL VPN gateway using a web browser, is authenticated, and is then presented with a web page that acts as the portal to the other services. 2) SSL Tunnel VPNs - An individual uses a web browser to securely access multiple network services, including applications and protocols that are not web-based, through an SSL tunnel. This commonly requires custom programming to allow the services to be accessible through a web-based connection.

233. D. Privacy Level Agreements (PLAs) are intended to be used as an appendix to Cloud Services Agreements to describe the level of privacy protection that the cloud service provider (CSP) will maintain. While Service Level Agreements (SLAs) are generally used to provide metrics and other information on the performance of the services, PLAs will address information privacy and personal data1 protection practices.

234. D. The project list describes Broad Network Access provides services over the network and accessed through standard mechanisms that promote use by heterogeneous thin or thick client platforms (e.g., mobile phones, tablets, laptops, and workstations). On-demand self-service is a characteristic as well, but not described in the question. The other answers do not apply.

235. B. SaaS applications are usually deployed as hosted services and are accessed via a network connecting SaaS consumers and providers. The SaaS consumers can be organizations that provide their members with access to software applications, end-users who directly use software applications, or software application administrators who configure applications for end-users. SaaS consumers access and use applications on-demand and can be billed on the number of consumers or the amount of consumed services. The provider installs and manages the software applications for the customer.

236. A. SSL Portal VPNs as a single standard SSL connection to a website to securely access multiple network services. PPTP extends PPP connections by providing a tunnel through networks that do not understand PPP – no confidentiality. IPsec provides encryption, data integrity, and system-based authentication. When something is encrypted, it creates confidentiality due to encapsulation. SSL Tunnel and Portals are web-based technologies. 1) SSL Portal VPNs - An individual uses a single standard SSL connection to a website to securely access multiple network services. The website accessed is typically called a portal because it is a single location that provides access to other resources. The remote user accesses the SSL VPN gateway using a web browser, is authenticated, and is then presented with a web page that acts as the portal to the other services. 2) SSL Tunnel VPNs - An individual uses a web browser to securely access multiple network services, including applications and protocols that are not web-based, through an SSL tunnel. This commonly requires custom programming to allow the services to be accessible through a web-based connection.

237. C. This question comes from multiple domains within the CISSP CBK. It is appropriate to use a web and packet filtering firewall for the organization's web applications, and IP addresses will need filtering. The authentication scheme is to use an SSL VPN over port 443. Port 80 is for unsecured traffic. Token and user-based authentication will not provide the level of protection that smart cards can use PKI technology. Key management is the best choice to manage any issues with keys.

238. D. The formula $n(n-1)/2$ $(45(45-1)/2)$ can be used for the key pairs. Symmetric cryptography uses AES, DES, Blowfish, and Skipjack as standard algorithms. RSA, Diffie-Hellman, and Digital Signature Algorithm are all used for Asymmetric Cryptography. Symmetric key cryptosystems are more efficient and can handle high data throughput rates; keys for symmetric-key cryptosystems are shorter than public-key algorithms, and symmetric key ciphers can be composed together to produce a stronger cryptosystem. Asymmetric key cryptosystems are suitable for digital signatures and key exchange.

239. C. The question covers multiple domains of the CISSP CBK. The components of an SQL database are schemas, tables, and views. A schema describes the structure of related tables and views. Tables hold the actual data in the database; they consist of rows and columns. Each row is a set of columns; each column is a single data element. Views are derived tables and may be composed of a subset of a table or the result of table operation (e.g., a join of different tables). The SQL standard describes facilities to perform four specific functions: Schema Definition defines the database structure, integrity constraints, and access privileges. Retrieval retrieves data from a database with a standard query interface. Data Manipulation populates and modifies the contents of a database by adding, modifying, or deleting rows and columns. Schema Manipulation modifies the structure, integrity constraints, and privileges associated with the tables and views in the database. Transaction Management is the ability to define and manage SQL transactions. Each of these components is related to certain security threats. Schema definition and manipulation relate to problems of inference and aggregation. Data retrieval tasks must conform to confidentiality policies. Data manipulation must conform to integrity policy. Transaction management contributes to maintaining the integrity of the database. When the schema is defined, wrong issues that arise for attacks, data manipulation, and integrity can occur. The schema defines the privileges and structures for the database requirements. Separation of duties is enforced through the Clark-Wilson Model – Prevent authorized personnel from making improper modifications. Maintain external and internal consistency is a Clark-Wilson duty, but it is designed to support well-formed transactions. SQL injections occur due to improper statements that are injected into a database.

25. Bonus Questions

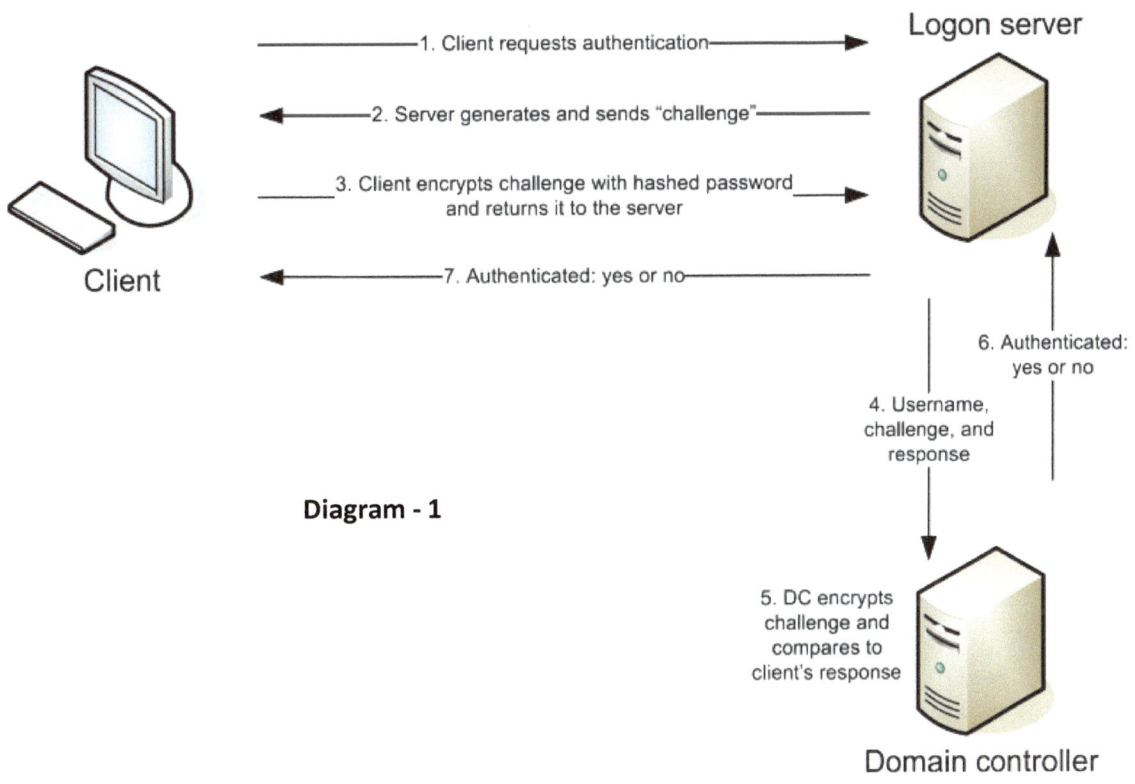

1. Client requests authentication

2. Server generates and sends "challenge"

3. Client encrypts challenge with hashed password and returns it to the server

7. Authenticated: yes or no

Logon server

6. Authenticated: yes or no

4. Username, challenge, and response

5. DC encrypts challenge and compares to client's response

Client

Diagram - 1

Domain controller

1. **When Step 3 is fully executed, what security principle (s) is achieved?**

   A. Pre-Authentication and Integrity

   B. Confidentiality and Availability

   C. Authorization and Pre-Authentication

   D. Integrity and Confidentiality

2. **If the above diagram was presented to senior management, what security concept would be important concerning the use of the diagram.**

   A. The organization's governance strategy supports challenge handshake protocols to counter attacks.

   B. The diagram represents an authentication method where handshaking is optional.

   C. The enterprise configuration standard use challenge-response for authentication.

   D. The threat posture for the organization use challenge responses to deter hackers.

3. **What would the outcome produce if Step 2 failed (Diagram -1)? Choose the best answer.**

   A. The authentication process would fail at Step 6.

   B. Step 7 would be a "no."

   C. The encryption process would never occur.

   D. The process would resort to password authentication.

Security Model Concept	Definition
Simple Security Rule	Subject cannot read data at a higher security level.
Star Property Rule	A subject cannot read data at a lower integrity level.
Simple Integrity Axiom	Subject cannot write data to an object at a lower security level.
Strong Star Property	Subject can perform read and write functions only to the objects at the same security level.

Table - Question 4

4. **Match the Security Model Concept to the appropriate definition.**

    A. A C B D

    B. C B A D

    C. D A C B

    D. A C D B

Security Device	Definition
Virtual Private Network (VPN) Firewall Intrusion Detection and Prevention (IDP)	Secures out-of-office connections with specific access control policies for groups and individual users. Authenticated user sessions from outside the office ensure data remains confidential during internet transit. Scans network traffic at the application level and seamlessly blocks malicious behavior with zero latency. C. Protects servers and workstations from a host of network-level attacks, including protocol anomalies, connection flooding, denial-of-service, SYN flooding, as well as packet fragmentation evasion techniques.

Table - Question 5

5. **Match the Security Device to the appropriate definition.**

    A. C B A

    B. B A C

    C. A B C

    D. A C B

BCP Metrics	Definition
Meantime to Repair (MTTR)	This refers to the maximum amount of time key business systems will be inoperable.
Recovery Time Objective (RTO)	The amount of time required that is necessary to bring a critical business function back to operation.
Recovery Point Objective (RPO)	
Meantime Between Failures (MTBF)	Maximum time in which data will be lost after a disaster. D. The measure of how long something is supposed to operate before failure.

Table - Question 6

6. **Match the BCP Metrics to the appropriate definition.**

   A. A B C D

   B. C A B D

   C. B A C D

   D. D A C B

Database File	Use	Location
File. Save	Saves all records with saved SSN	DB2
File.Store	Store user profiles	DB4
File.Delete	A dump repository for deleted PII	DB2

Table - Question 7

7. **A security control requires that all PII be deleted or protected through DLP methodologies for SEMAIS databases. Based on the control requirement, how should SEMAIS evaluate the control?**

   A. Test DB2 database files for PII and then implement DLP technologies such as Data In Transit.

   B. Verify that DB2 protects PII through configuration management practices such as Data In Use.

   C. Test DB4 to see if data leaks occur.

   D. Verify that PII exists for DB2 files. If there is PII, test the DLP technology for compliance.

8. **If there existed a task to permanently delete the PII, what organizational policy would support such a task?**

   A. Data Retention Policy

   B. Information Security and Compliance Standard

   C. The control framework policy

   D. Privacy Level Agreement Policy

9. **If the organization decides to transfer its services to a Cloud Service Provider, what specific documentation should control PII?**

    A. Data Retention Policy

    B. Information Security and Compliance Standard

    C. The control framework policy

    D. Privacy Level Agreement Policy

Service Operation Concepts	Definition
Event	Represents a change of state within a SIEM dashboard.
Alert	Represents a warning or notification indicated via log data.
Incident	An unplanned interruption where teams counter outside attacks.
	D. The unknown cause of one or more events.

Table - Question 10

10. **Match the Service Operation Concept to the appropriate definition.**

    A. C B A

    B. D A C

    C. A B D

    D. A C D

Attack	Definition
Backdoor	A hacker tries to decode a password or PIN through trial and error.
Spoofing	Designed to bypass intrusion detection systems.
Denial of Service	The attacker is in the middle of ongoing communication between two parties.
Brute Force	
	It prevents legitimate users from accessing services or information.

Table - Question 11

11. **Match the Attack to the appropriate definition.**

    A. A D C B

    B. B A C D

    C. B C D A

    D. D A C B

12. A service provider architect has designed a newer approach to Company A's multi-tenancy environment that hosts 100 applications. The architect is IaaS based, and the service provider is more concerned with ensuring the SaaS environment operates securely. The service provider architect has decided to focus on the service provider requirements and provide security recommendations for the IaaS environment due to recent cloud-based risks. Which of the following represents the best recommendation the architect can provide?

A. Incorporate a Software-based firewall that resides within the hypervisor layer, between the physical network interface and the instance's virtual interface.

B. Implement a Software-based firewall and VLAN architect to reduce asset visibility between tenants.

C. Implement the CIA triad for applications; and isolate the tenants.

D. Design an IaaS based segmentation policy.

Cloud Deployment Model	Definition
Private Cloud	Owned by specialized business units.
Community Cloud	Operated by a business, academic, or government organization.
Public Cloud	Owned based on shared concerns such as security requirements, policy, or compliance considerations.
	Composition of two or more distinct cloud infrastructures.

Table - Question 13

13. Match the Cloud Deployment Model to the appropriate definition.

A. C B A

B. B A C

C. B C A

D. A C B

Go to the Next Page

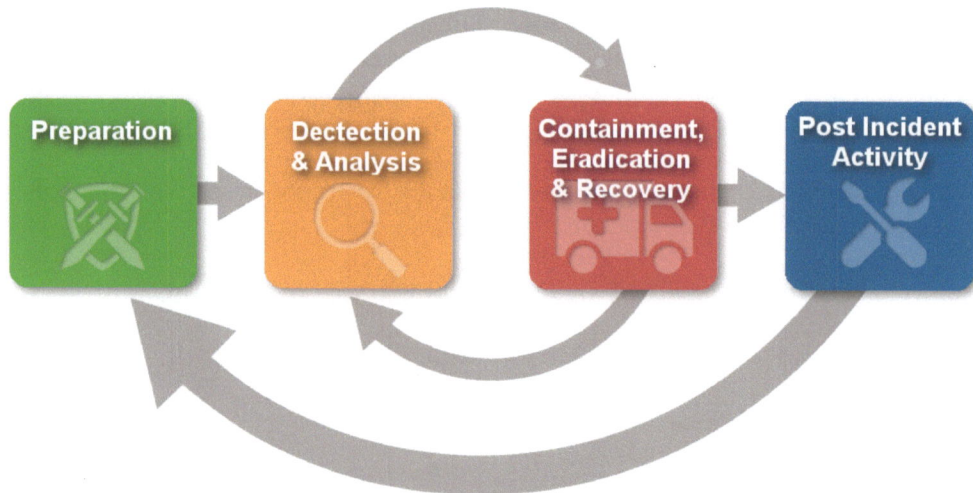

Diagram - 2

14. The communication guidelines for the IR activities failed during a training exercise. Which step will need to be adjusted for the IR phases?

   A. Detection

   B. Analysis

   C. Recovery

   D. Preparation

15. This is one of the most critical stages of incident response. After the system is restored and security is verified, normal operations can resume.

   A. Detection

   B. Analysis

   C. Containment

   D. Preparation

16. If you have identified domains or IP addresses known to be leveraged by threat actors for command and control, issue threat mitigation requests to block the communication from all egress channels connected to these domains.

   A. Detection

   B. Analysis

   C. Containment

   D. Preparation

Security Device	Definition
IaaS	The consumer has control over the deployed applications and configuration settings for the application-hosting environment.
SaaS	B. The capability provided to the consumer is to provision processing, storage, networks, and other fundamental computing resources where the consumer can deploy and run arbitrary software.
PaaS	C. The consumer does not manage or control the underlying cloud network, servers, operating systems, or storage.

Table - Question 17

17. **Match the Cloud Deployment Model to the appropriate definition.**

    A. C B A

    B. B C A

    C. C A B

    D. A C B

Go to the Next Page

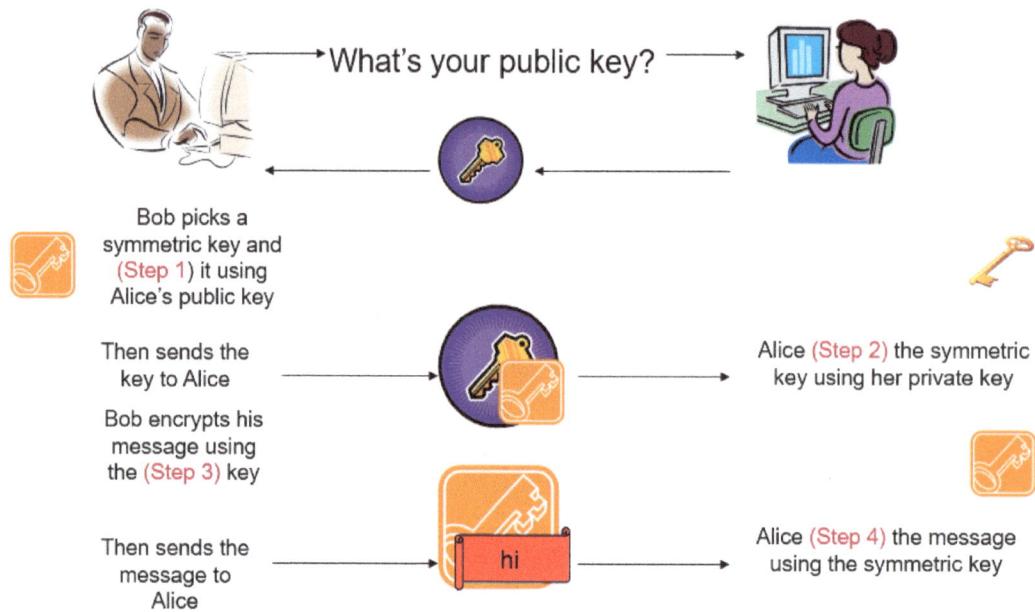

What's your public key?

Bob picks a symmetric key and (Step 1) it using Alice's public key

Then sends the key to Alice

Alice (Step 2) the symmetric key using her private key

Bob encrypts his message using the (Step 3) key

Then sends the message to Alice

hi

Alice (Step 4) the message using the symmetric key

Diagram - 3

18. **What should happen at Step 1 for the operation?**

    A. Decryption with Bob's Public Key

    B. Encryption

    C. Public Key Exchange

    D. Hash

19. **What should happen at Step 2 for the operation?**

    A. Decryption

    B. Encryption

    C. Public Key Exchange

    D. Hash

20. **What technology defines the complete PKI process for the diagram?**

    A. Asymmetric Cryptography

    B. Hashing and X.509

    C. Symmetric Encryption

    D. Digital Signature

Go to the Next Page

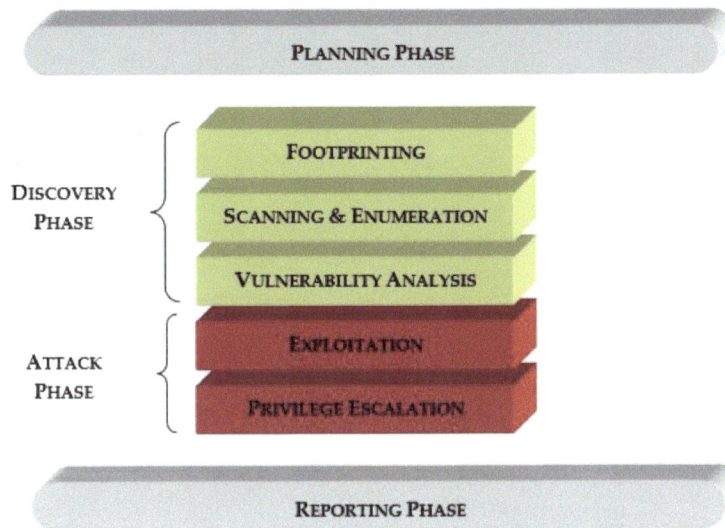

Diagram - 4

21. This process uses reconnaissance for gathering information about computer systems and their configuration.

    A. Scanning

    B. Vulnerability Analysis

    C. Footprinting

    D. Planning

22. The process establishes an active connection to the target hosts to discover potential attack vectors in the system, such as simple network management protocol (SNMP) and DNS.

    A. Exploitation

    B. Vulnerability Analysis

    C. Footprinting

    D. Enumeration

23. This phase can be dangerous if not executed properly. There are chances that running an the exploit may bring a production system down.

    A. Privilege Escalation

    B. Vulnerability Analysis

    C. Exploitation

    D. Enumeration

For questions 24-26, refer to the five testing strategies listed below:
- **Walkthrough Testing**
- **Simulation Testing**
- **Checklist Testing**
- **Full Interruption Testing**
- **Parallel Testing**

24. **Each business unit walks through the specific steps based on the DRP.**

    A. Simulation Testing.

    B. Parallel Testing

    C. Checklist Testing

    D. Parallel Testing

25. **Which of the following aligns with a Functional exercise?**

    A. You confirmed the effectiveness of the test.

    B. You are to determine whether critical systems can be recovered at the alternate processing site.

    C. You are tasked to identify whether backups operate in real-time.

    D. You are tasked to disrupt operations entirely.

26. **The exercise provides proof of the entire integration of the business continuity plans, relocation plans, and technical recovery plans.**

    A. Walkthrough

    B. Checklist

    C. Simulation Test

    D. Full Interruption

27. **A cloud customer has designed its services to accommodate its business operations strategy. Part of the strategy requires the architect to safeguard against vendor lock-in risks. Which is the best safeguard the organization can use to protect against vendor lock-in.**

    A. Create an SLA that describes how the CSP must safeguard data and access control.

    B. Design a backup strategy where software codes are vendor proprietary and portable.

    C. Design an SLA where services can be transferrable between service providers.

    D. Design portable and interoperable database programs; and scalable operations for the cloud.

28. **A loud provider owns and has designed an instance to host data storage. In the past, the CSP has been held through legal issues where customers' data was not transferrable to newer CSP storage platforms. To prevent the legal concerns from reoccurring, the CSP can use which specific policy?**

    A. Create an SLA that describes the SaaS Lock-in policy and the CSP responsibilities.

    B. Push for the customers to obtain better on-premise service.

    C. Create safeguards where DRM and privacy exist for in-house SLA requirements.

    D. Design IaaS services that prevent lock-in of resources and data.

29. **An extensive database company has decided to deliver a new customized database software program for its customer. The package consists of logs, databases, and configuration data for critical assets. Before the final release, the company notices that the data operate across three platform connections; and customers must manually manipulate the data. To resolve the issue, the product manager has assembled the development team and requested a quick solution. Which answer should the team provide as the best solution?**

    A. Integrate a design feature that operates via API calls and retest the interfaces.

    B. Design a minor program with a script that can export the missing data

    C. Create isolation points where the customer data can transfer without risks.

    D. Integrate security keys that onboard SSL, TLS, and JavaScript object notation (JSON).

26. Bonus Questions – Answers and Explanations

1. **D.** The security principles executed for the diagram are confidentiality and integrity. Confidentiality occurs due to the encryption process. Integrity occurs due to hashing. An asynchronous token device is based on challenge/response mechanisms. The authentication service sends the user a challenge value, which the user enters the token. The token encrypts or hashes this value, and the user uses this as her one-time password. Pre-authentication is not a security principle. When something is encrypted, the outcome is confidentiality.

2. **C.** Challenge Handshake Authentication Protocol (CHAP) is a process of authenticating a user to a network entity, any server, e.g., the web or internet service provider (ISP). CHAP is primarily used for security purposes. For example, users provide authenticated plain text passwords when accessing remote servers, authenticated before user access.

3. **C.** The encryption process is fully executed once the challenge-response is completed. Encryption algorithms provide confidentiality and drive key security initiatives, including authentication, integrity, and non-repudiation. Authentication allows for verifying a message's origin, and integrity proves that a message's contents have not changed since it was sent. Additionally, non-repudiation ensures that a message sender cannot deny sending the message. If step 2 failed, none of the above would occur.

4. **A.**
   Simple security property (SSP) — This property states that a subject at one level of confidentiality cannot read the information at a higher level of confidentiality. This is sometimes referred to as "no read-up."
   Star * security property — This property states that a subject at one level of confidentiality cannot write information to a lower level of confidentiality. This is also known as "no write-down."
   Strong star * property — This property states that a subject cannot read/write to an object of higher/lower sensitivity.
   Simple integrity axiom A subject cannot read data from a lower integrity level (referred to as "no read down").

5. **D.**
   Firewall Protects servers and workstations from a host of network-level attacks, including protocol anomalies, connection flooding, denial-of-service, SYN flooding, as well as packet fragmentation evasion techniques.

   Virtual Private Network (VPN) Secures out-of-office connections with specific access control policies for groups and individual users. Authenticated user sessions from outside the office ensure data remains confidential during internet transit.

   Intrusion Detection and Prevention (IDP) The IDP module integrated with the Firewall scans network traffic at the application level and seamlessly blocks malicious behavior with zero latency. Protection against newly emerging threats is provided by a database of vulnerability-class-based signatures and heuristic (expert system) anomaly-based behavioral analysis.

6. **C.**
   MTBF (Mean Time Between Failures) – a time determination for how long a piece of IT infrastructure will continue to work before it fails.

   MTTR (Mean Time to Repair) – a time determination for how long it will take to get a piece of hardware/software repaired and back online.

   RPO (Recovery Point Objective) – is the organization's definition of acceptable data loss.

   RTO (Recovery Time Objective) – is the organization's definition of the acceptable amount of time an IT system can be off-line.

7. **D.** A DLPS tool captures PII surrounding each file. It flags as violating a defined policy, which includes information identifying the File Owner and his or her immediate supervisor and any PII in the flagged file, which could pertain to FAA personnel or a member of the public. This PII is captured in DLPS as follows:

- DLPS reads the metadata associated with each file that appears to have violated a defined policy. This includes the File Owner name, access dates related to the file (created, modified, and accessed), and the access rights associated with the file.
- The DLPS tool maintains a connection with Active Directory. It will use this connection to capture the current business contact information of the File Owner defined in the metadata of the violating file. The tool will also capture the business contact information of the violating File Owner's immediate supervisor through the Active Directory connection.
- The business contact information collected includes: First and Last Name, Phone Number, LOB/SO, Email address
- DLPS also captures a sample of text from within the file flagged as violating a defined policy. The sample text could contain PII about an individual.

8. **A.** Organizations should develop comprehensive data retention policies and procedures for handling PII at the organization level, the program or component level, and, where appropriate, at the system level. Some types of data retention policies address foundational privacy principles, privacy rules of behavior, policies that implement laws and other mandates, and system-level policies. The foundational privacy principles reflect the organization 's privacy objectives. Foundational privacy principles may also be used as a guide against which to develop additional policies and procedures.

9. **D.** PLA is intended to be used as an appendix to a Cloud Services Agreement and describe the level of privacy protection that the CSP will provide. While Service Level Agreements ("SLA") are generally used to provide metrics and other information on the performance of the services, PLAs will address information privacy and personal data protection practices.

10. **C.** An event is an observed change to the normal behavior, environment, process, workflow, or person. Examples: router ACLs were updated; firewall policy was pushed. An alert is a notification that an event (or series of events) has occurred, sent to responsible parties to spawn action. Examples: the events above sent to on-call personnel. An event that negatively affects the confidentiality, integrity, and availability (CIA) of an organization impacts the business. Examples: attacker posts company credentials online, an attacker steals customer credit card database, the worm spreads through the network. Events are captured changes in the environment, alerts are notifications that specific events took place, and incidents are special events that negatively impact the CIA and cause an impact on the business.

11. **C.** A backdoor is a method of bypassing normal authentication procedures. Once a system has been compromised (by one of the above methods, or in some other way), one or more backdoors may be installed to allow easier access in the future. DOS is an attack used to deny legitimate users access to a resource such as accessing a website, network, emails, etc., or making it extremely slow. A Brute Force Attack is the simplest method to access a site or server (or anything that is password protected). It tries various combinations of usernames and passwords again and again until it gets in. This repetitive action is like an army attacking a fort. The act of spoofing is a scheme that tricks humans and networks into believing that a source of information is trustworthy when, in actuality, it is not. During a spoofing attack, a criminal will pose as a known and trusted source so they can mine for personal information and eventually wreak havoc on a business. This is sometimes called a Man-In-The-Middle Attack.

12. **B.** With the increasing adoption of cloud services by large enterprises that must host multi-tier applications, the datacenter network administrators need a flexible virtual networking topology to obtain the required isolation through network segmentation. This degree of independence between the virtual networks and the physical networks provided by overlay-based techniques also provides the scalability and configuration ease needed for maintaining the logical network segmentation within large datacenters. VLAN Segmentation reduces asset visibility and achieves tenant isolation. A software-based firewall is implemented within the hypervisor layer, between the physical network interface and the instance's virtual interface.

13. **D**. Deployment models describe the relationship between the cloud Provider and cloud Consumer(s) – for example, the Consumer may be one of many entities using a Provider's cloud service, it may have sole access to a particular service, or it may own and operate its cloud. There are four cloud deployment models: Public, Private, Community, and Hybrid. In a Public cloud, the cloud infrastructure is provisioned for open use by the general public. It may be owned, managed, and operated by a business, academic, or government organization, or some combination. It exists on the premises of the cloud provider. In a Private cloud, the cloud infrastructure is provisioned for exclusive use by a single organization comprising multiple consumers (e.g., business units). It may be owned, managed, and operated by the organization, a third party, or some combination, and it may exist on or off-premises. In a Community cloud, the cloud infrastructure is provisioned for exclusive use by a specific community of consumers from organizations with shared concerns (e.g., mission, security requirements, policy, and compliance considerations). It may be owned, managed, and operated by one or more of the organizations in the community, a third party, or some combination of them, and it may exist on or off-premises. In a Hybrid cloud, the cloud infrastructure is a composite of two or more distinct cloud infrastructures (Private, Community, or Public) that remain unique entities but are bound together by standardized or proprietary technology that enables data and application portability (e.g., cloud bursting for load-balancing between clouds).

14. **D; 15. C; 16. C**

The incident response process has several phases. The initial step involves establishing and training an incident response team and acquiring the necessary tools and resources. During preparation, the organization also attempts to limit the number of incidents by selecting and implementing a set of controls based on risk assessments. However, residual risk will inevitably persist after controls are implemented. Detection of security breaches is thus necessary to alert the organization whenever incidents occur. In keeping with the severity of the incident, the organization can mitigate the impact of the incident by containing it and ultimately recovering from it. During this phase, the activity often cycles back to detection and analysis—for example, to see if additional hosts are infected by malware while eradicating a malware incident. After the incident is adequately handled, the organization issues a report that details the cause and cost of the incident and the steps the organization should take to prevent future incidents.

17. **C**. Infrastructure as a Service (IaaS), the Cloud Provider is responsible for everything up to, but not including, the operating system. The Cloud Consumer is responsible for everything from the operating system up through the rest of the stack. Platform as a Service (PaaS), the Cloud Provider is responsible for everything up through the middleware & development environment. The Cloud Consumer is responsible for everything from the application up through the rest of the stack. Software as a Service (SaaS), the Cloud Provider is responsible for everything up through the application, and the Cloud Consumer is responsible for the application configuration, personalization, and application data.

18. **B; 19 A; 20 A.** How does this work? Bob sends Alice a message that Bob wants only Alice to be able to read. Bob encrypts his message with a secret key, so now Bob has ciphertext and a symmetric key. The key needs to be protected, so Bob encrypts the symmetric key with an asymmetric key. Remember that asymmetric algorithms use private and public keys, so Bob will encrypt the symmetric key with Alice's public key. Now Bob has ciphertext from the message and ciphertext from the symmetric key. Why did Bob encrypt the symmetric key with Alice's public key instead of his private key? Because if Bob encrypted it with his private key, anyone with Bob's public key could decrypt it and retrieve the symmetric key. However, Bob does not want anyone who has his public key to read his message to Alice. Bob only wants Alice to be able to read it. Therefore, Bob encrypts the symmetric key with Alice's public key. If Alice has done a good job protecting his private key, he will be the only one to read Bob's message.

21. C; 22. D; 23. C

The process of footprinting is a completely non-intrusive activity performed to get the maximum possible information available about the target organization and its systems using various means, both technical and non-technical. This involves searching the internet and querying various public repositories (databases, domain registrars, Usenet groups, mailing lists, etc.). The scanning and enumeration phase will usually identify live systems, open/filtered ports found, services running on these ports, mapping router/firewall rules, identifying the operating system details, network path discovery, etc. After successfully identifying the target systems and gathering the required information from the above phases, a penetration tester should try to find any possible vulnerabilities in each target system. During the vulnerability analysis phase, a penetration tester may use automated tools to scan the target systems for known vulnerabilities. These tools will usually have their databases consisting of the latest vulnerabilities and their details. During the exploitation phase, a penetration tester will find exploits for the various vulnerabilities found in the previous phase. There are many repositories on the internet that provide proof-of-concept exploits for most of the vulnerabilities. There are chances that running an exploit may bring a production system down. All exploits need to be thoroughly tested in a lab environment before actual implementation.

24. A; 25. B; 26. D.

- Tabletop Exercise or Structured Walk-Through Test: A preliminary step in the overall testing process and an effective training tool for individuals and groups, as well as validating comprehensive strategies, communication, and integrations. Tabletop exercises are excellent for training around group dynamics, notification, assembly, etc. The primary objective of the tabletop exercise is to ensure that critical personnel from all areas are familiar with the Business Continuity Plan and that it accurately reflects the organization's ability to recover from a disaster. Though not often used for Disaster Recovery Planning, tabletop exercises can provide these same benefits and review technical steps before performing a functional test.

- Walk-Through Drill or Simulation Test: It is also a preliminary step in the testing process; it is more involved than a tabletop exercise/structured walk-through test. This exercise uses a specific event scenario that is applied to the plan. These types of tests are usually used for Business Continuity plans and Emergency Management team plans.

- Functional Exercise, Drill, or Parallel Test: Involves personnel mobilization to other sites to establish communications and perform processing as outlined in the plans.

- For Business Continuity, this typically involves determining if employees can deploy the procedures defined in the Business Continuity plan.

- The goal is to determine whether critical systems can be recovered at the alternate processing site for disaster recovery plans.

- Once the individual Business Continuity and Disaster Recovery functional tests are successful, a parallel test for both may be conducted where the business functions relocate to an alternate site and use the recovered systems and applications.

- Full interruptions: The most comprehensive type of testing. In a full-scale test, a real-life situation is simulated as closely as possible. Comprehensive planning is a prerequisite to this type of test to ensure that business operations are not negatively affected. The exercise provides proof of the entire integration of the business continuity plans, relocation plans, and technical recovery plans. This type of exercise should only be attempted once the exercises described above have been completed and the organization is comfortable with the functional capability of the recovery strategies.

27. B LOCK-IN: There is currently little on offer regarding tools, procedures, or standard data formats or services interfaces that could guarantee data, application, and service portability. This can make it difficult for the customer to migrate from one provider to another or migrate data and services back to an in-house IT environment. This introduces a dependency on a particular CP for service provision, especially if data portability, as the most fundamental aspect, is not enabled.

This set of questions should be considered to understand the risks related to vendor lock-in.
- Are there documented procedures and APIs for exporting data from the cloud?
- Does the vendor provide interoperable export formats for all data stored within the cloud?
- In the case of SaaS, are the API interfaces used standardized?
- Are there any provisions for exporting user-created applications in a standard format?
- Are there processes for testing that data can be exported to another cloud provider – should the client wish to change provider, for example?
- Can the client perform their data extraction to verify that the format is universal and migrated to another cloud provider?

28. D. IaaSLock-in. IaaS lock-in varies depending on the specific infrastructure services consumed. For example, a customer using cloud storage will not be impacted by non-compatible virtual machine formats.
- IaaS computing providers typically offer hypervisor-based virtual machines. Software and VM metadata are bundled together for portability – typically just within the provider's cloud. Migrating between providers is non-trivial until open standards, such as OVF (11), are adopted.
- IaaS storage provider offerings vary from simplistic key/value-based data stores to policy-enhanced file-based stores. Feature sets can vary significantly; hence so do storage semantics. However, application-level dependence on specific policy features (e.g., access controls) may limit the customer's choice of provider.
- Data lock-in is the obvious concern with IaaS storage services as cloud customers push more data to cloud storage; data lock-in increases unless the CSP provides data portability.

29. A. A Cloud Application Programming Interface (Cloud API) is a type of API that enables the development of applications and services to provide cloud hardware, software, and platforms. A Cloud API serves as a gateway or interface that provides direct and indirect cloud infrastructure and software services to users. A Cloud API is the core component behind any public cloud solution. It is generally based primarily on the REST and SOAP frameworks and cross-platform and vendor-specific APIs.

APPENDIX A - ACRONYMS

3DES	Triple Data Encryption Standard
AAA (*aka Triple A*)	Authentication, Authorization, and Accounting
ACAS	Assured Compliance Assessment Solution
ACL	Access Control List
AES	Advanced Encryption Standard
AH	Authentication Header
AI	Artificial Intelligence
AJAX	Asynchronous JavaScript and XML
ALE	Annualized Loss Expectancy
AMTSO	Ani-Malware Testing Standard Organization
ANSI	American National Standards Institute
API	Application Program Interfaces
APT	Advance Persistent Threats
ARO	Annual Rate of Occurrence
ARP	Address Resolution Protocol
ASCII	American Standard Code for Information Interchange
ATM	Asynchronous Transfer Mode
AV	Asset Value
BCP	Business Continuity Plan
BIA	Business Impact Analysis
BLP	Bell-LaPadula
BOL	Bureau of Labor
CA	Certification Authority
CBC	Cipher Block Chaining
CBC-MAC	Cipher Block Chaining - Message Authentication Code
CBK	Common Body of Knowledge
CCTV	Closed Circuit Television
CDMA	Code Division Multiple Access
CDN	Content Delivery Network
CD-ROM	Compact Disc - Read Only Memory
CEO	Chief Executive Officer
CER	Crossover Error Rate
CERT	Computer Emergency Readiness Team
CHAP	Challenge Handshake Authentication Protocol
CI	Configuration Item
CIA	Confidentiality, Integrity, And Availability
CICA	Canadian Institute of Chartered Accountants
CIO	Chief Information Officer
CIRT	Computer Incident Response Team
CISO	Chief Information Security Officer
CISSP	Certified Information System Security Professional
CM	Configuration Management
CMAC	Cipher-based Message Authentication Code
CMDB	Configuration Management Database
CMMT	Capability Maturity Model Integration
CNO	Chief Networking Officer
COM	Component Object Model
COTS	Commercial-off-the-shelf
CPA	Chosen Plaintext Attack
CPTED	Crime Prevention Through Environment Design
CPU	Central Processing Unit
CSD	Computer Security Division
CSP	Cloud Service Provider
CSS	Cascading Style Sheet

DAC	Discretionary Access Control
DAST	Dynamic Application Security Testing
DBMS	Database Management System
DCS	Distributed Control System
DDoS	Distributed Denial-of-Service
DES	Data Encryption Standard
DevOps	Development and Operations
DISA	Defense Information Security Agency
DLP	Data Loss Prevention
DLPS	Data Loss Prevention System
DMZ	Demilitarized Zone
DNSBLs	Domain Name System Blacklist or DNS Blacklists
DoD	Department of Defense
DoS	Denial of Service
DRP	Disaster Recovery Plan
DRE	Data Rest Environment
DRM	Digital Rights Management
DRP	Disaster Recovery Plan
DSP	Discretionary Security Property
DSA	Digital Signature Algorithm
EAR	Export Administration Regulations
EF	Exposure Factor
EISA	Enterprise Security Architecture
EMI	Electromagnetic Interference
ePHI	Electronic Protected Health Information
ERR	Equal Error Rate
ESI	Electronic Stored Information
ESN	Electronic Serial Number
ESP	Encapsulating Security Payload
EU	European Union
EUD	End User Devices
EUM	End User Experience Monitoring
FAA	Federal Aviation Administration
FCoE	Fiber Channel over Ethernet
FDMA	Frequency Division Multiple Access
FedRAMP	Federal Risk and Authorization Management Program
FIPS	Federal Information Processing Standards
FISMA	Federal Information Security Management Act
FTP	File Transfer Protocol
GB	Gigabyte
GLBA	Gramm-Leach-Bliley Act
GRC	Governance, Risk, and Compliance
GSM	Global System for Mobile Communication
GUI	Graphical User Interface
HA	High Availability
HBSS	Host-Based System Security
HIDS	Host Intrusion Detection Systems
HIPPA	Health Insurance Portability and Accountability Act
HMAC	Hash-based Message Authentication Code
HR	Human Resource
HTML	Hyper Text Markup Language
HTTP	Hypertext Transfer Protocol
HTTPS	Hypertext Transfer Protocol Secure
HTTP-SSL	Hypertext Transfer Protocol- Secure Socket Layer
HVAC	Heating, Ventilation, And Air Conditioning
I/O	Input/Output

IAAA	Identification, Authentication, Authorization, and Accountability
IaaS	Infrastructure as a Service
IAFT	Information Assurance Technology Framework
IaM	Identity and Access Management
IBM	International Business Machines
ICMP	Internet Control Message Protocol
ICS	Industrial Control System
IDaaS	Identity as a Service
IdP	Identity Provider
IDP	Intrusion Detection and Prevention
IDS	Intrusion Detection System
IM	Infrastructure Management
IoT	Internet of Things
IP	Internet Protocol
IPPD	Integrated Product and Process Development
IR	Incident Response
IPS	Intrusion Prevention System
IPSec	Internet Protocol Security
IPT	Integrated Product Team
ISAS	International Service Availability Symposium
(ISC)²	International Information System Security Certification Consortium
ISDN	Integrated Services for Digital Network
ISMS	Information System Management System
ISO	International Organization for Standardization
ISSO	Information System Security Officer
ISP	Internet Service Provider
IT	Information Technology
ITAM	Information Technology Asset Management
ITAR	International Traffic in Arms Regulations
ITIL	Information Technology Infrastructure Library
ITL	Information Technology Laboratory
ITSEC	Information Technology Security Evaluation Criteria
IV	Initialization Vector
JSON	JavaScript Object Notation
JVM	Java Virtual Machine
KCA	Knowledge, Comprehension, and Application
KDFs	Key Derivation Functions
KMPS	Key Management Practices Statement
KMS	Key Management Specification
L2TP	Layer 2 Tunneling Protocol
LAN	Local Area Network
LDAP	Lightweight Directory Access Protocol
LEDs	Light-Emitting Diodes
LOB	Line-of-Business
MAC	Mandatory Access Control
MD	Message Digest
MitM, MiM, or MitMA	Man-In-The-Middle Attack
MTA	Mail Transfer Agent
MTBF	Mean Time Between Failure
MTTR	Mean Time to Repair
NAT	Network Address Translation
NCP	National Checklist Program
NDA	Non-Disclosure Agreement
NIC	Network Interface Card
NIDS	Network Intrusion Detection System
NIJ	National Institute of Justice

NIST	National Institute of Standards and Technology
NSA	National Security Agency
OASIS	Organization for the Advancement of Structured Information Standards
OECD	Organization for Economic Cooperation and Development
OFDMA	Orthogonal Frequency Division Multiple Access
OLTP	Online Transaction Processing
OS	Operating System
OSI	Open Systems Interconnection
OTP	One-time Pad
OWSAP	Open Web Application Security Project
P2P	Peer-to-Peer
PaaS	Platform as a Service
PACS	Physical Access Control System
PAP	Password Authentication Protocol
PBX	Private Branch Exchange
PC	Personal Computer
PCI-DSS	Payment Card Industry Data Security Standard
PCs	Personal Computers
PDA	Personal Digital Assistant
PDCA	Plan–Do–Check–Act
PDF	Portable Document format
PGP	Pretty Good Privacy
PII	Personally Identifiable Information
PINs	Personal Identification Numbers
PKC	Public Key Cryptography
PKI	Public Key Infrastructure
PMTU	Path Maximum Transmission Unit
PPP	Point-To-Point Protocol
PPTP	Point-To-Point Tunneling Protocol
PSE	Packet Switching Exchange
PSK	Pre-Shared Key
PVC	Permanent Virtual Circuit
QA	Quality Assurance
RA	Registration Authority
RABC	Role Based Access Control
RADIUS	Remote Authentication Dial-in User Service
RAID	Redundant Array of Independent Disks
RAM	Random Access Memory
RARP	Reverse Address Resolution Protocol
RDS	Remote Desktop Services
REST	Representational State Transfer
RFC	Request for Comment
RMF	Risk Management Framework
RNGs	Random Number Generators
ROM	Read Only Memory
RPO	Recovery Point Objective
RSA	Rivest-Shamir-Adleman
RTO	Recovery Time Objective
RTUs	Remote Terminal Units
RuBAC	Rule-Based Access Control
RUM	Real User Monitoring
SaaS	Software as a Service
SAML	Security Assertion Markup Language
SAN	Storage Area Network
SAS	Statement on Auditing Standards
SAST	Static Application Security Testing

SAT	Security Assessment and Testing
SCADA	Supervisory Control and Data Acquisition
SCIF	Sensitive Compartmented Information Facility
SCM	Security Configuration Management
SDH	Synchronous Digital Hierarchy
SDLC	System Development Life Cycle
SDN	Storage Defined Network
SEMAIS	Secure Managed Instructional Systems
SHA	Secure Hash Algorithm
SIEM	Security Information and Event Management
SIP	Session Initiation Protocol
SKA	Shared Key Authentication
SKC	Secret Key Cryptography
SLA	Service-Level Agreement
SLE	Single Loss Expectancy
SME	Subject Matter Expert
SMPT	Simple Mail Transfer Protocol
SMURF	Simulation and Modeling Underlying Radio Frequencies
SNMP	Simple Network Management Protocol
SOAP	Simple Object Access Protocol
SOC	Security Operational Center
SONET	Synchronous Optical Networking
SPI	Stateful Packet Inspection
SPML	Service Provisioning Markup Language
SPOFs	Single Point of Failures
SQL	Structured Query Language
SSP	Simple Security Property
SSH	Secure Shell
SSL	Secure Socket Layer
SSN	Social Security Number
SSO	Single Sign-on
STIGs	Security Technical Information Guides
SVC	Switched Virtual Circuit
SWGDE	Scientific Working Group on Digital Evidence
SYN	Synchronize
TACACS	Terminal Access Controller Access Control System
TCP	Transmission Control Protocol
TCP/IP	Transmission Control Protocol/Internet Protocol
TCP/SYN	Transmission Control Protocol/Synchronize
TCSEC	Trusted Computer System Evaluation Criteria
TDMA	Time Division Multiple Access
TELNET	Telecommunications Network
TFTP	Trivial File Transfer Protocol
TIER	Trust and Identity in Education and Research
TIFF	Tagged Image File Format
TLS	Transport Layer Security
TOCTOU	Time of Check/Time of Use
TOGAF	The Open Group Architecture Framework
UDP	User Datagram Protocol
UPS	Uninterruptible Power Supply
URL	Uniform Resource Identifier
USB	Universal Serial Bus
UTP	Unshielded Twisted Pair
VBScript	Visual Basic Script
VLAN	Virtual Land Area Network
VM	Virtual Machine.

VoIP	Voice Over Internet Protocol
VPN	Virtual Private Network
VSAN	Virtual Storage Area Network
WAF	Web Application Firewall
WAN	Wide Area Network
WEP	Wired Equivalent Privacy
Wi-Fi	Wireless Fidelity
WiMAX	Worldwide Interoperability for Microwave Access
WPA	Wi-Fi Protected Access
WWW	World Wide Web
XACML	Extensible Assess Control Markup Language
XML	Extensible Markup Language
XSS	Cross-Site Scripting

SEMAIS
Cybersecurity Consulting

Please contact **workforcedevelopment@semais.net**
for any questions.

Arthur D. Hart

Chief Executive Officer

**Secure Managed
InstructionalSystems, LLC
(SEMAIS)**

semais@semais.net
www.semais.net

3350 Riverwood Pkwy., Suite 1900
Atlanta, Georgia 30339

Office: 800-497-3376
Cell: 404-709-1702